INNOVATIONS IN
PENSION FUND MANAGEMENT

INNOVATIONS *in*

PENSION

FUND

MANAGEMENT

ARUN S. MURALIDHAR

STANFORD ECONOMICS + FINANCE
An Imprint of Stanford University Press

Stanford University Press
Stanford, California
©2001 by the Board of Trustees of the
Leland Stanford Junior University

Printed in the United States of America on acid-free,
archival-quality paper.

Library of Congress Cataloging-in-Publication Data
Muralidhar, Arun S.
    Innovations in pension fund management/Arun S. Muralidhar.
        p.   cm.
    Includes bibliographical references.
    ISBN 0-8047-4521-8 (alk. paper)
        1. Pension trusts—Management. 2. Pension trusts—Investments. 3. Pension
trusts—Evaluation. I. Title.

    HD7105.4.M87 2001
    332.67'254—dc21   2001049224

Original Printing 2001

Last figure below indicates year of this printing:

10   09   08   07   06   05   04   03   02   01

Designed by James P. Brommer
Typeset by Interactive Composition Corporation

To Mina and Murali

CONTENTS

The following are coauthors of papers on which some of the chapters are based: Sudhir Krishnamurthi (Chapters 1, 2, and 3), Ronald van der Wouden (Chapters 2, 3, 4, and 5), Robertus Prajogi (Chapters 5 and 12), Masaki Tsumagari (Chapter 6), Kemal Asad-Syed (Chapters 7 and 8), Paolo Pasquariello (Chapter 8), Arturo Balana (Chapter 9), Robert Weary (Chapters 6, 9, and 12), Shaila Muralidhar (Chapter 10), and Khin Mala U (Chapter 14).

LIST OF FIGURES AND TABLES

Tables

Chapter 7

Figures

Chapter 8

Tables

Chapter 9

Figures

PREFACE

BACKGROUND

I joined the World Bank in 1992, after completing my PhD at the M.I.T. Sloan School of Management, to work with the derivatives and liability management team. I was fortunate to be associated with Afsaneh Mashayekhi Beschloss and Sudhir Krishnamurthi in this team. In early 1995, Afsaneh was asked to head up the pension investment area and convinced Sudhir and me to join her. The benefit of having no prior experience in asset management is that we started with a clean slate. We visited plan sponsors (corporate and public) and investment managers around the world to adopt best practices and began to question the largely asset-only focus in the industry-possibly because of our liability-based background. In addition, risk management had always been a keen issue for us in managing derivative portfolios—in the asset management area, risk management was treated much more casually.

Afsaneh and Sudhir assembled a relatively unique team to invest the World Bank's pension assets—at one point boasting four PhDs in a staff of seven—and emphasized research and innovation. As Afsaneh's responsibilities evolved to incorporate other internal assets, I was fortunate to be asked to head up the Research and Analytics area for the entire Investment Department. We assembled a talented, enthusiastic team with global experiences. Most of the articles that form the essence of this book are co-authored with colleagues from this team (Kemal Asad-Syed, Masaki Tsumagari, Arturo Balana, Ronald van der

Wouden, Cybele Suarez, and Robert Weary), good testament to the fun we had in questioning conventional wisdom. As the reader will notice, every aspect of managing funds (from establishing investment objectives to evaluating derivatives and leverage) has a new practical or theoretical twist. For example, the M^3 measure and the "luck or skill" measure mark the culmination of many years of thinking on the topic, and the fact that some plan sponsors are evaluating its use is once again a compliment to the fantastic people I have been lucky to work with over the years

PURPOSE OF THE BOOK

The book is designed to help investors, regardless of the institutions they work for, establish formal processes for efficient management of funds. We have tried to integrate best practices worldwide, gained through meetings with plan sponsors and investment managers and our own work on the topics to create material of practical relevance. I have attempted, in putting this book together, to highlight both sides of the investment issue—plan sponsor and investment manager—to facilitate decision-making.

The case study approach is used wherever possible, as practical exposition is more important to fund administrators. Theoretical concepts are either provided in the Appendices or referred to in the text for those who are interested in these aspects. The comments of many plan sponsors are interspersed throughout the book—and the Acknowledgment is testimony to the number of people who have contributed to the final text. In many cases, the "innovation" is a shift in paradigm, rather than a totally different way of doing business. This is most evident in the material on risk management and peer comparison. It is our hope that by addressing the key decisions that sponsors need to make on asset allocation, risk management, and performance evaluation, and demonstrating keys to successful implementation that this book will assist plan sponsors to achieve their objectives more efficiently. It is clear that the state-of-the-art is evolving daily. This book gives a unique perspective of innovative ideas to manage portfolios today.

DISCLAIMER

All information contained in the book are composed of the author's views and theoretical applications developed throughout the author's educational and professional career, and do not represent the views of J.P. Morgan Chase & Co. or any of its affiliates ("JPMC"). They also do not represent the views of the World Bank Group ("WGB") or any of its affiliates. Accordingly, all views, hypotheses, conclusions, recommendations and errors thereof, reflected in the book are those of the author's. The author's ability to write this book in his role with JPMC shall not be construed as an endorsement by JPMC, and any references to JPMC contained in the book are included for general information purposes only. The author's ability to write this book using insights gained at the WBG shall not be construed as an endorsement by WBG, and any references to WBG contained in the book are included for general information purposes only.

ACKNOWLEDGMENTS

This book is the culmination of a series of collaborations with several individuals to whom I owe an enormous debt of gratitude. This research would have never been undertaken if I had not been convinced/coerced by Afsaneh Mashayekhi Beschloss and Sudhir Krishnamurthi to convert from being a derivatives trader to an asset management professional in 1995. In addition, they provided guidance and an incredible opportunity to revamp the World Bank's asset management function. The lessons from this experience form the backbone of this book. Gary Perlin, too, provided invaluable guidance, assistance, and friendship and was always willing to entertain my crazy ideas. However, Joelyn Flomenhaft, former editor of the *Journal of Pension Plan Investing* and a dear friend, not only encouraged me to write numerous articles on pension fund management topics, but also convinced me that I need to put together an abstract for a book and provided valuable guidance.

Among the many colleagues and friends who coauthored papers interspersed throughout the book, I have to recognize Sudhir Krishnamurthi (Chapters 1, 2, and 3), Ronald van der Wouden (Chapters 2, 3, 4, and 5), Robertus Prajogi (Chapters 5 and 12), Masaki Tsumagari (Chapter 6), Kemal Asad-Syed (Chapters 7 and 8), Paolo Pasquariello (Chapter 8), Arturo Balana (Chapter 9), Robert Weary (Chapters 6, 9, and 12), Shaila Muralidhar (Chapter 10), and Khin Mala U (Chapter 14). Their contributions exceed their participation in specific papers and it is a pity that all these names do not appear on the cover of the book.

In addition, many colleagues have been generous with their time and provided valuable guidance and assistance, including, Robert Katz, Krishnan Nagarajan, Cybele Suarez, Pamela Na, Esther Moon, Garrett McDonald, P. S. Srinivas, David Wilton, Kristin Gilbertons, Sue Wan Chua, Tsuyoshi Fukui, Jim Park, S. Sem, John Gandolfo, and Eleanor Valencia (World Bank). We are also grateful to the many industry participants who educated us on many topics—Jamil Baz (Deutsche Bank), Leah Modigliani (Morgan Stanley), Stanley Kogelman (formerly with Salomon Brothers Asset Management and Goldman Sachs Asset Management), Guus Boender, Fred Heemskerk and Martijn Vos (ORTEC Consultants) Wai Lee (CSAM), Francis Vitagliano, the actuaries at Buck Consultants, R. Ambarish (West Deutsche Asset Management), the custodial teams at State Street and Northern Trust, consultants at Barra Rogers Casey, Watson Wyatt, Cambridge Associates, Callan Associates, Wilshire Associates and Frank Russell, the risk management team at Bankers Trust (especially Michelle McCarthy and Neil Paragiri), Sanjay Santhanam and Samir Varma (Chaos Systems LLC), Thomas Philips (Paradigm Asset Management), Michael Peskin (MSAM), Dmitri Shishkoff, George Jabbor (George Washington University), Cees Dert (ABN Amro Asset Management), Srinivas Pulavarti (Johns Hopkins University), David Blake (Birkbeck College), Andrew Lo (MIT), Walter Bodden, Tom Palameta, Tim Hebert (Daimler Chrysler—Canada), David Services (Towers Perrin—Canada), Bernhard Radtke and Mark Schmid (Daimler Chrysler—US), Robin Diamonte, Bill Raver and Robert Hunt (Verizon), Landis Zimmerman and Narv Narvekar (University of Pennsylvania Endowment), Karin Brodbeck and Mannfred Lehman (Nestle), Eric Busay (CalPERs), Kirk Brown and Nancy Eckl (AMR Investments), Frank del Vecchio, James Merrill, and Mary Ann Florez (GMIMCO), Steve Healey and David Nixon (EDS), Kevin McCormack and Tom Harvey (Bellsouth), Lisa Johnson, Sheyla Peterson, and David Axelson (UPS), Dekia Scott (Southern Companies), Michael Pradko and Verne Sedlacek (Harvard Management Company), Paul Laubscher and Ray Kanner (IBM), and Roger Paschke (Oil Insurance). In addition, many individuals around the world have been generous in sharing their knowledge on pension fund management or reserves management, including Jaime Villasenor (Mexico), Iker Zubizaretta and Adrian Asciano (Venezuela), Gion Cavegn, Erich Muur and Dewet Moser (Switzerland), Cagatay Ergenekon (Turkey), Sung Hwan Shin (Korea), Dr. Chia Tai Tee, Yeoh Lam Keong and Irene Goh (Singapore), Rupert Thorne (United Kingdom), Joe Silvera and Kirit Patel (United Arab Emirates), and Dr. R. Thilianathan (Malaysia).

I was fortunate to have the keen advice of my brother Sanjay Muralidhar throughout the process, and many improvements and ideas are thanks to him. I am also fortunate to have married into a family of outstanding communicators, and the editorial work of Jeanette Fernandes (my mother-in-law) and Shaila Muralidhar (my wife) has hopefully made a fairly technical set of topics more enjoyable reading. Shaila also deserves high praise for allowing me to use our personal time to finish this project—her patience saved the day.

At the end, there are two mentors to whom I owe the inspiration of undertaking this work—Lester Seigel, who is always there to show me new ways of understanding difficult material (and providing an existential view of topics in finance), and my friend, mentor, coauthor, surrogate father, and constant guide, Franco Modigliani—his constant enthusiasm to learn and share his knowledge (at all hours of the day!) never ceases to amaze me.

Finally, my thanks to the entire team at Stanford University Press, especially Ken McLeod, Kate Wahl, the editorial team of Anita Wagner and Rick Reser, designer James P. Brommer, and Judith Hibbard, as well as the production team at Interactive Composition Corporation, for exceptional work in taking a manuscript with many errors and poor formatting to deliver a high-quality finish.

A. S. M.

FOREWORD

Franco Modigliani

Corporate and public pensions are being reformed worldwide, with an increasing emphasis toward funded systems, whether they are defined benefit or defined contribution, with assets managed by professionals. Other institutional investors too, including country central banks, are increasingly using external managers or mutual fund companies to manage assets. Hence there is a need for guidance on the several decisions these investors have to make, from setting investment policy to hiring the best managers to oversee the management of their assets. This book accomplishes this lofty task.

My early papers on savings used simple models to demonstrate the benefits of setting aside funds to finance a future stream of commitments. This was one of the earliest representations of a funded pension system. As any pension fund administrator can affirm, a fairly sophisticated understanding of finance and economics is required to put these ideas on savings and investment into practice. This book achieves the goal of assisting fund administrators by demonstrating the fine interplay between how much one sets aside during one's working life (contribution policy) and how those monies are invested (investment policy). There has been a tendency to use simple mean-variance asset allocation models to set investment policy. This book demonstrates the need to take into account the benefit stream that has to be financed and the

Franco Modigliani is Institute Professor Emeritus, M. I. T. Sloan School of Management and winner of the Alfred Nobel Prize in Economics (1985).

multiple objectives that have to be satisfied. By incorporating the feedback effects of contribution policy decisions on investment policy, it demonstrates more efficient outcomes. This book also examines the impact of innovative methods of strategic asset allocation, such as the use of leverage and dynamic asset allocation, and debunks the notion that simple derivative strategies can protect clients from major market meltdowns. It also highlights the importance of dynamic contribution policies. A number of these principles have been incorporated in my joint work with Arun on reforming social security systems—a testament to the broad applicability of these principles.

This volume goes further, addressing issues I have examined recently with my granddaughter, Leah Modigliani: how to measure the performance of an investment manager or mutual fund, and more specifically, how to adjust for risk. In this book, my measure of risk-adjusted performance has been extended to account for the unique risks to which participants in the pension industry are exposed. Where principal-agent problems exist (i.e., committee overseeing investment staff or investment staff overseeing external managers), this book demonstrates that adjusting for differences in volatility may be inadequate and that investors need to understand how risks (tracking error) are generated. By explicitly incorporating the risk that managers' performance is not highly correlated with their benchmarks, this book not only develops a risk-adjusted measure consistent with a simple evaluation of skill, but also gives guidance on portfolio construction across active and passive management. Once again, these principles can be applied by any investor and not only by funded defined benefit schemes.

Arun worked as my teaching assistant at the Sloan School of Management between 1989 and 1992 and gathered the academic perspective on capital markets and institutions. However, his practical experiences trading derivatives and managing the investment funds of the World Bank, coupled with his extensive exposure to the asset management function and sophisticated clients in the private sector, have allowed him the opportunity to bring theoretical tools to practical life for the average user. The style of the book is simple, yet the technical reader has access to the chapter appendices where more complicated equations are derived.

This book is a must-read for any investor who seeks to establish simple, yet rigorous processes to manage assets. The case study approach favored here is used to highlight simple applications to the numerous different decisions investors must make, including strategic asset allocation, tactical and manager allocations, risk management, and performance attribution. This contribution may well prove the start of more innovative research in the area of pension fund management.

I

GENERAL OVERVIEW

1

MANAGING INVESTMENT
FUNDS EFFICIENTLY

Arun S. Muralidhar

The key investment issues that institutional investors must focus on are introduced in this chapter. These issues include (1) the need for knowledgeable and experienced personnel, (2) selection and implementation of the correct asset mix for the portfolio, and (3) monitoring performance and risks of the portfolio. Fund administrators have to set a long-term investment policy benchmark that enables them to meet future obligations (manage asset-liability risk) and they must ensure efficient implementation of the investment policy (manage implementation risks). To achieve these objectives, an appropriate organizational structure is required.

OVERVIEW

Global institutional investors include a broad brush of organizations, such as pension funds (both corporate and governmental systems), endowments, life and casualty insurance companies, and central banks. Investment professionals responsible for implementing asset portfolios in any of these organizations face several challenges. On the one hand, there is a paucity of resources—monetary and human capital/head count—due to internal budgetary constraints, yet on the other hand these organizations control vast sums of money.

A number of organizations have sought to leverage their relationships with large investment management companies or consulting companies. The most notable example is GTE Corporation (currently Verizon), which institutional-ized its arrangement with four major investment management "strategic partners."[1] However, sponsors of such investment pools face the problem that only a few individuals in investment management companies have the exper-tise to deal with different types of institutional investors as well as the ability to resolve various investment issues encountered by sponsors. These issues in-clude strategic asset allocation, risk management, portfolio construction, and performance measurement and attribution. Investment management compa-nies also struggle as they face increasing demands from institutional investors, and may be forced into an activity in which they have no comparative advan-tage in an attempt to satisfy large investors.

This book attempts to take on this challenge by sharing my experience, and those of my colleagues, in managing pension portfolios. The analysis in this book is developed largely in the context of pension funds, as the theoretical aspects of pension fund management are clearly articulated. It attempts to show the similarity of various investment management principles adopted by different types of institutional investors. The book highlights critical fund management issues and provides innovative solutions to problems faced by fund administrators. It provides innovative, yet simple, models that institu-tional investors can develop for themselves to measure, monitor, and manage risks and performance, and thereby enable effective decision making on asset allocation, manager selection, and manager retention.

Regardless of the type of investment fund, there are three keys to success: (1) experienced and knowledgeable personnel, (2) selection and implementa-tion of the correct asset mix for the portfolio, and (3) effective monitoring of risk and performance of various investment decisions. In a recent survey of 80 pension fund CEOs, 98 percent cited poor process as a barrier to excel-lence, 48 percent indicated they were affected by inadequate resources, 43 per-cent cited lack of focus or poor mission, and 35 percent cited insufficient skills (Ambachtsheer, Capelle, Scheibelhut 1998). The same survey concluded that improved organization design, effective governance, and clarity of goals and strategic positions would improve pension fund performance.

For any institutional investor, an efficient investment program is critical, as marginal improvements in asset performance can prove to be a much more

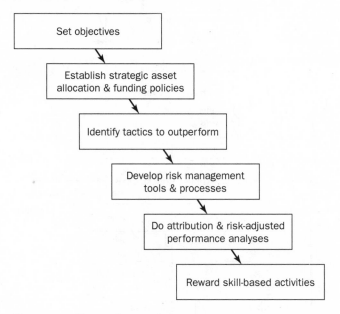

Figure 1.1   Keys to Success

politically viable alternative to increasing contributions or reducing benefits (in a pensions context), increasing government contributions to reserves (central banks), or reducing transfers to university or charitable organizations' budgets (endowments). Efficiency can be viewed from two perspectives: (1) incurring the lowest cost for performing the various functions and (2) reducing the economic cost of the overall organization through surpluses generated by these funds. These two are interlinked, but this chapter focuses on the latter.

The key steps are summarized in Figure 1.1. This book considers innovative approaches to each of these steps, and for simplicity, it assumes that external managers are selected to implement portfolios. To achieve these objectives, however, an appropriate organization structure is required.

GOVERNANCE AND ORGANIZATION STRUCTURE

To ensure effective management of assets, it is crucial that the organization vested with the authority to oversee these assets has the appropriate governance and internal structure. With regard to governance, the structure highlighted

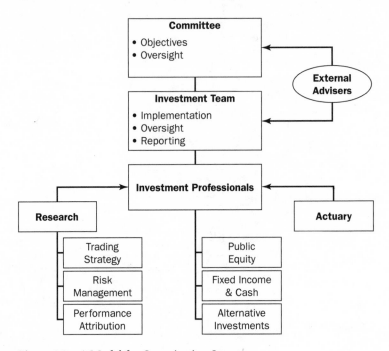

Figure 1.2 A Model for Organization Structure

in Figure 1.2 is a useful model. Ambachtsheer (1997) suggests that the critical aspects to effective governance are knowledgeable trustees, clarity of mission, and a visible, accountable chief investment officer (CIO).

The overall responsibility for developing the long-term asset mix, providing guidelines for investment strategy, and reviewing performance of the fund is that of a board or an oversight committee. It is the responsibility of the investment team to manage the funds to the long-term benchmark within these guidelines. External experts who serve in an advisory group can advise both the oversight committee and investment staff on investment issues. The investment team should include a research group to measure risk and performance and to generate and evaluate trade ideas to assist investment professionals.

This separation of the governance function from actual implementation of the investment function helps to ensure that personal agendas of members of the governing committee are not implemented without acceptable testing of potential returns from such investments. In government organizations, an appropriate structure and the use of external advisory groups could insulate investment decisions from political agendas. These issues are discussed in more detail in Ambachtsheer and Ezra (1998). In addition, the Canadian Pension Plan Board, responsible for investing Canada's pension monies, has developed a very interesting structure. It ensures representation of appropriate groups, selection of competent individuals, and delegation of duties that other country pension systems could learn from.

Composition and Responsibility of Oversight Committee

Clearly, the composition and responsibilities of this group are critical to the success of any pension fund. It is important to make sure all interested parties are represented on the oversight committee (Figure 1.3). In the case of a pension fund, this would include labor, retirees, and employers, and have scope to include other individuals, such as academicians or researchers, with expertise in asset management or pension finance. It is difficult to form an oversight committee in which every member has the same degree of financial sophistication; however, past financial experience of members is important in setting objectives and evaluating the quality of work performed by investment staff. If it is not possible to include external experts in the committee, these individuals could serve on an advisory board.

The major responsibility of the oversight committee is to articulate the objectives of the fund and ensure that the long-term asset mix is selected so as to achieve the objectives of the fund. In the case of a pension fund, this

---

Composition
- Internal (Labor, Employers)
- External (Academics, Researchers, Government)

Responsibility
- Clarify Objectives
- Set Investment Policy
- Approve Funding Amounts
- Monitor Investment Performance

Figure 1.3 Oversight Committee: Composition and Responsibilities

could include minimizing the funding shortfall (i.e., assets insufficient to cover liabilities) or providing acceptable annuities. In addition, the committee should periodically review this policy. The benchmark should be articulated clearly and, at a minimum, should specify the target allocation to each asset class, the underlying market indices for measuring asset performance (e.g., Standard and Poor's [S&P] 500 index for U.S. equities), and the maximum permissible deviations from the target weight. In addition to setting policy, the committee is responsible for laying down broad investment guidelines by which assets are to be managed to this benchmark, reviewing the performance of the investment team in implementing these guidelines, and assessing the risks taken to achieve these results. An example of an effective benchmark is provided later in Table 1.2.

Composition and Responsibility of Investment Team

Ideally, the investment (and research) team is composed of individuals with either an advanced degree or training in economics, finance, or accounting. As indicated earlier, a visible, accountable CIO with vision complements such a team. However, these qualifications are not always necessary as is borne out by investment management companies in which some of the most successful investors have liberal arts backgrounds in history or languages. It is, nevertheless, useful to have at least a few individuals who have quantitative skills, which are required[2] for the analysis of benchmarks, risk, and performance. Finally, in the case of a pension fund, it is useful, but not critical, to have an actuary closely aligned to the investment function. In many pension funds, the actuary reports to the benefits administrator, but as demonstrated later in the book, it is crucial that the actuary ensure that the investment benchmark chosen covers the critical liability risks.[3]

The key responsibility of the investment group is to implement the portfolio as per the guidelines of the oversight committee and to outperform the investment benchmark (Figure 1.4). Equally important, though more mundane, is the task of periodic reporting to the committee on the performance and risks of the fund and achievement of investment objectives. This team also serves the oversight committee by making recommendations on the long-term benchmark, funding policy, investment in new strategies (e.g., private

Composition
- Finance Professionals
- Accountant
- Quantitative Specialists
- Actuaries

Responsibility
- Funding & Investment Recommendations
- Investment Management
- Investment Research & Risk Management
- Performance Evaluation & Reporting

Figure 1.4   Investment Team: Composition and
Responsibilities

equities or hedge funds), and development of innovative investment products
(e.g., derivative strategies); by measuring and monitoring the risks of the investment portfolio; and by evaluating the performance of various investment
decisions.

Many institutions complement the work of internal staff by maintaining a
formal or informal external advisory group composed of finance experts. This
group could include individuals in charge of research or strategic partnerships
at investment management firms with whom business is conducted. This
advisory group could perform useful functions for the oversight committee
and the investment team. Where the financial sophistication of the oversight
committee members is not adequate, training for the committee and the
expertise of the external advisory group could be very useful.[4] Finally, this
advisory group could prove invaluable in directing the investment team to
other organizations with state-of-the-art risk management or performance
evaluation practices. A relatively underutilized resource available to any investment team is the vast community of other institutional investors. The difficulty is to identify institutions sophisticated enough to have implemented
innovative solutions for various investment problems. This is where investment management firms and external advisers are extremely helpful.

The presence of high-level investment professionals is critical to outperforming the long-term benchmark. The difficulty that organizations face is
competitive salaries offered by financial institutions that attract the brightest
minds away from typical salary scales of pension funds and the public sector.

There are positive and negative aspects to this brain drain. The negative is that some of the best professionals are lost to the industry, but on the flip side, an alumni roll that suggests an institution is able to select and train people who become successful can be an attractive recruiting tool. The World Bank's Treasury faces a similar situation: it has been fortunate to hire excellent staff from around the world who realize that success at the bank can translate into better opportunities on Wall Street. More importantly, the bank has been able to retain top talent by delegating substantial responsibility to bright junior staff, who would not get such opportunities elsewhere.

SETTING APPROPRIATE INVESTMENT AND FUNDING POLICIES

In some countries, even developed countries like Japan, a number of privately managed corporate pensions do not have a clearly specified benchmark or investment policy. This has led to poor investments and potentially severe underfunding problems.

There is no dearth of research in support of the fact that investment policy contributes over 80–90 percent of total investment returns.[5] In the United Kingdom, Blake (2000) finds the contribution to total return (from strategic asset allocation) is as high as 99.5 percent. Unfortunately, most funds spend less than 10 percent of their time and effort in determining the benchmark. More importantly, it is critical to set the investment asset mix to ensure that the long-term objectives of the institutional investor are met. One aspect that has been relatively ignored in previous research is the importance of the simultaneous establishment of funding and investment policy. Ambachtsheer and Ezra (1998) emphasize both policies, but many others have only focused on investment policy. Chapters 3, 4, and 5 cover the key aspects of setting an appropriate investment and funding policy and discuss how some innovative extensions allow for significant benefits to investors.

Essentially, the liabilities of any institutional investor may be regarded as the obligations or raison d'etre of the organization. In the context of pensions, a pension fund exists to be able to pay retirees their benefits. Moreover, key variables such as inflation and interest rates affect not only liabilities but also asset returns.

There are two ways to finance future benefits: through future contributions or a *funding/contribution policy* and through future asset returns or *investment policy.* Since these two are so closely interconnected, it is important to understand the implications of any investment policy decision for present and future contributions and vice versa. Figure 1.5 highlights this interplay among liabilities, investment policy, and contribution policy. This chart motivates the recommendation to align the actuary closely with the investment team.

The objectives of a pension fund need to be clearly specified to ensure that they are met over the short- and long-term (Figure 1.6). Chapter 3 addresses these in more detail and demonstrates how oversight committees can be assisted in setting objectives.

On the funding policy side, the two critical objectives for the pension fund would be to maintain an appropriate funded ratio (i.e., the ratio of assets to

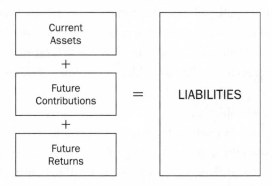

Figure 1.5   The Pension Fund Balance Sheet

Funding Policy
• Funded Ratio (Level & Volatility)
• Contribution Rate (Level & Volatility)

Investment Policy
• Expected Return & Risk
• Performance Relative to Benchmarks
• Performance Relative to Peers
• Guaranteed Rate of Return
• Impact on Net Income

Figure 1.6   Pension Fund Objectives

liabilities), and to maintain a conservative funding policy (i.e., having a stable and preferably declining contribution rate). The reason these are important is that large changes in either the funded status or contributions could lead to a political outcry that no organization would want. Therefore, it is important to measure and monitor the funded ratio in both the short- and long-term. This ratio is affected by changes in liabilities, either from changes in demographics or changes in wage or price inflation, and asset performance. The risk of being severely underfunded because of either poor contribution policy or asset performance is termed asset-liability risk. An additional objective for the sponsor of the fund (e.g., a corporate entity) might be to ensure that pension income (or expense) is at reasonable levels and has minimal volatility. For example, a sudden reduction in pension earnings could affect corporate earnings, thereby affecting the stock price. However, these outcomes depend largely on funding and investment policies.

Pure investment policy objectives could include a targeted rate of return, a targeted level of risk, and performance relative to either peers or the investment benchmark. Hence, it is important to ensure that expected return objectives are also achieved. The key is to select a portfolio of assets that not only achieves these targets but simultaneously minimizes the risk of a shortfall between assets and liabilities.

Researchers have evaluated objectives through a different categorization, but essentially with the same goal of highlighting the complexity of articulating and ranking objectives. Mennis and Clark (1983) distinguish between absolute return strategies (stabilize contributions, cover vested liabilities with assets at the end of some time period, exceed inflation by some target percentage) and relative return objectives (exceed a risk-free rate by a specified amount, exceed some composite market index, exceed the performance of peers). They also highlight investment risk objectives (desirable probability of a low rate of return, desirable probability of stabilizing contributions, acceptable volatility of portfolio, and tolerable decline in asset value for a particular period).

In summary, an investigation into setting a long-term asset allocation involves articulating objectives, understanding the liabilities—which in the

Table 1.1
Objective identification and ranking by oversight committee

Objective	Relative Importance to Committee	Targets
Maximize expected return	First	10%
Other Objectives:		
Asset-Liability Management		
Funded ratio	Second	100%
Contribution rate and volatility	Third	10%
Pension income	Fourth	Maintain
Real rate of return	Fifth	4%
Performance		
Relative to peers	Sixth	±2%
Relative to the benchmark	Seventh	±3%

case of a pension fund are pension benefits or replacement rates (i.e., the ratio of retirement annuity to a measure of salary or a measure of what fraction of income is replaced at retirement)—and identifying asset classes in which investments can be made. Table 1.1 provides an example of how objectives can be articulated and ranked, and Chapter 3 demonstrates how these objectives can be specified.

This hypothetical committee aims to achieve a 10 percent expected return, which in turn will raise the funded ratio. The committee would also like to ensure that the probability the funded ratio declines below 100 percent is minimized. Further, the contribution rate of the sponsor should not rise above 10 percent of salaries, and the annualized real rate of return should exceed 4 percent. Pension income should be maintained at current levels. Such performance should ideally be achieved with an average tracking error (standard deviation of excess returns versus any benchmark) not exceeding 2 percent per annum vis-à-vis a prespecified peer group and an annualized 3 percent tracking error relative to the asset benchmark. The last item specifies the range for tactical asset allocation that the committee is willing to permit. This is clearly a more complicated list of objectives than plans have traditionally articulated, but it attempts to crystallize and rank objectives and place quantitative targets against which the achievement of these goals can be measured. (Chapter 3 discusses the selection of optimal portfolios based on such complex objectives.)

The end result of this process should be a clearly specified asset portfolio that minimizes the risk of not achieving these objectives. In addition, it should provide broad investment guidelines for the investment team to implement.[6] The foregoing discussion may make it appear that the selection of an overall investment benchmark is a fairly easy procedure. This is not so. It usually requires a fairly sophisticated group of individuals to work with the oversight committee to specify, rank, and understand various objectives. For example, another committee could rank outperformance of peers higher than achievement of a real return objective. This need for sophisticated perspectives can be met by soliciting the advice of outside experts.

Constraints and Benchmark Specification

A major issue to be highlighted is investment restrictions that must condition a strategic asset allocation exercise. Four constraints normally affect the average institutional investor: (a) limits to investing in equities; (b) limits to investing in international assets; (c) forced investment in government debt securities; and (d) no leverage. It should be noted that more than one constraint can apply to an investor. For example, for a long time Japanese pension investors were governed by the 5:3:2 rule that required a minimum of 50 percent in government debt, no more than 30 percent in equities, and no more than 20 percent invested abroad.

Even in developed countries (e.g., France and Germany), there may be objections to investing pension fund monies in equity markets; at an aggregate country level, the U.S. Social Security system is one such example. The risk of using only one type of security to manage the risk of volatile liabilities is that unless these assets have characteristics identical to those of the liabilities, the pension funds are exposed to extreme asset-liability risk. In other words, if future cash flows are known, then appropriate bonds can be purchased to immunize liabilities. However, if these cash flows are uncertain, especially because of changes in salary, price, and asset inflation or demographics, fixed income securities or government bonds would be a poor hedge. As finance theory has shown, a more diversified pool of assets may have better properties to meet future liabilities than portfolios invested in just one asset.[7]

With regard to investing abroad, capital or investment controls can often preclude such investment alternatives (e.g., Canada, Switzerland, and Japan). Why is investing abroad so important? Investors are aware that investing abroad is likely to pay off in the long run because of the diversification benefits of investing in opportunities not perfectly correlated to the domestic market. In addition, where local markets are small and illiquid, changes in investment policy will have an enormous impact on local markets. For example, investing in the Canadian equity market was effectively a view on just one stock—Nortel, Inc. Hence investing abroad would take some pressure off local markets. However, investing abroad requires foreign exchange, which may be a scarce commodity, and initial purchases of foreign currency could put pressure on the local currency if these capital outflows are not offset by compensating inflows. It is not an enviable position to be in, having to decide whether your pension funds should invest abroad, but clearly a gradualist approach would be the best way to tackle this issue. Chapter 5 examines the impact of constraints on international investing for Canadian investors and demonstrates the cost of such constraints.

The combination of constraints on equity investment and international investing is implicitly or explicitly a means by which regulators ensure that funds invest in government securities. Currently, a number of countries are relaxing these rules, but for a long time it was the practice for government bonds to be the only investment vehicle for pension funds because of the perceived safety from default risk, with less regard to the achievement of a retirement wealth objective.

Another common constraint is the lack of leverage either in strategic asset allocation or in the implementation of specific portfolios. Laws, or perceptions that leverage is risky, often preclude it. However, recent research has demonstrated that leverage can actually reduce risk both on a strategic and on a tactical basis. Chapters 4 and 9 cover this in greater detail.

At the end of the day, regardless of whether constraints are internal (i.e., created by the oversight committee) or external and imposed by regulators, it is important to arrive at some estimate of the impact of such constraints on

Table 1.2
An example of a good benchmark

Asset Class	Benchmark	Target (%)	Range (%)
U.S. equities	Wilshire 5000	50	40–60
Non-U.S. equities	MSCI EAFE	20	10–30
U.S. fixed income	Salomon BIG	10	5–15
Non-U.S. fixed income	Salomon World	5	0–10
Private equities	Brinson Partners	6	2–8
Real estate	NCREIF Property	6	3–10
Cash	6-month LIBOR	3	0–5

the optimal portfolio. It is also beneficial to ensure that when such regulatory, legislative, economic, or political controls are lifted, the long-term benchmark is adjusted to take advantage of such opportunities.

Assuming that the pension plan has been able to identify a long-term asset mix, with clearly articulated target investment levels, it is critical to specify ranges around these levels.[8] Ranges are important for two reasons: (1) to prevent constant rebalancing to the benchmark arising from market movements, and (2) to facilitate tactical asset allocation. These can be viewed either negatively as constraints or positively as guidance from the committee as to the desirability of minimizing cost while creating opportunities for returns. More important, the market indices by which performance of a specific asset class are measured need to be clearly articulated. Fund administrators have some discretion in this area, and the discussion in Chapter 6 covers some interesting innovations that can be considered for more cost-effective implementation. Table 1.2 provides an example of a clearly articulated investment benchmark for a typical U.S.-based pension plan.

EFFICIENT IMPLEMENTATION OF INVESTMENT POLICY

One of the most important, yet least attractive, steps in effective implementation of investment policy is to ensure reliable custodianship of all assets purchased on behalf of the fund, rather than angling for fancy asset allocation models or financial experts. The reason is that good custody arrangements, whether through a local or global custodian, ensure the security of the assets

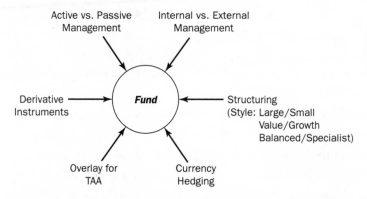

Figure 1.7   Implementation of Investment Policy

purchased on behalf of the fund. Once assets are safeguarded from fraud and theft, a good custodian can be very useful in ensuring that basic accounting and reporting is performed. At a higher level of sophistication, the custodian can be used to ensure guideline compliance, performance attribution, and risk management reporting.

Knowing that assets are secure, the investment team next needs to develop tactics to implement the investment policy. These tactics, depicted in Figure 1.7, range from the choice between active and passive management and the choice between internal and external management, to style and sector biases, the choice between balanced and specialist mandates, currency hedging, use of futures overlays for tactical asset allocation (TAA), and the use of derivatives (e.g., surplus options; derivatives are discussed in Chapters 4 and 6).[9]

The next two subsections focus on the decision between active and passive management, and on the decision between investing internally and using external managers.

Active Versus Passive Management

What is meant by active versus passive investment and how does one decide between these alternatives? In a nutshell, passive investment is the process by which an investor creates a portfolio that exactly replicates a market index. For example, to replicate the S&P 500 U.S. equity index, the investor would buy all 500 securities in the S&P index in the exact proportion of the index. An active investor, on the other hand, could choose to select securities not included in the index and weight them by any proportion. The passive portfolio, if maintained accurately, would produce returns largely identical to that of the benchmark, whereas one would expect the active portfolio to outperform the index over the long term.

There are different degrees of active and passive management, and combinations of the two are feasible and desirable. Most managers charge meager fees for passive investments and much higher fees for active investments. The risk of an active portfolio is that there are periods when it underperforms the benchmark and other periods when excess returns are quite volatile. Philips (1999) indicates that the active decision should be based on inefficiencies in markets, and that the cost of active management should be low enough to warrant trying and depends on whether it is possible to find competent active managers. In many asset classes it is difficult to find competent and consistent managers. In such asset classes, sponsors may prefer passive or enhanced index managers. Alternatively, they may choose to rotate managers based on some tactical analysis. This choice between active and passive management has been hotly debated by various product providers and academicians. Chapters 9–12 cover this in greater detail.

Internal Versus External Management

The choice between internal and external management is another critical issue that is not mutually exclusive. In internal management, all investment decisions are made in-house, whereas in external management, in-house staff select the portfolio and investment managers. The advantage of internal management is that investment returns can be achieved at a lower cost and with greater control (Ward 1999). However, in public sector enterprises, managers who perform well are often recruited into the private sector. Implementing passive portfolios can be handled internally and it is a good way to develop investment skills in-house.

Several institutional investors in the United States that have the resources to compensate their staff adequately have found that internal managers often outperform external managers at a lower cost. However, it is useful to use external managers as a benchmark for internal staff. It could be valuable to expose internal staff to alternative investment strategies. This model is followed by large institutions and central banks.

Another benefit of using external managers is to leverage the research capabilities of external managers in the areas of asset allocation and risk management. Chapters 9–12 focus largely on tools to help investors evaluate the performance of external managers, though the principle is largely the same for internal managers. From an implementation point of view, it tends to be easier to track internal managers on a daily basis and more difficult to track external managers due to lack of proximity.

Finally, either choice has agency problems: namely, the objectives of the agent chosen to manage assets on behalf of a principal should be appropriately aligned with those of the principal.

MONITORING PERFORMANCE AND RISKS OF INVESTMENT DECISIONS

A pension plan is exposed to two broad risks; namely, (1) asset-liability risk, the risk that the portfolio selected by the oversight committee does not meet funding policy and investment policy targets, and (2) implementation risks, the risks that internal staff and external managers underperform their respective benchmarks. Gibson (1997) refers to these risks as Level I and Level II risks, respectively. For funds that hire external managers, the implementation risk can be subdivided into tactical and active risk as demonstrated in Figure 1.8.

	Asset-Liability Risk (Committee)	Tactical Risk (Staff)	Active Risk (Managers)
Measure	Funded Ratio/ Contribution Rate	Attribution & Value-at-Risk Models	Tracking Error & Value-at-Risk Models
Monitor	Annually	Monthly	Monthly
Manage	Strategic Allocation	Tactical Allocations	Manager Allocations

Figure 1.8   Pension Fund Risks

Asset-liability risk should be monitored annually by reviewing the funded status and implications for funding policy. If the risks are too high, the committee must review whether the investment policy benchmark is still appropriate. Chapter 3 discusses models to measure, monitor, and manage this risk. Implementation risks should be monitored more frequently and managed through tactical shifts. Models to measure these risks are provided in Chapters 7 and 8, and techniques to manage them form the backbone of this book.

Monitoring performance is as important a function as any other and is dealt with in greater depth in Chapter 9. It diagnoses the success and failure of investment strategies implemented to determine the action that needs to be taken in the future. Performance needs to be monitored frequently, at least monthly (in some cases daily), by the investment team and reported at least quarterly to the oversight committee. Performance reports should include the performance of the actual portfolio versus the benchmark over short and long periods (say 3 to 5 years), on a before- and after-fee basis. In addition, performance should be measured on an absolute and risk-adjusted basis. Chapters 10 and 11 extend this framework and discuss how the performance of multiple manager portfolios can be evaluated. These chapters provide innovative approaches for manager selection and retention based on the skill of the managers.

Staff can develop the format for reports, with the actual production of the reports delegated to the custodian. Reports to the oversight committee should be simple and concise, whereas internal reports can be more detailed. The second aspect of these reports is performance attribution or analysis to understand sources of value added relative to the benchmark.

For example, a pension fund could have a quarterly return of 5.5 percent and could be ranked the top-performing pension fund for similar size. What accounts for this good performance? The quick analysis in Figure 1.9 reveals the following. The benchmark returned 2.0 percent, internal staff added another 0.5 percent through tactical asset allocation and other strategies, internal staff added another 1.0 percent by picking the correct managers, and the external managers beat their benchmarks by 2.0 percent, for a total return

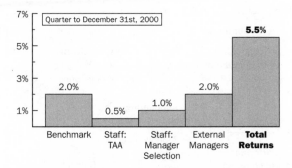

Figure 1.9 Performance Attribution: A Simple Example

of 5.5 percent during the quarter. The sponsor must perform this analysis down to the level of individual managers and accordingly rectify negative factors by changing strategies or terminating managers.

A record of good asset performance should enable a sponsor to reduce the contributions or offer higher replacement rates. Hence, monitoring performance is a critical function. For those funds in which peer comparison is important, Chapter 14 discusses the shortcomings of current methodologies. It proposes a new methodology that ensures that the peer universe is appropriate and that there is adequate information in the analysis.

OTHER IMPLEMENTATION ISSUES

Other important implementation issues include reviewing the contracts and guidelines for managers. It should be emphasized that the development of contracts and guidelines has been an area in which staff must put considerable effort. The contract and guidelines are the legally sound way to ensure that the mandates implemented by external managers are in line with the risk tolerance of the oversight committee and that adequate indemnification is provided should there be fraud or negligence by the external manager. In addition, these contracts should specify requirements for risk management, accounting reports, and most important, performance reporting to staff

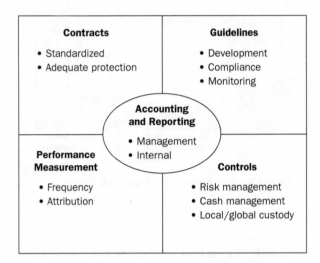

Figure 1.10 Implementation Issues for Each Manager
and for the Entire Portfolio

(Figure 1.10). Mashayekhi and Muralidhar (1996) highlight these issues and introduce innovative approaches to risk control and performance attribution in the context of currency programs.

In reviewing one fund, an advisory group discovered that the investment team received performance reports only quarterly. Typically, external managers have to report the performance of the fund and reasons for both under- or outperformance within a few business days of the end of each month. If performance lags behind benchmarks either for the entire portfolio or for specific managers, then corrective measures can be taken by changing allocations or replacing managers. An important point is that risk and performance monitoring requires fairly sophisticated computer software. Given the importance of risk management and performance evaluation to the overall stability of the pension program, at least one staff member should be designated and trained to perform this function effectively. Chapters 7 and 8 demonstrate how risk should be evaluated at an overall fund level and then provide tools to allow sponsors to decompose risks from various investment decisions. This decomposition can be conducted at any level—asset class, manager, or even security.

SUMMARY

By highlighting issues encountered by fund administrators, this chapter lays the foundation for the rest of the book. To recapitulate, fund administrators must ensure that governance and organization structures separate the oversight committee from the implementation function and set clear responsibilities and goals for each group. The oversight committee must then frame a long-term investment policy based on an explicit statement of objectives. This policy must be reviewed periodically to ensure that balance sheet risks are managed. The investment staff should implement the portfolio by using an appropriate mix of tactics. Finally, the investment staff should monitor performance and risks to ensure that the funds are managed efficiently.[10] Clearly, all these functions require competent staff and regular training as the state of the art is evolving daily. Following these simple steps is likely to lead to the achievement of objectives and significant gains for the institutional investor or plan sponsor.

CENTRAL BANK RESERVES MANAGEMENT—

A SIMILAR PERSPECTIVE

The management of central bank reserves is very similar in principle to the pension fund—though more interesting and less researched. The reserves of the central bank are maintained to defend the domestic currency or provide valuable foreign exchange to pay for imports or service debt. Therefore, the objective for the reserve management team is to ensure that the assets are invested in safe and liquid instruments. However, if the level of reserves falls below a particular level, the reserves should be topped up, which may or may not be expensive for the country depending on its credit status. In addition, central banks in emerging markets may like to borrow long-term so that they do not need to return to the market frequently and at a time that is disadvantageous. This, in turn, creates a host of problems as they then incur negative carry between the borrowing rate and the investment rate (credit spread), and a duration mismatch between long-term borrowing and short-term investing.

Therefore, although a higher level of reserves may appear to provide greater credibility in terms of being able to defend a currency, it is expensive to do so. Hence central banks need to optimize the timing, size, and duration of borrowings and simultaneously optimize the size and investment strategy of the reserves pool. The endowment problem is not very different: administrators have to simultaneously optimize multiple, competing objectives. These competing objectives for a central bank are highlighted in Figure A1.1.1.

Return and Cost
- Maximize Expected Return
- Minimize Volatility of Returns (Capital Preservation)
- Minimize Cost of Reserves
- Minimize Volatility of Cost of Reserves
- Cover Central Bank Expenses

Uses
- Guarantee Debt Coverage
- Guarantee Import Coverage
- Ability to Intervene in Currency Markets

Figure A1.1.1 Objectives for Management of Central Bank Reserves

Central banks also have unusual constraints—most notably the forced holding of gold, even for developed countries, and no investment in equities (with the exception of the Hong Kong Monetary Authority). This makes the job of reserves management and optimal benchmark selection extremely challenging and interesting. However, the implementation of these mandates is largely similar for central banks and pension funds, especially as central banks increasingly hire investment firms to manage reserves.

NOTES

1. For further details see the three Harvard Business School case studies entitled "GTE Corporation (A), (B), (C)," listed in the References at the end of the book.

2. See Logue and Rader (1997), Chapter 14.

3. For other key functions of the actuary see Mennis and Clark (1983).

4. See Ambachtsheer and Ezra (1998), Chapters 4–7.

5. See Brinson, Singer, Beebower (1991).

6. Some authors (Bailey 1997) would go as far as to suggest that the investment policy should not only specify mission, risk tolerance, investment objectives, and policy asset mix, but also specify investment management structure and performance evaluation.

7. See Logue and Rader (1997), Chapter 3.

8. Tsumagari (1998) presents a very interesting model to establish ranges around the long-term allocation.

9. See Logue and Rader (1997), Chapter 11 on the internal versus external debate; Ambachtsheer and Ezra (1998), Chapter 10 on the active versus passive, internal versus external, and specialist versus balanced debates; Kehrer (1991) on active versus passive and TAA; and Nakovick (1999) on TAA, global multiasset managers, and derivatives.

10. See also Logue and Rader (1997), Chapter 14.

2

THE SIMILARITIES OF DEFINED BENEFIT AND DEFINED CONTRIBUTION SCHEMES

Arun S. Muralidhar

Two main points are the focus of this chapter. First, a combination of defined benefit (DB) and defined contribution (DC) plans is preferable to stand-alone DB or DC plans. Each plan has its own characteristics—and advantages—and a combination of the two (hybrid plans) is good for both employers and employees.

Second, although DB and DC plans look very different with respect to risk sharing (i.e., who bears the risk), the process adopted for investments is similar. The individual or group bearing the risk is the one that makes the investment decisions. The key point is, in all types of plans, the process used by the decision maker to come up with an investment policy is identical. The differences, if any, between the investment policy of a DB and a DC plan come about due to the differences in time horizon, objectives, and risk appetite of the participants, not because of the process. In addition, the process by which managers are selected and evaluated is identical across both schemes.

OVERVIEW

The popular press has recently carried extensive discussions on the privatization of social security schemes, and a number of companies are beginning to

Adapted from Sudhir Krishnamurthi, Arun S. Muralidhar, and Ronald van der Wouden. "Pension Investment Decisions." Investment Management Department Working Paper 98-001, The World Bank, May 1998.

reform their own pension systems. At a country or company level, there is essentially a choice between two types of pension plans: defined benefit (DB) and defined contribution (DC) (including provident fund type plans).

Defined Benefit Plans

In the DB pension plan, participants and/or sponsors make contributions, and these contributions could change over time. The scheme then provides a defined benefit—a *prespecified annuity* in either absolute currency or as a fraction of a measure of salary (e.g., 50 percent of final salary or the average of the last five years of salary). The guaranteed pension benefit could be in either real or nominal terms. The ratio of annuity or benefit to a measure of salary is known as the replacement rate.

Defined Contribution Plans

Under the DC scheme, participants and/or sponsors make *prespecified contributions*. These contributions could be specified in either absolute currency or as a fraction of a measure of salary (e.g., 5 percent of annual pretax salary). The participants invest the contributions in assets. However, the pension depends entirely on the asset performance of accumulated contributions. As a result, two individuals with identical contributions could receive very different pensions. Bader (1995), Bodie, Marcus, and Merton (1988), and Blake (2000) provide more detailed descriptions of DB and DC plans.

Funding Methods

There are several ways in which DB or DC plans can be funded. In general, country social security systems are pay-as-you-go (PAYG) DB schemes, which tax current participants to pay retiree benefits. However, corporate or occupational DB or DC schemes tend to be funded (both partially and fully). Funding requires allocating funds prior to retirement in order to service future liabilities. Some researchers (Logue and Rader 1997) suggest that DC plans are always fully funded. This assumes retirees are indifferent to the annuity they receive, which is clearly not true. Other researchers (Muralidhar and Van der Wouden 1998b) have suggested that DC plans are underfunded if the assets in the plan are insufficient to deliver a target replacement rate.

Outline

Essentially, in a DC plan, the participant bears the risk that the pension is below a target level. In a DB plan, because the benefit is guaranteed, the sponsor bears the risk of poor asset performance.[1] Though these schemes may appear to be very different, there are a number of similarities, as demonstrated in Krishnamurthi, Muralidhar, and Van der Wouden (1998a).

This chapter draws extensively from the cited paper and makes two main points: First, a combination of DB and DC plans is preferable to a wholly DB or a wholly DC plan. Both DB and DC plans have their own characteristics— and advantages—and a combination of the two (a hybrid plan) is good for employers and employees.[2] This has also been highlighted by other researchers such as Bodie, Merton, and Samuelson (1992). Second, though DB and DC plans look quite different with respect to risk sharing (i.e., who bears the risk), the process adopted for selecting optimal investment portfolios is similar.[3] The individual or group bearing the risk is the one that makes the investment decisions. As a result, some general finance principles broadly apply to both types of plans. The differences, if any, between the investment policy of a DB and DC plan occur due to the differences in time horizon, objectives, and risk appetite of the participants, not because of the process. In addition, as demonstrated in Chapters 9–11, the process by which managers are selected and managed is similar across these plans.

It is important to pay attention to these generalized conclusions in either designing or managing pension plans, as *they are likely to improve pension outcomes without direct monetary costs.* The most important point is that the appropriate investment policy for a DB or participant in a DC plan will have to be developed on an asset-liability basis. Time and effort spent on such modeling will more than pay for themselves through increased efficiency gains.

ISSUES CONCERNING PENSION PLANS

Why Have Pension Plans?

Even before the appropriate form of pension plans is debated and the similarity of the investment policy process is traced, it is worthwhile to record the reasons for the existence of pension plans. There is a plethora of literature on the subject, and researchers have undertaken a wide range of empirical studies (World Bank 1994). For example, Logue and Rader (1997) suggest that plans can be set up for insurance against uncertainty about retirement income, to create tax-efficient means of saving, and to create motivating contracts. These conclusions may be restated under three main headings.

First, *redistribution and social insurance* have proved to be particularly valid for countries. This is equivalent to a social obligation to ensure that all their citizens, especially the old, have resources to meet their basic needs. Pension schemes are also a redistribution mechanism for transferring resources from the well-to-do to the poorer segments of society. This argument suggests a means-tested safety-net scheme with DB characteristics.

Second, *private savings should be encouraged.* As economic theory has demonstrated, countries need savings for capital formation, and individuals need savings to support themselves in the nonearning phase of their lives.[4] Using a variety of incentives (such as tax credits and deferrals) and mandated contribution rules, governments are able to encourage citizens to step up their savings rates. These tend to be plans managed by individuals.

Third, *the desired behavior is induced.* At a macro level, a pension scheme allows individuals to adopt a life-cycle model of consumption.[5] This involves saving during one's youth in order to provide for one's old age. At a company level, pensions are a deferred wage and payable only if the employee exhibits desirable characteristics such as integrity and honesty. In addition, companies are able to induce behavior by offering matching contributions to ensure that their employees can retire without anxiety. Pensions can be structured so as to attract employees to join an organization, stay longer (typical corporate DB), retire early, and so on. Regardless of the reason, in principle, the philosophy behind a funded pension scheme is to set aside funds today, and invest them appropriately, to support some future consumption (liability).

In addition to pension plans, organizations may adopt other plans for retiree benefits, including retiree medical health plans. Chapter 3 demonstrates that retiree medical plans are a more complex version of the average pension plan.

Investment Characteristics

There is a perception, since DB and DC plans appear to be different, that different approaches to establish investment policies need to be taken. For example, Logue and Rader (1997) argue that relative to DB plans, DC plans are mortal, subject to taxes, exposed to inflation, and do not change with changes in interest rates. It will be demonstrated that these differences make liability modeling more difficult, but do not necessarily affect the process. It is important to understand the investment characteristics of DB and DC plans to better appreciate their relative pros and cons and, in turn, the logic of hybrid plans (Figure 2.1). Bader (1995) presents a detailed list of the advantages of DB and DC plans from the perspective of plan sponsors and participants.

DB plans pool investment risk across a large number of individuals of different ages and with different time horizons. Therefore, there is pooling of risk within a cohort and across cohorts. The plan sponsor who bears the investment risk of the plan has a much longer time frame and a much higher risk-bearing capacity than individuals in the plan. In other words, in a DC plan the time horizon is the life of one individual, whereas in DB plans, the time horizon is much longer, if not infinite. For these reasons, DB plans on average can take on more risk, generate higher returns, and their asset allocation

Defined Benefits	Defined Contributions
• Pools investment risk	• Allows individual to select the investment policy
• Plan sponsor bears risk	• Individual bears risk
• Provides stable benefits	• Enables better matching of cash flows with needs
• Provides insurance against longevity	• Allows bequeathing of wealth
Combination makes sense for both sponsor and individual.	

Figure 2.1   Investment Characteristics of Defined Benefit and Defined Contribution Plans

policy should change more slowly than those of individual plans. However, it appears that in the United States, DC plans are more invested in equities and international assets than DB plans.[6] DC plans, by contrast, enable individuals to tailor their portfolio to the risk they wish to bear and to participate in all the gains and losses of their plan.[7] Pooling assets suggests that investment management fees will be much lower in DB plans, though plan sponsors will need to maintain larger investment teams than in DC plans.[8]

DB plans provide stable retirement income based on salary as opposed to DC plans that offer less predictable retirement incomes because of the dependence on investment performance. However, by their very nature, DB plans are less flexible (i.e., individuals cannot reduce contributions) and unresponsive to meeting the cash flow needs of individuals before and after retirement.

DB plans provide insurance for longevity. The possibility of the money running out before the individual dies is largely nonexistent unless the sponsor defaults and there is no insurance coverage. Insurance is usually provided by agencies such as the Pension Benefit Guarantee Corporation (PBGC) in the United States. However, individuals who contribute during their entire lifetime and die soon after retirement will not have had the opportunity to leave a pool of funds for their heirs. DC plans do not make provision for insurance, but bequeathing monies to heirs in the event of premature death is possible only in DC plans.

Their differing investment characteristics render a mix of DB and DC plans ideal for both companies (countries) and their employees (citizens), as very few individuals are likely to be satisfied by the characteristics of any one type of plan. For example, Bodie, Marcus, and Merton (1988) argue that a hybrid minimum floor plan, where the DB is a floor, may dominate any one plan. Further, Muralidhar and Van der Wouden (1998a) recommend that countries implement contributory defined benefit (CDB) plans in which the contributions of the participant grow at a guaranteed real rate of return (guaranteed by the government). This plan engenders many of the advantages of DC plans (funded, individual accounts, the possibility of borrowing), and at the same time provides insurance through the guarantee. They also suggest that individuals should complement such plans by investing additional funds in DC plans for supplementary savings. The corporate analog to the CDB plan is the cash balance plan.

It is important to note that choosing between DB or DC plans also has noninvestment implications. For example, DC plans require a well-educated, financially literate group to ensure that replacement rates are adequate at retirement, whereas DB plans need strong governance structures to ensure sufficient funds, that are soundly invested to meet future liabilities. The relative mix of DB and DC plans is likely to be employer and country specific. For the interested reader, Muralidhar (1999c) provides a more theoretically rigorous approach to why hybrid pension schemes are preferable at the country level.

INVESTMENT POLICY PROCESS FOR DB AND DC SCHEMES

The Process

Chapter 1 introduced the pension funding equation (Figure 1.5). Simply put, the sum total of present assets, future contributions (funding policy), and future asset returns (investment policy) must equal present and future liabilities. To maintain the stability of a pension fund, regardless of whether it is for an individual (i.e., DC) or a group of individuals (i.e., DB), appropriate funding and investment policies need to be developed.

Both DB and DC plans have to make investment policy decisions, and allocate their assets across different securities and instruments. The only difference is the decision maker. In the former, it is a centralized expert group, whereas in the DC plan it is the individual. In either case, it is important that the process of arriving at the appropriate investment policy is disciplined. The key is to identify the liabilities and articulate a strategy to meet the objectives of the individual in DC plans and the sponsor in DB plans.

Identifying the appropriate investment policy is a four-step process, as shown in Figure 2.2. The first two steps, modeling liabilities and setting objectives, are specific to the plan or individual, and the manner in which they are modeled can vary between a DB and a DC plan. The next two steps, modeling asset classes and future returns, are more market-related and unlikely to vary significantly within the same regulatory environment in the same country for either DB or DC plans. This chapter examines the first two stages to demonstrate the similarities of both plans. This sets the stage for the remaining chapters that are written largely in the context of a DB

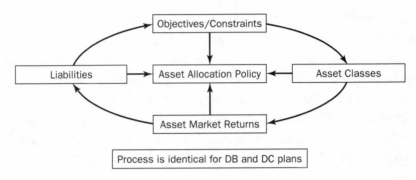

Figure 2.2 The Investment Policy Process

pension plan, but whose application to a DC plan is a simple extension of the same.

In theory, the specification of liabilities is straightforward, but in actual practice it is not so. For corporate pension plans, well-trained actuaries are needed and actuarial models can be very complex. For participants in DC pension schemes, there has recently been a proliferation of Web-based products that help individuals chart their future liability to account for uncertainties, inflation, and tax issues.[9] In addition, getting decision makers to explicitly define their objectives and articulate risk-return trade-offs is a challenge. Time is required to educate the decision makers to understand their choices and the consequences of choosing one objective or target over another. These are some of the practical difficulties faced by investors in the investment policy process.

Liabilities

The fundamental reason for determining a funding/contribution policy and an investment policy is to ensure sufficient assets to meet liabilities. A DB plan has to pay benefits to the current retirees and has outstanding obligations to participants in the plan (future retirees) who are accruing certain benefits rights. Since there are many current and projected participants in a DB plan, it is possible to identify the plan's liability at any future point. Therefore, if administrators choose to have fully funded DB plans, they must achieve projected minimum asset levels at any given future point. In a DC plan,

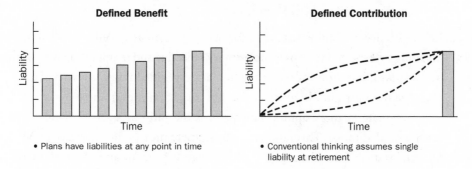

Figure 2.3 Liabilities in DB and DC Plans

conventional thinking assumes a single liability at retirement. This liability is the annuity (replacement rate) or the present value of retirement payments that would be sufficient to ensure the individual a certain standard of living after retirement.

At first glance, the DB and DC structures may seem totally different. The DB structure appears to have multiperiod targets and the DC structure appears to have a single target wealth that must be achieved on the date of retirement. For example, the current offering of Web-based software evaluates DC asset allocation strategies assuming that the goal is to achieve a terminal replacement rate. However, it is more realistic to assume that each individual participant in a DC plan has, at intermediate points prior to retirement, specific targets for retirement assets (Figure 2.3). These targets are levels that make the individual comfortable about reaching a desired replacement rate with a particular level of risk of falling short of this target. These targets are naturally different for each individual, but the role of the institution offering the DC plan is to give people guidance as to which targets are realistic and desirable and how they can be achieved. Increasingly, models for making such evaluations are being developed and will gradually offer such intermediate targets. In fact, Financial Engines™ has patented software that allows individuals to adopt a less sophisticated variant of this structure.

DB and DC plans both impose liabilities at each stage of an individual's life. Hence, from the perspective of liabilities, DB and DC plans may be perceived as largely similar.

Objectives of DB and DC Plans

In the absence of liabilities, an investor operates in an asset-only framework. Maximizing expected returns is the primary objective and maintaining volatility (standard deviation) of returns within a prespecified range is a secondary objective or constraint. In an asset-liability context, however, these measures are inadequate. A more appropriate target is the ratio of assets to liabilities (or the funded ratio). This ratio is an appropriate measure for indicating the financial status of the plan/individual (see Figure 2.4). For an individual in a DC plan, the funded ratio will be the ratio of the expected replacement rate to the targeted replacement rate. A funded ratio of 1 or higher indicates good financial status in a DB plan (in the DC case, it is a replacement rate equal to or greater than target), which indicates that the plan is able to pay all obligations, present and future. A funded ratio substantially lower than 1 indicates a bad financial situation, which must be avoided as it would require drastic remedial actions, including large increases in contributions. Unlike Logue and Rader (1997), this approach suggests that DC plans would be underfunded if the projected benefit were less than the target.

In a multiperiod asset-liability framework, intermediate funding targets and acceptable contributions rates act as subobjectives and add complexity to the problem. Plan sponsors want to ensure a healthy financial status during existence of the plan. A subobjective would be to minimize the risk or the probability that assets are lower than liabilities (or a funding ratio less than 1). Another subobjective would be to ensure optimal contribution policy for the participants, thereby minimizing the level of contributions and year-to-year volatility of these contributions.

Figure 2.4   Objectives of Both DB and DC Plans

Chapter 1 provided an example of how objectives can be expressed, along with target values (Table 1.1). These objectives are the same for an individual in a DC plan and administrators in a DB plan, and risk can be defined as not achieving specific target values.

Management of Assets

There are two sets of tools currently available to investors to select managers or mutual funds to meet their investment objectives. The first group attempts to solve the asset allocation and manager/fund selection problem simultaneously. One example of this would be the services of Financial Engines™.[10] This is a service offered to DC plan participants. Although the basics underlying the model are patent protected and confidential, it appears that an attempt is made to forecast relationships between funds and key asset classes. Thereafter, the models project future asset class returns (and thereby future portfolio performance of mutual funds) to determine the feasibility of achieving a specific retirement wealth goal. This process assumes that the relationships between funds and asset class benchmarks are stable, which may not be true with manager changes at mutual fund companies and style drifts. The efficacy of a mutual fund or portfolio of funds is established by whether or not an investment/retirement goal is achieved.

The second approach is more popular and even used by large institutions that manage defined benefit funds. In this process, first an optimal asset allocation is determined using an asset-liability model or based on the recommendations of an investment adviser. It is generally believed that asset allocation accounts for approximately 90 percent of the investment return. Thereafter, the investor seeks the best fund managers for these asset class allocations. In such a situation, the asset allocation decision provides the anchor to achieve the target retirement wealth and the selection of funds aims at providing a return higher (and with potentially lower risk) than that of the benchmark. We assume that this is the process used by investors as it is the most prevalent method for managing defined benefit and defined contribution portfolios.

Differences Between DB and DC Plans

This chapter has demonstrated that the investment policy process for pension funds is similar for DB and DC plans because the process for specifying liabilities and setting objectives is similar. However, there are some differences between a DC and DB plan that will affect the outcomes of investment policy.

Given that a DB plan can be viewed as the composite of many individual plans, with new entrants joining regularly after the plan is initiated, the time horizon is longer than individual DC plans. As a result, the risk-return trade-off will change more slowly in DB plans, as DC plans mature at a faster rate. This effect will influence the investment policy and the ability to take risk will decrease more rapidly in a DC plan than in a DB plan.

Generational risk sharing in DB plans makes it possible for such plans to bear higher risk and generate higher expected returns. Generational risk sharing includes the intergeneration effect and the intrageneration effect (or the ability to share risk between generations and within a generation). This generational risk sharing makes an efficient DB plan more socially optimal (from an investment point of view) than a DC alternative. There is a variant of the DC plan called a provident fund (PF), popular in Commonwealth countries. Under a PF scheme, individual contributions are pooled and participants are paid an annual dividend, which is usually the rate of return on the assets.

Provident funds also have some of the generational risk-sharing attributes prevalent in DB plans. Consequently, if structured appropriately, PFs could be more optimal than individual DC plans from a macro investment perspective. The two main disadvantages of PFs are (1) individuals bearing the risk are usually disconnected from the decision makers and have no control over the level of risk taken, and (2) participants are unable to choose their investment policies. This disadvantage can be addressed to some extent by offering a series of subfunds within a PF framework, with each subfund offering a different risk profile (also called life-cycle funds targeted to different age cohorts).

SUMMARY

Hybrid plans are better than either DB or DC plans. This is because each plan has its advantages and disadvantages and it is rare for a participant to be entirely satisfied with the characteristics of any one plan. In most developed countries, individuals have access to a social security or corporate DB plan and, in addition, have private savings equivalent to a DC scheme. Hence, current political moves to replace country DB systems with DC systems may actually leave participants worse off as they will lose the benefits of the hybrid scheme.

A more important factor is that the investment policy process is the same for both DB and DC plans. The next chapter highlights the process by which an entity establishes an asset allocation strategy. However, the objectives, time horizon, and liabilities make the actual asset allocation different across plans and over time. Finally, the method through which managers are selected and evaluated to manage specific asset pools is identical and is covered in detail in later chapters.

NOTES

1. Muralidhar and Van der Wouden (1998b) demonstrate how the risks of a DB plan and a DC plan can be evaluated when both have the same target replacement rate.

2. The same would be true for country pension systems.

3. Clearly, pay-as-you-go systems are not likely to face these issues unless they run surpluses, in which case some of these insights apply.

4. Modigliani and Ando (1963) and Modigliani and Brumberg (1954).

5. See Modigliani and Ando (1963).

6. See Mantel and Bowers (1999).

7. Blake (2000) states that "[a] DB scheme is invested in a portfolio containing: the underlying assets (and so, in part, a DC scheme) *plus* a put option *minus* a call option on these assets."

8. Blake (2000) examines other noninvestment related differences such as portability loss and cost of annuities. This paper finds that in the United Kingdom, total contributions into DC schemes tend to be much lower than with DB schemes.

9. See for example www.Financialengines.com.

10. Other companies such as M-Power offer similar services, but Financial Engines seems to enjoy the most press because of its affiliation with William Sharpe, a 1990 Nobel laureate in economics.

II

THE IMPORTANCE OF
ASSET-LIABILITY MANAGEMENT:
THREE CASE STUDIES

3

AN ASSET-LIABILITY ANALYSIS
WITH IMPLICATIONS FOR
SETTING OBJECTIVES

Arun S. Muralidhar

Overseers of pension funds, insurance companies, endowments, and central banks often use an asset-only analysis to invest liquid funds. These strategies are very likely to be suboptimal for the solvency of the fund. This chapter provides a framework for developing an optimal investment strategy by accounting for the multiple objectives (often driven by liability considerations) of fiduciaries of such funds. It highlights asset-liability considerations to assist decision makers in setting objectives and adopting appropriate investment and funding policies to protect surpluses.

OVERVIEW

The key purpose of this chapter is to assist with setting objectives and establishing investment benchmarks. The asset-liability analysis of a plan discussed in this chapter attempts to relate the choice of objectives to the asset allocation for the plan. It is based on work highlighted in Krishnamurthi, Muralidhar, and Van der Wouden (1998b), and seeks to explain the interrelationships between different objectives and how changes in objectives affect the asset

Adapted from Sudhir Krishnamurthi, Arun Muralidhar, and Ronald van der Wouden. "An Asset-Liability Analysis of Retirement Plans." Investment Management Department Working Paper 98-004, The World Bank, May 1998.

allocation of a plan. Once the objectives of a plan are specified, asset classes in which the plan can be invested have to be articulated and forecasts need to be made. The process of then determining the final strategic asset allocation (SAA) is relatively straightforward. In addition, this chapter demonstrates the importance of integrating funding policy decisions into investment policy analysis.

BACKGROUND ON TYPES OF PLANS

The previous chapter discussed three types of pension plans: defined benefit (DB), defined contribution (DC), and provident funds (PF). This section expands the scope of plans to include retiree health benefit plans. These plans are very similar to insurance plans and provide retirees with funds for post-retirement medical treatment.

In general, any plan can be either revocable or irrevocable, and can be used either for pensions or to meet other liability obligations. These plans may be either funded or not. Under a revocable trust, the assets of the plan are assets of the sponsor and may be used by the sponsor, at its discretion, for purposes other than funding pension benefits (such as medical benefits). Irrevocable plans do not allow the plan sponsor to claw back surpluses for purposes other than funding benefits.

Many large U.S. corporations offer medical benefits to their employees. These plans include the Voluntary Employee Benefit Associations (VEBAs) and 401(h) plans.[1] Companies book this expense annually and create a reserve on their balance sheets. However, they seldom fund these benefits, as the law does not mandate it and there is seldom any tax advantage (such as Federal Accounting Standard [FAS] 106) to doing so. Further, in bankruptcies, creditors can attach the reserve set aside and retirees could lose their medical benefits. However, under some circumstances it is advantageous to transfer pension surpluses to such plans. There is growing pressure in the United States to reform current laws that facilitate prefunding of such plans to protect benefits.

Although certain aspects of a medical plan are similar to a pension plan, in that they can receive annual contributions from the plan sponsor and have assets invested in capital markets, they are quite different in other aspects and closer to catastrophic risk insurance plans. They differ because they have volatile and unpredictable liabilities and cash outflows. For these reasons, the SAA of a medical benefit plan is likely to be quite different from that of a pension plan. This chapter highlights the asset-liability issues for a revocable medical plan, as it is the most expansive type of retirement plan. Funded retiree health plans are not common, but it is a useful illustration as the analysis for an irrevocable pension plan can be seen as a stylized version of the more generic model presented here. In addition, Chapter 2 demonstrated that the technique to determine an optimal asset allocation and funding policy is similar for DB and DC plans. This will become more evident in the course of this chapter. In addition, as highlighted in Chapter 1, the analysis for any fund that is maintained to service a "liability" can be seen as largely similar.

In this analysis, leverage is not considered in the passive benchmark. The impact of leverage is evaluated in the next chapter. Its inclusion is shown to improve the performance of the passive benchmark in an ALM context.

RISKS

Financial entities, such as pension plans and insurance companies, have risks that affect both the assets and liabilities of their balance sheets. Most risks are similar across organizations, and some are specific to a particular entity.

At the broadest level, a retirement (medical) plan is exposed to the three risks discussed below.

- *Asset risk:* This risk captures the volatility in asset values arising from movements in the prices of the securities held by the plan. A drop in value of plan assets adversely impacts the funded status of the plan, and could, in severe cases, lead to plan insolvency.

- *Liability risk:* This risk captures the volatility in liability values. Changes in liabilities could arise due to changes in salary growth, inflation, mortality, or the difference between actual active and retired plan participants versus those assumed. If liabilities increase, the funded status of the plan is adversely affected, and could, in severe cases, lead to plan insolvency.

- *Usage risk:* This risk is unique for a medical plan and makes these plans different from regular pension plans, especially when the number of participants is not very large. In pension plans, all retired participants are given a benefit every month, and the value of these payoffs is fairly stable. Consequently, the annual cash outflows from the plan are predictable. On the other hand, in medical benefit plans, a small number of participants, such as those in poor health, get most of the benefits. Small changes in the number of medical insurance beneficiaries, or the value of their payoffs due to rising medical costs, can significantly change the annual cash outflows from the plan.

Usage risk is also applicable to other insurance or crisis management funds. In the context of central bank reserves, a speculative attack on the currency could be seen as a sudden discrete event that would adversely impact reserves. Alternatively, for a catastrophic risk insurance company, a sudden calamity can be seen as a discrete, volatile impact on liabilities. In other words, the cash outflows of the plan are neither stable nor predictable. This places additional solvency risks on these plans. As a result, these plans need to have higher funded ratios, on average, than comparable pension plans.

This chapter assumes that the actuary evaluates liabilities. It evaluates the remaining three aspects of setting an investment policy; namely, setting objectives, selecting asset classes, and forecasting future returns and asset class relationships. Thereafter, a set of stylized liabilities are used to demonstrate certain investment "truths" applicable to all types of plans.

OBJECTIVES, RISK MEASURES, AND RISK TOLERANCE

In an asset-only framework, the key objective is to maximize expected returns and the volatility (standard deviation) of returns is usually used as a measure of risk. Essentially, investors pick a portfolio on the efficient frontier—a combination of all portfolios with the highest expected return for given levels of risk—to satisfy their specific objective. This is demonstrated in Figure 3.1.

In an asset-liability context, however, this measure is inadequate. Although pension plans have become more sophisticated, they do not fully integrate assets

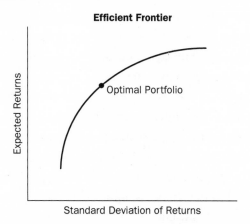

Figure 3.1   Investment Policy—The Traditional
Approach

and liabilities in the decision-making process.[2] The presence of liabilities is the
only reason for the existence of pension plans. Ignoring liabilities would, hence,
lead to a very narrow and potentially incorrect analysis. Figure 3.2 demonstrates
the development of assets and asset-liability ratios of pension plans in the
United States between 1980 and 1996, and indicates the importance of liabilities.

This illustration clearly shows that during the 1980–1996 period, on aggregate, pension plans benefited from high returns, but the aggregate ratio of

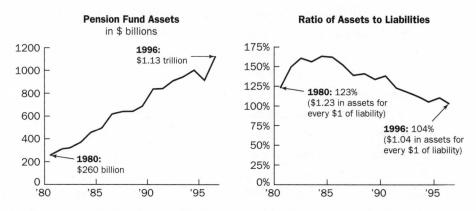

Figure 3.2   The Importance of Optimal Investment Policy: U.S. Pension Funds,
1980–1996. Source: PBGC.

assets to liabilities (the funded ratio) declined. One can question the suitability of the investment policies of these plans given their liability structures. More recent research by Chung, Granito, and Prajogi (2001) has shown that 1999 was a favorable year for the 200 largest corporate pension plans and that funding performance was the highest since the mid-1980s. However, the projected benefit obligation (PBO) of the average plan was expected to have decreased by 18 percent to 108 percent, and half the plans were expected to be underfunded in 2000. The prospects for 2001 are not favorable due to low expected returns and lower interest rates.

The funded ratio is a useful tool that indicates whether a DB or DC plan has sufficient assets to cover its liabilities, and the extent to which the plan is dependent on the plan sponsor to meet its liabilities. Funded ratios required in a medical plan would generally need to be higher (in excess of 100 percent) than those needed for traditional pension plans due to usage risk.

One of the decisions that an oversight committee needs to make is the appropriate level for the target-funded ratio. This is the ratio below which the committee would have concern about the "fundedness" of the plan. In other words, the oversight board or committee should seek to restrict the probability of the plan's funded ratio falling below this target to a low percentage, say 5 percent to 10 percent a year.

The key objective of the oversight committee is to ensure that the funded ratio is suitably close to 100 percent. For medical plans this may not be the case as there are no tax advantages to prefunding a plan *unless it is a revocable plan, in which the return from investments is greater than the opportunity cost of capital.* However, for simplicity it is assumed there is no tax penalty for doing so. In other words, a funded status of 100 percent or more helps to ensure that existing plan assets are adequate to meet the pension or medical insurance liabilities of all existing staff for past and future service.[3]

For example, if the target-funded ratio is 105 percent (which implies a 5 percent increment for usage risk), then an actual funded ratio less than 105 percent is assumed to reflect a solvency deficiency. The risk tolerance of the plan is the probability that a solvency deficiency occurs. A risk tolerance of 5 percent implies the probability of the actual funded ratio below the target of 105 percent is 1 out of 20. Leibowitz, Bader, and Kogelman (1996) call these "shortfall risks."

To establish the strategic asset allocation of a plan, the first step is to ascertain the objectives of the plan. There are a number of possible objectives; Menssen (1997) suggests that these could include (1) a 3–5 percent excess over consumer price inflation during a rolling 10-year period; (2) outperform a benchmark over a rolling 5-year period; and (c) outperform the median fund over a rolling 5-year period. The strength of this example is in the use of clearly articulated short- and long-term horizons, but it is by no means an exhaustive list. Others, such as Gibson (1997), worry about risks and suggest that funds should (1) cover pension liabilities at lowest cost; (2) ensure a surplus; (3) minimize surplus volatility and improve credit ratings; and (4) maximize shareholder value (or contribute to net income).[4] Logue and Rader (1997) emphasize the correlation of cash flows of the sponsor and the pension fund. For example, an airline with extensive operations in Japan would have lower profitability if the Japanese yen appreciates. At such times, making contributions would be difficult. However, if the pension fund has exposure to Japanese yen, then there is a possibility that the funded ratio would increase, negating the need for contributions. One instrument that could be used to clarify these objectives is a questionnaire such as the one in Figure 3.3.

There is a direct relationship between asset allocations and achievement of objectives. Therefore, an iterative process can be used to track the achievement of various objectives through different asset allocation decisions, and vice versa (covered later in the chapter). In other words, a portfolio with 80 percent in equities and 20 percent in bonds would have a high probability that the funded ratio target is achieved, but this portfolio may lead to an unacceptable volatility of contributions.

In reality, most decision makers are not sure what specific levels to pick and how to ensure that these levels represent a consistent trade-off across competing objectives. Classic finance theory requires a specification of various objectives and quantitative levels for each objective, but reality and good governance makes this an iterative process. The investment team can propose different combinations of portfolios and the objectives they achieve, and allow members of the board to pick the combination they feel most accurately represents the interests of those they serve. This iterative process allows the principal decision makers to identify the relative importance and target levels

POLICY QUESTIONNAIRE FOR THE OVERSIGHT COMMITTEE

I. *Identify and Rank Objectives*

Rank the following objectives over both the short (ST) and long term (LT), on a scale of 1 to 10 (1 is unimportant, 10 extremely important):

Asset objectives	ST	LT
• Maximize expected returns	—	—
• Minimize volatility of portfolio returns	—	—
• Ensure a real rate of 3%		
• Ensure performance in top quartile of peer universe	—	—
• Ensure fund performance within +/−3% of benchmark	—	—

Asset-Liability objectives		
• Maintain existing funding status	—	—
• Minimize company contributions	—	—
• Minimize volatility of contributions	—	—
• Maximize pension income	—	—
• Minimize volatility of pension income	—	—
• Ensure contributions when the sponsor can make them	—	—

II. *Establish and Quantify Constraints*

At what levels whould you have serious concerns for the following objectives? For example, 3% for expected returns over the LT, or 95% for funded status.

Asset objectives		
• Maximize expected returns	—	—
• Minimize volatility of portfolio returns	—	—
• Ensure a real rate of 3%	—	—
• Ensure performance in top quartile of peer universe	—	—
• Ensure fund performance within +/−3% of benchmark	—	—

Asset-Liability objectives		
• Maintain existing funding status	—	—
• Minimize company contributions (in % of salary or currency)	—	—
• Minimize volatility of contributions	—	—
• Maximize pension income	—	—
• Minimize volatility of pension income	—	—
• Maximum contribution when economic conditions are unfavorable	—	—

Figure 3.3 An Instrument to Establish Objectives

for the following key variables over the long and short horizons (defined by each sponsor):

- Funded ratio
- Risk tolerance (probability of actual funded ratio being below target)
- Basic contribution rate

- Flexibility in funding (minimum and maximum contribution rates)
- Guaranteed rate of return
- Peer comparison (and appropriate peer benchmark)
- Pension income

The impact of revocability on asset allocation policies is covered later in the chapter.

INVESTMENT AND FUNDING STRATEGIES

It is commonly felt that investment and funding policies are independent, yet both are important to achieve pension excellence.[5] The oversight committee selects the investment policy and funding policy, which are interdependent in achieving the level and volatility of the target funded ratio. The investment policy describes the way in which assets of the plan must be invested, and the funding policy proposes the manner in which annual contributions to the plan are to be determined. An effort must be made to integrate these two policies to meet the objectives of the committee.[6]

The interdependence of these two policy variables is trivial: one way to increase the funded status is to increase contributions, but this is expensive. Further, increases in contributions could have tax implications (Bader 1995). Alternatively, a plan sponsor could take more investment risk to get higher expected returns, but this increases the probability of significantly higher contributions in the future while lowering the average contribution rate. Unfortunately, few plan sponsors optimize investment and funding policy jointly. This may happen for at least two reasons: organizationally, the reporting line of the benefits administrator is different from that of the investment head; or models used by consultants and actuaries are incapable of performing such joint optimizations. To illustrate the latter, World Bank staff evaluated several models with various limitations before selecting a model that could perform joint optimizations. These issues are discussed in the subsection on models, and a comparison of models is provided in Appendix 3.1.

Choosing the optimal funding and investment policy is an iterative process and the benefits of joint optimization are significant. An asset-liability study could use any time horizon (such as 1 year or 50 years) to determine optimal policies for this horizon. For convenience, a long-term horizon of 9 consecutive years was used (2001–2010) to determine the results presented here, with a short-term horizon of 1 year used iteratively.

Investment Policy

One may choose a static or dynamic approach to investment policy. The static approach would rebalance the portfolio every year back to an initial allocation; the dynamic approach would permit the asset allocation to change to a new optimal allocation annually based on the funded ratio of the plan.[7] Our analysis indicates that the dynamic approach could increase the performance of the plan without increasing the risk, as demonstrated in Chapter 4.[8]

Both approaches require an asset allocation to be set for the first year (year 2001 in our example). However, the dynamic approach requires an asset allocation rule to be identified for portfolio reallocation across asset classes depending on the funded status of the plan.

The asset allocation analysis may be done with or without constraints on the amount invested in different asset categories. It may be useful to set limits on some asset classes to ensure that the model does not propose politically unrealistic allocations.

Funding Policy

An important decision that has not been given due attention is the choice of funding policy of the plan. Many assume the difference between liabilities and assets must equal the present value of contributions. Hence, this is a "plug" variable. If the plan suffers from losses on its investments, it has the *ability* to cover these losses (when required) by increasing the contributions of the sponsor. This means that the willingness to make higher contributions could cover higher losses on the investment side, which could lead the plan to take on more investment risk. One can visualize the greater willingness to tolerate asset risk through contributions as a form of hedge against poor investment decisions. Consequently, the decision on the funding policy has a direct impact on the investment policy and they must be evaluated and set simultaneously.

As with the investment policy, the plan could choose between a static and dynamic funding approach. In the static approach, the plan would maintain a fixed contribution rate, whereas the dynamic approach permits the contribution rate to vary annually based on the funded status of the plan. It is critical to analyze a large number of funding policies (static and dynamic approaches) and the sensitivity of investment policies to changes in funding policy.

Our analysis for this specific fund indicates that funding policy changes do not significantly change investment policy—they are less important for medical plans than for regular pension plans.[9] Moreover, the use of a dynamic asset allocation strategy is more important than changing funding policies to meet the objectives of the plan. Finally, permitting annual changes in the contribution rate (the dynamic approach) is better than maintaining a fixed contribution rate (the static approach).[10] Several different funding policies have been analyzed to demonstrate these results but these results could be reversed for another plan with a different maturity and liability profile.[11]

ASSET CLASSES, RETURNS, AND MODELS

The next step is to identify the various asset classes (or the opportunity set) from which the recommended investment strategy is to be developed. Thereafter, some assumptions need to be made about the future returns from investing in these asset classes, and how the returns will evolve over time.

Identifying Asset Classes

The definition of any investment opportunity as an asset class is subjective, and practitioners must use good judgment and common sense to identify asset classes. Classic candidates include domestic equities, domestic bonds, international developed market equities (hedged and unhedged), emerging market equities (unhedged), foreign bonds (hedged and unhedged), real estate (domestic and foreign), and private equity (which incorporates many variants).

Three important criteria must be used to decide whether an investment opportunity is an asset class. First, the overall market for an investment opportunity must be sufficiently large for the plan to make a meaningful allocation, say 5 percent of its total assets. Allocations less than 5 percent do not provide significant diversification benefits and can be viewed as tactical allocations to enhance returns. Cash allocations are usually the exception to this rule, as plans may need cash to service pension payments, depending on the maturity of the plan. Second, assets in the investment opportunity must be sufficiently dissimilar from assets in other asset classes so that the correlation is low (less than 0.90). Finally, external investment managers must offer products targeted to the investment opportunity (on a low-cost passive and high-fee active basis). Sharpe (1990) restates some of this and suggests other criteria, including the following: (1) the number of asset classes must be small; (2) an asset class should explain major variability in returns; and (3) asset classes must have a measurable return and beta.

Establishing the Future Economic Environment

All asset allocation exercises require two major capital market inputs. First, the expected long-term returns for different asset classes over a given time horizon; and second, the variance-covariance matrix for returns across asset classes, indicating how tightly or loosely returns of different asset classes move over time. This matrix and expected returns are used to generate the asset returns for each asset class for a number of future periods. All nominal expected returns for assets can be numerically represented as the aggregate of three components: (1) inflation; (2) expected real risk-free rate (in this case, the real return to domestic fixed income); and (3) expected equity risk premium (Figure 3.4). All major consultants follow this technique.[12] The assumption

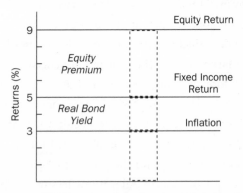

• Volatility and correlation based on historical numbers
• Undertake sensitivity analysis of all assumptions

Figure 3.4 Establishing Forward-Looking Return Assumptions

that all domestic or international asset classes within a group (such as fixed income) have the same expected return tend to provide well-diversified asset allocations that are more resilient to errors in predicting return premiums.[13]

Models for Conducting Analyses

The most common approach to evaluate policy options for investment funds is to use the mean-variance optimization technique. The recommended models for a SAA exercise are multiperiod, multiple objective, and with dynamic optimization (and/or simulation).[14] In addition, these models must be able to incorporate both assets and liabilities under the same framework.

Two key macroeconomic variables have an impact on the present value of liabilities—interest rates and inflation. These variables also affect asset valuations and influence the performance of any asset allocation strategy. A good asset-liability model explicitly incorporates assets and liabilities as a function of these economic variables. This assists in the selection of optimal portfolios and determines optimal contribution policies to satisfy the objectives of the pension plan.

The importance of multiperiod, multiobjective requirements is discussed below. Other options are discussed in Appendix 3.1. Table A3.1.1 in the appendix highlights and summarizes the pros and cons of the different model approaches.

Single Period Versus Multiperiod

A single-period model assumes that objectives are met at the end of the investment horizon. The multiperiod models assume that decisions can be made over the long term even though intermediate, short-term objectives must be met. There are generally two advantages to multiperiod models. First, they can never perform worse than a single-period model (with greater choice in the multiperiod model, the worst outcome would be a "buy and hold," which is equivalent to a single-period recommendation). Second, multiperiod models allow for the consideration of intermediate goals in addition to the final horizon goal.

Single Objective Versus Multiple Objective

The mean-variance method assumes a single objective—optimization of returns for a given level of risk (or vice versa). Given the host of issues in managing pension funds highlighted earlier, these models cannot adequately capture the trade-offs that a plan sponsor must make. Hence, mean-variance models are likely to provide suboptimal recommendations on investment policy. Multiple-objective models can jointly optimize investment and funding policy.

The superiority of these approaches is demonstrated in the following case study.

A CASE STUDY OF AN ASSET-LIABILITY ANALYSIS FOR A RETIREE MEDICAL BENEFIT PLAN

In this section, a step-by-step process is outlined to demonstrate how an asset-liability study might be conducted.

Setting Objectives

As highlighted in Chapter 1 and previous sections, an oversight committee must choose from several competing objectives and, ultimately, has to rank the short-listed objectives. For the purpose of this analysis, a target guaranteed rate of return is not considered.[15] In addition, though peer comparison is used extensively in pension funds in the United States and United Kingdom, it reflects embarrassment risk rather than economic or financial risk. This is addressed in greater detail in Chapter 14. The analysis uses a combination of levels for the remaining variables.

The detailed results of this analysis are included in Tables A3.2.3–6 of Appendix 3.2. For the purpose of illustration, hypothetical liabilities are assumed for a medical insurance plan and it is assumed that the committee has a single time horizon of 9 years, at the end of which the achievement of objectives is evaluated. The analysis is based on the following possible objectives and corresponding targets and risk measures:

1. Target-funded ratio of 105 percent and 100 percent[16]
2. Risk tolerance of 5 percent and 10 percent[17]
3. Fixed basic contribution rate of 1 percent and 3 percent of gross salaries
4. Minimum contribution rate of 0 percent when the funded ratio is above 135 percent and a maximum rate of 5 percent when the funded ratio is below 75 percent.

One could very easily impose some of these objectives over a shorter time and evaluate the efficacy of any investment or funding policy.

Asset Classes and Forecasted Returns

This case study groups assets in three broad categories: equities (domestic U.S., international unhedged, and emerging markets), fixed income (U.S., non-U.S. hedged into U.S. dollars, high-yield bonds, inflation-indexed bonds, and cash), and alternative investments (real estate and private equities).

To deal with the uncertainty and impact of capital returns, 10,000 different scenarios of the economic environment have been created. Each scenario represents the development of these returns over a period of 9 years. An investment policy is evaluated for each scenario and the impact of the particular policy is captured by risk measures, which take into account the behavior of the policy in each scenario.

The model generating the scenarios assumes each economic factor follows a random walk. In addition, the statistical relationships between economic factors are preserved in the simulations.[18] The most important characteristics of the scenarios generated are depicted in Table 3.1.

Embedded in Table 3.1 are the assumptions of an expected real risk-free rate of 1.2 percent (the difference between the expected inflation and the return on

Table 3.1
Characteristics of the Economic Variables

	Annual Expected Nominal Value (%)	Standard Deviation (Annual Volatility) (%)
Price inflation	4.0	3.0
U.S. equity	10.5	15.0
Non-U.S. equity (unhedged)	10.5	19.7
Emerging markets equity	10.5	23.3
U.S. fixed income	6.5	5.2
Non-U.S. fixed income (hedged)	6.5	12.6
High yield bonds	8.0	9.8
Inflation-indexed bonds	6.5	4.0
Real estate	7.0	18.0
Private equity	10.5	27.0
Cash	5.2	1.4

cash), a bond premium of 1.3 percent (the difference between cash and U.S. fixed income), and an expected real equity risk premium of 4 percent (the difference between the expected return on equity and fixed income). The correlation between these asset classes is provided in Table A3.2.2 of Appendix 3.2.[19]

Constraints

In this analysis, the total allocation to emerging markets, high-yield bonds, and index bonds combined is bound at 10 percent of the portfolio, and total investments in equity is capped at 90 percent. The percentage of alternative investments, including real estate and private equity, is fixed at 10 percent of the portfolio. This is not required, but is used to make final allocations more realistic.[20]

Percentage of Equity

Assume a fund with the initial asset allocation shown in Table 3.2. The amount of permissible investment risk is critical to defining the optimal strategic asset allocation. This analysis uses the amount allocated to equity as a measure of the investment risk. In other words, a high allocation to equity implies a high-risk investment policy, and vice versa. Consequently, the percentage

Table 3.2
Initial Allocation Across Asset Classes

	Current Allocation 68% Equity (%)
Equity	
U.S. equity	30.0
Non-U.S. equity	33.0
Emerging markets	5.0
Fixed Income	
Global fixed income	18.0
High yield bonds	4.0
Indexed bonds	0.0
Cash	0.0
Alternative Investments	
Real estate	5.0
Private equity	5.0

allocation to equity is a key investment policy statistic. This approach contrasts with others that build liability indices as a composite of fixed income portfolios (Ryan 1997). The techniques presented here are more sophisticated than the simplistic approaches that identify the duration of liabilities and implement duration-based strategies. As demonstrated earlier, objectives can be more complex and duration unnecessarily constrains the analysis.

Tables 3.3 and 3.4 report results for the various parameter choices using the optimization models. Table 3.3 presents the optimal percentage allocation to equity in the first year, and by construct the intermediate years, with a target funded ratio of 105 percent. In this table, where the contribution policy can vary between 0 and 5 percent, four scenarios are evaluated based on two options for two objectives: a risk tolerance of the funded ratio falling below target of 5 percent and 10 percent (that is, once in 20 years or once in 10 years, respectively); or an initial contribution rate of 1 percent and 3 percent. Table 3.4 provides the results for a target funded ratio of 100 percent with the same simulations.

Table 3.3
Optimal Percentage Allocation to Equity for Funded
Ratio Target of 105%

	Initial Contribution Rate	
Risk Tolerance[a]	1%	3%
5%	55	65
10%	85	90

Note: Range of contributions: minimum 0%, maximum 5%.
[a]Probability of actual funded ratio below target in any year.

Table 3.4
Optimal Percentage Allocation to Equity for Funded
Ratio Target of 100%

	Initial Contribution Rate	
Risk Tolerance[a]	1%	3%
5%	80	90
10%	90	90

Note: Range of contributions: minimum 0%, maximum 5%.
[a]Probability of actual funded ratio below target in any year.

Tables 3.3 and 3.4 show that total allocation to equity increases with a lower target funded ratio. Moreover, total allocation to equity increases with the contribution rate.[21] Finally, equity allocation increases with risk tolerance, where risk tolerance is defined as a greater willingness to have an actual funded ratio below target.

An additional effect (Appendix 3.2, Table A.3.2.3) is that a willingness to increase the maximum funding rate from 5 percent to 10 percent, which suggests a more flexible funding policy, also increases the total allocation to equity. This result is most evident for a target funded ratio of 105 percent and a risk tolerance of 5 percent. The rationale is that a flexible funding policy serves as a hedge against asset risk and therefore permits a higher risk posture. Bodie, Merton, and Samuelson (1992) provide a similar result, except that they perceive changes in future contributions to be driven by labor supply decisions rather than changes in the contribution rate. Their result can be viewed as a result applicable to an individual in a DC pension plan. This confirms an earlier statement that a number of investment "truths" are identical across different types of plans.

The accompanying box summarizes some of these simplistic results, which are called "investment truths."

INVESTMENT TRUTHS

The optimal allocation to equity or ability to take risk increases when

■ *The committee lowers the target funded ratio.*

■ *The committee raises its risk tolerance.*

■ *The committee is willing to set a high initial contribution rate.*

■ *The plan adopts a flexible funding policy (is willing to permit higher maximum contribution rates).*

Table 3.5
Dynamic Asset Allocation Rule

Equity level of the initial allocation (Year 2001)	55%	65%	85%	90%
Change in equity percentage allocation for a 1% increase in funded ratio	1.75%	1.25%	0.25%	0%

Dynamic Investment Approach

In a static investment policy approach, the asset allocation of the plan for 2001 remains fixed for the ensuing years. On the other hand, a dynamic approach possibly implies variations in asset allocations for each year after 2001.

After determining the allocation for year one, a rule determines how to re-allocate the portfolio. This rule seeks to maximize terminal wealth without in-creasing the risks to the plan relative to a static investment strategy. Table 3.5 demonstrates the rules obtained from jointly optimizing the funding and in-vestment policies. It highlights the optimal impact of a 1 percent increase in funded ratio on the percentage allocated to equity across different initial eq-uity levels for different equity percentages in Table 3.6.

Table 3.5 shows the allocation to equity is unaffected by an increase in the funded ratio when the initial allocation is 90 percent, the maximum permis-sible level of equity. On the other hand, it shows that for other equity levels the total allocation to equity increases as the funded ratio of the plan increases. When the funded ratio increases, the plan builds a reserve, which enables it to take on more risk.[22] The plan can bear more risk because potential additional losses can be covered by this reserve. However, the lower the initial allocation to equity, the larger the change in equity allocation per unit change in funded status. Chapter 4 discusses dynamic investment policies in detail, demonstrat-ing their potential superiority over static investment policies.

Allocation Across Asset Classes

Tables 3.3 and 3.4 provided different alternatives for the total allocation to equity. This case study uses the total allocation to equity as a measure of investment risk undertaken by the plan. This section presents a breakdown of

Table 3.6

Optimal Allocation Across Asset Classes for Given Levels of Equity

	Allocation (%) by Equity Level				
	Current: 68% Equity	55% Equity	65% Equity	85% Equity	90% Equity
Equity					
U.S. equity	30.00	26.25	34.00	46.50	47.00
Non-U.S. equity	33.00	18.75	21.00	31.00	37.00
Emerging markets	5.00	10.00	10.00	7.50	6.00
Fixed Income					
Global fixed income	18.00	15.00	6.50	0.00	0.00
High-yield bonds	4.00	10.00	10.00	3.75	0.00
Indexed bonds[a]	0.00	10.00	8.50	1.25	0.00
Cash	0.00	0.00	0.00	0.00	0.00
Alternative Investments					
Real estate	5.00	5.00	5.00	5.00	5.00
Private equity	5.00	5.00	5.00	5.00	5.00

[a]The indexed bonds used in the analysis generate a guaranteed return of 2% above the inflation rate.

the total equity component across different equity asset classes (U.S., international developed, and emerging markets) and provides details on other asset classes.[23]

For simplicity, Table 3.6 repeats the current allocation in order to compare it to allocations for four different equity percentages (55 percent, 65 percent, 85 percent, and 90 percent).

The asset allocation for the 65 percent equity case, relative to the current allocation of 68 percent, brings out two interesting points. First, the allocation to emerging markets is higher, and the allocation to non-U.S. equities is lower. Second, allocations to indexed bonds and high-yield bonds are higher, and the allocation to investment-grade global fixed income funds is lower.

The higher allocations to emerging markets and high-yield bonds can be attributed to the diversification effect of these categories. In addition, although not shown here, analysis suggests the allocation to indexed bonds would be even higher if the artificially imposed constraint is dropped. The main reason behind this strong effect is that the indexed bonds hedge inflation risk, which is strongly correlated to the increase in medical costs. Chapter 5 discusses similar implications for assets with attractive asset-liability properties.

Other Key Summary Statistics

Strategic asset allocation decisions affect a number of important asset-liability variables beyond those described in the earlier sections. Tables A3.2.4–7 in Appendix 3.2 give details on the impact of various asset allocation strategies on four of these variables. The key results are summarized here:

- Expected average portfolio returns increase with the allocation to equity (Table A3.2.4).

- The expected funded ratio increases at the end of the time horizon (that is, end-of-year 2010) with the allocation to equity (Table A3.2.5). This is trivial, as higher equity allocations lead to higher average returns and, hence, a greater accumulation of surplus.

- The expected average contribution rate declines with an increasing allocation to equity (Table A3.2.6).[24] Essentially, if asset-liability risks are managed and higher returns are earned, the funded status improves, requiring lower future contributions.

- Expected probability of underperforming a U.S. plan[25] declines with higher equity allocations up to a point, as increases in equity imply an increase in volatility (Table A3.2.7). Given the equity premium, more equity relative to the peer group implies a greater likelihood of outperformance. However, the variance of performance vis-à-vis the peer group also increases.

Irrevocability and Impact on Results

If the plan is made irrevocable, the asset-liability analysis suggests that as a plan gets more funding the need to invest in equities declines. In other words, if the plan sponsor cannot capture increased returns, the accompanying increased volatility implies greater downside risk. Hence, the allocation to equity (described in Table 3.5) is likely to taper off much faster if the plan is irrevocable. Likewise, the desire to take on more risk is less than that of a revocable plan, unless the plan is able to transfer the surplus to another plan, thereby lowering the overall cost of offering retiree benefits. In this case, the risk-taking ability would be the same, because the sponsor is able to capture the surplus implicitly.

SUMMARY

The main conclusions of this case study highlight the "truths" of asset-liability analyses. The results are useful to assist individuals in governance roles within a fund in establishing effective objectives. The analysis arrives at three main conclusions for DB and DC pension plans, as well as retirement plans other than pension plans.

> *Willingness to contribute at higher and/or more flexible rates permits the plan to bear additional risk, and in turn, a higher allocation to equities.*

In an unconstrained setting, a higher allocation to equity reduces the average expected contribution to the plan.[26]

> *Willingness to have shortfalls in target funded ratios leads to higher equity levels.*

A willingness to tolerate a higher probability of the actual funded ratio being below target leads to higher levels of equity for the plan. A higher equity level leads to higher funded ratios, lower expected contributions to the plan, and a higher likelihood of outperforming peers.

> *Allocation across asset classes, or diversification, will improve efficiency.*

The analysis indicates that emerging market equities and high-yield bonds offer good diversification characteristics and usually come up against their artificially imposed permissible levels. Allocations to inflation indexed bonds are particularly desirable due to their high correlation with medical costs. Hence, some assets are preferable from a purely asset perspective, and others are desirable from an asset-liability perspective.

As demonstrated by the case study, objectives (and constraints) determine the final asset allocation policy. However, committee members may not want to pick levels for variables in a vacuum, so it may be useful to provide tables of results similar to those in the case study (and Appendix 3.2) to demonstrate that reasonable portfolios achieve objectives and unnecessary constraints are expensive (they lead to higher average contributions). This process allows committee members to evaluate their comfort zone and establish a correspondence between objectives and asset allocation. This creates a more effective dialog between the committee and staff and allows for the selection of the optimal strategic asset allocation, which minimizes the various asset-liability risks to the sponsor.

EVALUATING MODELS AVAILABLE TO PLAN SPONSORS

A PRIMER ON OPTIMIZATION AND SIMULATION MODELS

The optimization method is theoretically the most rigorous of any method as it seeks to optimize the various objectives given constraints. These models tend to be complicated and can be black boxes because one is not able to discern what caused a particular result. In addition, such models do not permit the evaluation of hypothetical "what-if" type scenarios. For example, if an optimizer suggests a 50-50 bond-equity mix, the plan sponsor is unable to evaluate whether a 60-40 portfolio or 55-45 portfolio would closely approximate the results of the optimized portfolio. In addition, optimizers tend to require calibration of various parameters, which can make the results somewhat arbitrary.

Simulation technologies are simpler and based on the assumption that future economic scenarios can be simulated based on some initial assumptions. The plan sponsor can then evaluate multiple options to find the most feasible option for committee acceptance. The difficulty is the user largely visualizes the "optimal" portfolio and this makes portfolio selection more time consuming.

Software packages now offer simulation, optimization, and joint simulation-optimization capabilities, thereby facilitating a more user-friendly analysis. For details on the various techniques and their advantages and disadvantages, see Boender and Heemskerk (1995) and Boender (1997).

Table A3.1.1 summarizes the simulation and optimization methods along with mean-variance methods.

Table A3.1.1

Comparing Mean-Variance, Dynamic Simulation, and Optimization Models

Mean-Variance	*Monte Carlo Simulation*	*Dynamic Programming*
• Single- or Multiperiod	• Multiperiod	• Multiperiod • Single vs. Dual Policy Optimization
Background **Method** —Simple optimization to trade off between expected return and risk → efficient frontier: $E(r_p) - \sigma_p^2/\lambda$	**Method** —Multiple simulations are performed to determine multiple paths for all the asset returns. —Model is provided information on the portfolios ex-ante and the portfolio performance is simulated over each path. —Portfolios are ranked ex-post based on the distributional aspects of each of the objectives.	**Method** —Output of a scenario generator is used to populate a multistage, multi-node tree. —Identify the best contingency plan for each node, and then outputs the probabilities of breaching the various constraints in the objective function.
Objective —Maximizing expected return for a given level of risk or —Minimizing risk for a given level of expected return	**Objective** —Any specification of multiple objectives —Can be set up to rebalance in every period to starting weights or weights determined by some rebalancing equation, e.g.: Equities $= -0.51 + 1.7 \times$ funded status	**Objective** —Ability to determine both the optimal funding and investment policy based on the ordinal ranking of the various objectives.
Pros **Investment/Funding Policy** —Simple specification of objectives. **Time/Technical Intensity** —Analysis is not time intensive.	**Investment/Funding Policy** —Defines risk parameters individually—increases transparency for typical decision makers **Stability of Optimal Portfolio** —Permits meaningful trade-offs between short, intermediate, and long-term goals —Ability to rebalance enhances stability of optimal portfolios. —Detailed analysis can be conducted on the impact of each objective given that as many as 10,000 simulations can be performed.	**Investment/Funding Policy** —Since the optimizer is able to determine the optimal investment policy and contribution rate policy jointly, the probability of achieving all the ALM objectives jointly is high. —Defines risk parameters individually—increases transparency for typical decision makers. **Stability of Optimal Portfolio** —Multiperiod, multiobjective specification ensures stability of optimal portfolio. —Permits meaningful trade-offs between short, intermediate, and long-term goals.

Table A3.1.1 (*Continued*)

Mean-Variance • Single- or Multiperiod	*Monte Carlo Simulation* • Multiperiod	*Dynamic Programming* • Multiperiod • Single vs. Dual Policy Optimization
	Contingency Plans —Provides for dynamic strategies and contingencies. **Multiple Asset Specification** —Multiple asset specification makes these models more robust.	**Contingency Plans** —Possible to extract a dynamic rebalancing rule. Hence the oversight committee can be provided with contingency plans for future years that are independent of emotion. **Optimization vs. Simulation** —Best method because it optimizes dual/conflicting policy objectives.
Cons **Investment/Funding Policy** —Cannot handle multiple objectives and ignores liabilities. Investors do not equate risk with total variability of portfolio returns. —Defines risk as a terminal wealth surprise regardless of direction (i.e., good vs. bad). —Funding policy cannot handle liabilities. **Stability of Optimal Portfolio** —Oversensitivity to forecast errors in the inputs. —Sensitive to the horizon period and the estimates of the riskless assets (e.g., USFI). —Effectively, those models are error optimizers, i.e., selecting assets where expected return is overestimated and volatility is underestimated. —Portfolios close to the optimal on the efficient frontier can be very different in composition. —In a single-period model, doesn't trade off between short- and long-term goals. Possible in a multiperiod model. —Ignores the dynamic nature of the world.	**Investment/Funding Policy** —Difficult to jointly optimize both funding and investment policy. Usually, one is fixed (funding policy) and the second is optimized. **Optimization vs. Simulation** —These models are optimized manually and hence the true optimal portfolio may be missed. **Time/Technical Intensity** —Can be time-consuming.	**Optimization vs. Simulation** —Dynamic optimization is a technically difficult exercise. —Requires extensive experience. —Time-consuming process. —The user should be able to evaluate what assumptions and constraints are driving model and be able to interpret the dynamic rebalancing rule.

ADDITIONAL DATA FOR THE CASE STUDY

Table A3.2.2
Correlations Between Asset Class Returns

Asset Classes	Correlations							
	USEQ	NUSEQ	USFI	NUSFI	HY	RE	PE	Cash
U.S. equities	1.0	0.5	0.4	0.1	0.5	0.1	0.4	0.1
Non-U.S. equities	0.5	1.0	0.2	0.4	0.2	0.1	0.1	−0.2
U.S. fixed income	0.4	0.2	1.0	0.2	0.3	0.0	0.0	0.1
Non-U.S. fixed income	0.1	0.4	0.2	1.0	0.0	0.0	0.0	−0.1
High yield bonds	0.5	0.2	0.3	0.0	1.0	0.0	0.0	−0.2
Real estate	0.1	0.1	0.0	0.0	0.0	1.0	0.0	0.1
Private equity	0.4	0.1	0.0	0.0	0.0	0.0	1.0	0.0
Cash	0.1	−0.2	0.1	−0.1	−0.2	0.1	0.0	1.0
Inflation	−0.3	−0.2	−0.1	−0.2	−0.3	−0.2	−0.2	0.3

Table A3.2.3
Optimal Percentage of Equity by Funded Ratio Target, Risk Tolerance, and Funding Policy

Funded Ratio Target (Risk Measure)	Probability of Not Meeting Target Ratio (Risk Tolerance)	Contribution Policy					
		Fixed 1%	(0 - 1 - 10)[a] %	(0 - 1 - 5)[a] %	(0 - 3 - 5)[a] %	(0 - 3 - 10)[a] %	Fixed 3%
110%	5%	NA[b]	35%	NA[b]	NA[b]	50%	NA[b]
	10%	NA[b]	75%	45%	65%	90%[c]	50%
105%	5%	NA[b]	75%	55%	65%	85%	50%
	10%	60%	90%[c]	85%	90%[c]	90%[c]	85%
100%	5%	55%	90%[c]	80%	90%[c]	90%[c]	80%
	10%	90%[c]	90%[c]	90%[c]	90%[c]	90%[c]	90%[c]

[a]This notation means (minimum rate - basic rate - maximum rate). The basic rate is the annual contribution rate at the current level of funded ratio for the plan. If the funded ratio reaches levels higher than 135% the contribution rate can decrease to the minimum rate, but funded ratio levels lower than 115% could result in contribution rates as high as the maximum rate.

[b]NA means that no equity level would meet the given level of risk tolerance. Even the allocation that resulted in the lowest possible risk would have a risk higher than the risk tolerance level.

[c]Due to restrictions on the amount invested in the asset categories, 90% is the maximum permissible allocation to equity.

Table A3.2.4
Expected Average Return for Different Equity Levels by Funding Policy

Percentage Equity	Contribution Policy					
	Fixed 1%	(0 - 1 - 10) %	(0 - 1 - 5) %	(0 - 3 - 5) %	(0 - 3 - 10) %	Fixed 3%
30	8.43%	8.42%	8.42%	8.59%	8.59%	8.62%
40	8.85%	8.85%	8.85%	8.98%	8.99%	9.01%
50	9.23%	9.23%	9.23%	9.33%	9.34%	9.35%
60	9.58%	9.59%	9.58%	9.64%	9.64%	9.66%
70	9.89%	9.89%	9.89%	9.92%	9.92%	9.94%
80	10.14%	10.13%	10.14%	10.15%	10.15%	10.16%
90	10.32%	10.32%	10.32%	10.32%	10.32%	10.32%

Table A3.2.5
Expected Funded Ratio at the End of the Time Horizon (Year 2010)

Percentage Equity	Contribution Policy					
	Fixed 1%	(0 - 1 - 10) %	(0 - 1 - 5) %	(0 - 3 - 5) %	(0 - 3 - 10) %	Fixed 3%
30	118.3	124.1	121.4	127.1	129.4	127.5
40	121.8	127.5	124.8	130.0	132.5	130.7
50	124.9	130.6	127.8	132.6	135.2	133.6
60	127.8	133.6	130.7	134.9	137.6	136.2
70	130.3	136.1	133.1	137.0	139.8	138.5
80	132.4	138.2	135.0	138.6	141.7	140.3
90	133.7	139.8	136.4	139.8	143.0	141.6

Table A3.2.6
Expected Average Contribution Rate for Different Equity Levels by Funding Policy

Percentage Equity	Contribution Policy					
	Fixed 1%	(0 - 1 - 10) %	(0 - 1 - 5) %	(0 - 3 - 5) %	(0 - 3 - 10) %	Fixed 3%
30	1.00%	2.92%	2.04%	3.03%	3.80%	3.00%
40	1.00%	2.83%	1.97%	2.93%	3.70%	3.00%
50	1.00%	2.79%	1.92%	2.83%	3.61%	3.00%
60	1.00%	2.75%	1.89%	2.74%	3.53%	3.00%
70	1.00%	2.72%	1.84%	2.66%	3.48%	3.00%
80	1.00%	2.72%	1.80%	2.58%	3.45%	3.00%
90	1.00%	2.74%	1.78%	2.54%	3.43%	3.00%

Table A3.2.7
Expected Probability of Underperforming the Average U.S. Plan[a]

Percentage Equity	Contribution Policy					
	Fixed 1%	(0 - 1 - 10) %	(0 - 1 - 5) %	(0 - 3 - 5) %	(0 - 3 - 10) %	Fixed 3%
30	55.2%	55.2%	55.24%	53.82%	53.9%	53.6%
40	52.3%	52.4%	52.36%	50.93%	51.0%	51.0%
50	49.2%	49.1%	49.20%	48.27%	48.2%	48.0%
60	44.9%	44.5%	44.71%	43.78%	43.7%	43.6%
70	40.8%	40.8%	40.71%	40.93%	41.1%	40.8%
80	39.5%	39.5%	39.60%	39.64%	39.7%	39.6%
90	41.1%	41.1%	41.07%	41.07%	41.1%	41.1%

[a]Assuming a peer plan that invests 60% in U.S. equity, 30% in global fixed income, and 10% in alternative investments.

1. For an excellent discussion on funding retiree health plans, see England (2001).

2. There are still a number of pension plans that develop their policy decisions on mean-variance types of analyses, or some consensus benchmark like the WM 50.

3. It is useful to determine what an increase in the funded ratio by 5 percent in one year would mean in terms of an additional sponsor contribution as a percentage of gross salaries.

4. Chung, Granito, and Prajogi (2001) demonstrate that the best performing plans went from a modest drain on earnings-per-share in 1991 to a meaningful contribution in 1999 and 2000.

5. Ambachtsheer and Ezra (1998), Chapters 3 and 4.

6. See Dert (1995) and Krishnamurthi, Muralidhar, and Van der Wouden (1998a).

7. This conclusion was made assuming that the plan sponsor would not withdraw any assets from the plan. If the sponsor were to withdraw assets from the plan when the funded ratio reaches certain levels, then the ability to take on higher risk on the investment side will be limited.

8. See Krishnamurthi, Muralidhar, and Van der Wouden (1998a), Peskin (1997), Dert (1995), and Boender (1998).

9. This is mainly due to the fact that the total contributions are low relative to the total market value of assets.

10. Our research showed that a dynamic funding approach would reduce the risk significantly, while ensuring the same or even higher wealth of the plan relative to a static approach.

11. These funding policies were extracted from a number of different policies as being the ones that were most effective for different investment policies. At the same time, these policies give the reader more insight into the impact of the different ways of making contributions to the plan.

12. The only minor difference is where models simulate yield curves rather than returns and as a result the equity premium is normally the premium to the yield on the long duration bond. See Mulvey and Ziemba (1999).

13. The reference here is to geometric returns.

14. There is a class of models that use hybrid simulation-optimization techniques and such a model was used for the case study in this chapter and the next.

15. Muralidhar and Van der Wouden (1998a) show the impact of making this the sole objective of a national pension plan.

16. A target ratio of 105 percent assumes an additional amount of 5 percent for usage risk. The results are robust even if the target ratio is lowered.

17. A probability of 5 percent would mean that the odds in any year of experiencing an actual funded ratio lower than the target would be a chance of 1 out of 20. A probability of 10 percent implies a chance of 1 out of 10.

18. See Dert (1995) for a technical discussion of performing such analyses. These are standard simulation techniques.

19. Justification for these assumptions is provided in Krishnamurthi, Muralidhar, and Van der Wouden (1998a).

20. The data assumptions for means, correlations, and standard deviations are identical to those used in Muralidhar and U (1997).

21. This shift arises by assuming this particular set of liabilities. For other liabilities, the direction would be the same, but not the same magnitude.

22. On the one hand, a higher funded status can come from an increase in the market value of the assets, which can be the result of good returns in any asset categories (e.g., fixed income). On the other hand, it can be a result of lower than expected increases on the liability side.

23. Other authors have suggested liability partitioning (Mennis and Clark 1983), whereby liability pools are broken out (e.g., for retirees and actives) and separate asset allocations established. This is likely to be inefficient from an overall sponsor's perspective as it does not allow for diversification of liability risk and as a consequence asset-liability risk.

24. In an asset-liability environment, the average contribution does not always decrease as the allocation to equity increases. The main reason for this result is that this particular plan is reasonably well funded at the beginning of the time horizon.

25. This statistic provides a peer comparison to a regular U.S. pension plan that invested 60 percent in U.S. equity, 30 percent in global fixed income and 10 percent in real estate and venture capital. However, a medical plan shows more resemblance to an insurance company.

26. However, the impact of such a flexible funding policy is limited for a medical plan because contributions are a small fraction of the total assets of the plan.

4

OPTIMAL

ALM STRATEGIES

Arun S. Muralidhar and Ronald van der Wouden

This chapter focuses on the practical implications of certain "alternative" investment strategies for pension plans. It compares these strategies and describes the situations under which they can lead to efficiency gains for pension plans in an ALM context. We demonstrate that relatively simple strategies can achieve substantial efficiency gains. In a seemingly counterintuitive result, leverage strategies, both static and dynamic, are risk reducing and hence outperform basic and derivative-based strategies. This occurs because dynamic leveraging replicates, more cost effectively, any derivative strategy in an ALM context. More important, when asset-liability markets are incomplete, asset-liability strategies will outperform asset-only strategies.

OVERVIEW

Over the last few years, institutional investors in the West have benefited from continuously rising stock markets and reasonably solid economic performance. Money has been pouring into capital markets and there has been substantial wealth accumulation. Institutional investors, such as pension plans,

Adapted from Arun Muralidhar and Ronald van der Wouden. "Optimal ALM Strategies for Defined Benefit Plans." First published in *The Journal of Risk,* Volume 2, Number 2. Copyright Risk Waters Group 2001.

have benefited from the unusually high returns. However, the recent financial turmoil in different regions around the world and the hesitation over the fundamental justification of these high returns have tempered expectations. As a consequence, and because pension plans are becoming more sophisticated in determining their investment strategy, these plans are looking increasingly for alternative investment opportunities, either to lock in their previous asset gains or to extend the choice in allocating their assets. In addition to extending into nonmarketable asset classes, pension plans are contemplating derivative strategies on their current asset positions. In spite of their relative complexity, it appears that pension funds in the United States have entered into these transactions in substantial volume.

This chapter focuses on the practical implications of certain alternative investment strategies for pension plans. Each of these strategies could be optimal, depending on the practical and regulatory constraints imposed on pension funds. This chapter compares these strategies and describes the situations under which these investment strategies can lead to efficiency gains for pension plans in an asset-liability management (ALM) context. These simulations demonstrate that relatively simple strategies can achieve substantial efficiency gains.

Outline

The analysis in this chapter is based on a hypothetical defined benefit pension plan, which makes annual benefit payments many years into the future and has inflows from contributions made by the sponsor of and participants in the plan. Since the investment horizon of pension plans is normally long term, strategies are evaluated over a period of 9 years. The choice of horizon is merely for simplicity and does not affect the results; however, we assume that plans review their investment policy annually. In a subsequent section, a more elaborate description of the investment strategies that are being compared is provided. The discussion in Chapter 3 showed the benefit of dynamic funding strategies, and this chapter formally demonstrates their importance. However, in a departure from previous research, leverage (to determine optimal strategies) is permitted. This is done as analyses are often conducted with leverage unintentionally precluded.[1] This may be a reflection of the fact that regulations in some countries preclude leverage in asset allocations.

The chapter is structured as follows. The different investment policy strategies are first described and then developed in greater detail. Subsequent sections then describe the assumptions on the economy and the pension plan's investment and contribution policy. This is followed by an overview of the methodology that has been used for analyzing the investment strategies and the results. Thereafter, extensions to the analysis are covered, concluding with recommendations for optimal strategies for pension funds. As indicated earlier, these principles can be more broadly applied to any investment problem, whether for an insurance company or a central bank managing reserves.

Strategies to Be Evaluated

There are three critical distinctions for the strategies: (1) static versus dynamic investment policies; (2) with and without derivatives; and (3) leveraged versus unleveraged portfolios. The static versus dynamic strategy has been highlighted in Chapter 3 in the context of a plain-vanilla ALM study; the analysis is extended here and the strategies are defined as follows.

The static investment strategy proposes a fixed allocation throughout the investment horizon, whereas the dynamic investment strategy focuses on the ability to revise the asset allocation from one period to the next. Derivative/ optioned investment strategies are based on the ability to acquire a long put position on the domestic equity portion of the portfolio (either on a static or dynamic basis). And leveraged investment strategies are based on the ability to construct portfolios that leverage cash or other investment-grade fixed income (either on a static or dynamic basis).

A CASE STUDY FOR A U.S.-BASED DEFINED BENEFIT PENSION PLAN

This section describes the environment used for the analyses, first the plan-specific issues and then the assumptions made on capital returns and volatility. In addition, assumptions are made on policy issues that deal with the restrictions and freedom the pension plan managers have in constructing its policy. The policy assumptions help to prevent investment policies from being impractical or unrealistic.

Plan-Specific Issues

This case study is based on the demographic profiles (i.e., length of employment, life expectancy, salary growth, mortality, and entry and exit rates) of participants of the pension fund of the World Bank Group Staff Retirement Plan. We have created a hypothetical plan based on these demographics, and the hypothetical plan is assumed to be a defined benefit scheme that entitles the employee, after 35 years of service, to a replacement rate of approximately 70 percent of his or her final salary. The benefits are unconditionally indexed to price inflation, and the liabilities of the plan are measured under the closed group method.[2] Further, a real discount factor of 4 percent is used for discounting the liabilities. It is critical to evaluate liabilities and funded ratios using the actuarial funding method. Otherwise recommendations on asset allocation and funding will not be synchronized with the recommendations of the actuaries.[3]

For the purposes of our analysis, a 125 percent initial ratio of asset to liabilities is assumed. Sensitivity to the initial funded ratio is evaluated and reported later. The maturity of the plan, measured by the ratio of present value of liabilities to total salary, is approximately 10. This value is significant as it suggests that a 1 percent change in liabilities, all else being equal, will require a 10 percent change in contributions (as a ratio to salaries) to maintain the funded status.

Asset Classes and Future Economic Environment

The standard techniques highlighted in Chapter 3 for simulating returns are used here. Further, the assumptions about asset class returns, volatility, and correlations are also maintained. For simplicity a long-term simulation horizon of 9 years is assumed and shorter-term constraints are ignored. The most important characteristics of the generated scenarios are depicted in Table 4.1. Currency-hedging issues are dealt with in Chapter 5.

Policy Issues

Once again a distinction has been made between two tools available to pension funds for managing their plan, namely, the investment policy and the contribution policy. Some restrictions on the use of these tools have been incorporated into the analysis to prevent the policies from becoming unrealistic.

Table 4.1
Characteristics of the Economic Variables

	Annual Expected Arithmetic Return (%)	Standard Deviation (Annual Volatility) (%)
Price inflation	4.0	3.0
U.S. equity	10.5	15.0
Non-U.S. equity (unhedged)	10.5	19.7
Emerging markets equity	10.5	23.3
U.S. fixed income (hedged)	6.5	5.2
Non-U.S. fixed income	6.5	12.6
High yield bonds	8.0	9.8
Inflation-indexed bonds	6.5	4.0
Real estate	7.0	18.0
Private equity	10.5	27.0
Cash	5.2	1.4

Investment Policy

The investment team can allocate investments of the pension fund to nine different asset classes (Table 4.1), which give a fair representation of the current investment opportunities for U.S. pension plans. In addition, the allocation to several classes has been fixed at a certain percentage to avoid significant allocation changes, from one period to the next, in asset classes that are illiquid.[4] An alternative way to manage this in the simulations would have been to increase transaction costs. Table 4.2 gives an overview of the levels at which certain asset classes are fixed.[5]

Derivative strategies could be used at a strategic level to protect any shortfall in return or alternatively on a tactical level to generate additional returns. In this chapter, the derivative strategy has been used for the former reason. The use of derivatives for tactical reasons is discussed in Chapter 6. Since derivatives on surpluses are not readily available in the market, the assumption in the analyses is that the plan sponsors have the ability to acquire a long put position on the U.S. equity portion of the portfolio. These options positions will be financed by liquidating U.S. equity positions with a market value equal to the premium on the options.

Although the pension plan in the analysis is constrained to long put positions only, a distinction has been made between a static and a dynamic

Table 4.2
Fixed and Floating Allocations

	Fixed/Floating	Allocation (If Fixed) (%)
U.S. equity	Floating	
Non-U.S. equity (unhedged)	Floating	
Emerging markets equity	Fixed	5.0
U.S. fixed income	Floating	
Non-U.S. Fixed Income (hedged)	Floating	
High-yield bonds	Fixed	2.0
Real estate	Fixed	7.0
Private equity	Fixed	3.0
Cash	Floating	

derivative strategy. (These strategies will be explained later in more detail.) Further, the possibility of acquiring a derivative position on one asset class (i.e., U.S. equity) is analyzed. There are two reasons for this: (1) to keep the transaction as transparent and simple as possible, and (2) the perceived tendency of institutional investors to focus on derivative strategies in one asset class only. This may be partly a reflection of the fact that the U.S. equity market tends to be one of the largest allocations for pension funds in the United States, and the equity market had indicated a susceptibility to a correction in 2000 and 2001.

Contribution Policy

In general, pension plans have the ability to revise the contribution rate from one year to the next. In Chapter 3, the benefit of such flexibility was demonstrated. However, this rate is often determined by either actuarial projections or accounting rules. In occupational pension plans, the contributions are made by the employer, and in some plans, by the employee. Generally the employee's portion of this amount is a fixed rate, whereas the employer's may be flexible and has therefore to be determined from one period to the next. There are, however, some practical limitations on the flexibility and levels of these contribution rates. Limitations on the flexibility could arise because of the nature of an organization or for tax reasons. For example, in an organization that is budget driven, it is difficult to accept a significant increase in the contribution rate, as it jeopardizes other activities.

It has already been pointed out that the initial funded ratio of the hypothetical pension plan is 125 percent. The contribution policy is so framed that at this funded ratio level the basic total contribution rate will be 7 percent,[6] which can be seen as the fixed portion that the employees are contributing. If the funded ratio falls below 110 percent, this rate will be increased; on the other hand, if the funded ratio increases to levels above 140 percent, this rate will be decreased. We assume that increases in the contribution level from one year to the next cannot exceed 5 percent, once the contribution rate exceeds the basic contribution of 7 percent. In addition, we restrict the contribution level to no higher than 25 percent.[7]

METHODOLOGY

The following is a description of the alternative investment strategies and an explanation of the methodology for comparing the different strategies.

Alternative Strategies

In this section, a number of different investment strategies are discussed.

Static and Dynamic Investment Strategy

Chapter 3 provided a description of these strategies and they are briefly reviewed below. A static investment strategy implies a set of allocations according to which the portfolio is rebalanced annually. Since the strategies are evaluated in a multiperiod context it is possible to change the allocation annually. The dynamic approach permits the asset allocation to change to a new optimal allocation every year based on the funded ratio of the plan.[8] The logic behind this method is that if the financial situation of a pension plan improves, then the ability to rebalance to a more risky portfolio is more feasible because of the increase in the risk-bearing capacity of the plan. Consequently, by taking on a more risky position, the expected return also increases. Chapter 6 recognizes that there will be difficulties in implementing dynamic strategies (for market reasons) and suggests ways to overcome these constraints.

Static Put Derivative Strategy

In the static derivative approach, the plan purchases a long put option on each unit invested in U.S. equity. This option has a maturity of one year, and the exercise price is set at the same level of the underlying asset at the moment the option is purchased (i.e., the derivative is at-the-money). This option position is purchased each year, regardless of the financial status of the plan. Consequently, even if the pension fund is significantly overfunded, the option position is still in place. This is essentially a naïve stock-versus-cash allocation decision.

Dynamic Put Derivative Strategy

Derivative strategies are easy to implement. In contrast to the static derivative strategy, the dynamic derivative strategy takes the financial status of the pension plan as the basis for entering into the transactions. The maturity of this option is also one year; however, the exercise price of the option is determined in a dynamic way. At the beginning of every year, the strategy makes a projection of the liability development during the course of the year and the funded ratio of the plan at the end of the year. The strategy then estimates the return it has to achieve on the U.S. equity portion of the portfolio in order to "ensure" a funded ratio of 100 percent at the end of the year. Consequently, the exercise price of the long put option is determined by these projections. The only additional restriction is the total amount that can be spent on option premiums. This amount is restricted to 10 percent of the total asset value that is allocated to U.S. equity. Application of this strategy implies that the derivative strategy is dependent on the financial status of the plan.[9] This is a sophisticated liability-based stock-versus-cash allocation strategy.

Leverage Opportunities

The discussion also covers the impact of allowing leveraged positions in the asset allocation. Since the investment horizon of the pension plan is generally long term, leveraging certain asset classes can be considered as a way to generate extra returns. In the strategies with leverage possibilities, we allow negative positions up to −100 percent in cash, U.S. fixed income, non-U.S. fixed income, U.S. equity, and non-U.S. equity. Negative positions are offset by increased allocations to other asset classes. Leveraging can be conducted in a static or a dynamic approach. It is interesting to note that allowing leverage enables the possible investment strategies to be extended and hence results in an expansion of the efficient frontier. However, in many countries, leveraging assets is not permitted, as it is considered to be speculative.[10]

Risk Measures, Objectives, and the Framework for Comparison

As highlighted in Chapter 3, the ratio of assets to liabilities is generally used as an indication of the financial status of the plan. It is often argued that investors worry that the return generated on an investment could be below a certain hurdle rate or threshold. This section describes the various objectives and risk measures used for the analysis.

Risk Measures

We use the funded ratio of the plan as the target, with a threshold of 100 percent. The appropriate strategy would be to minimize the probability that the funded ratio will be lower than 100 percent at any time (since it is impossible to preclude these situations completely, due to the uncertainty of the returns and the liabilities). Consequently, the probability that the funded ratio in any year is lower than 100 percent is used as a measure of the risk taken by the plan. However, this measure does not indicate the extent to which the funded ratio is below this threshold. In order to capture this, we use the downside deviation as a risk measure. The downside deviation represents the volatility of the shortfall when the funded ratio is lower than the threshold and hence indicates the extent to which the funded ratio is lower than this threshold.[11]

In this chapter we focus primarily on the downside deviation risk measure and the probability of not achieving a threshold for the funded ratio of 100 percent. These are generic measures for all plans and lend themselves to comparisons across plans, unlike comparisons of investment return, which do not normalize for different liabilities.

Objectives

Before presenting the results, we briefly address the possible objectives of a pension plan, which are quantified and used to compare different investment strategies. One of the main objectives is to minimize the occurrence and extent to which the funded ratio of the plan is lower than 100 percent. In addition, plans should try to maximize wealth and minimize the contributions made by the plan sponsor. These objectives are in some sense opposed to each other; however, in selecting the "right" investment strategy an oversight committee must make a trade-off between these objectives.

Comparison

The method used to compare different investment strategies is completely dependent on the objectives and consequently closely related to the risk measures used.

In general we make a distinction between three main objectives for overseers of a pension plan: (1) maximization of the funded ratio (i.e., maximization of the wealth of the plan), (2) minimization of the level and volatility of the contributions, and (3) minimization of the occurrences of underfunding (i.e., minimization of downside risk).

First, controlling the volatility of contributions is important for plans, because it is difficult for plan sponsors to budget for large increases in contribution rate from one period to the next. This is incorporated in our analysis by constraining the annual contribution rate increases to 5 percent once the contribution rate reaches levels higher than the basic rate of 7 percent. Further, in order to reduce the complexity of viewing the problem in a three-dimensional space, the additional assumption is made that the contribution rate can be negative (i.e., the sponsor can extract the surplus and liquidate assets to repay itself and/or participants). This would effectively make the plan revocable (Chapter 3).

This simple modification ensures that the maximization of wealth objective will now indirectly appear in the average contribution rate. This follows because maximization of the wealth implies that the funded ratio of the plan will be as high as possible. However, if one assumes that once the surplus of the plan reaches a certain level the extra surplus will be given back to the plan sponsor, the wealth of the plan is maximized by maximizing the amount that will be paid back to the plan sponsor (i.e., minimizing the contribution level).

As a result, the focus is the risk of the plan and the average contribution rate. The objective will now be to minimize the contribution rate for every level of risk or to minimize the risk at every level for the contribution rate.

In the previous chapter the percentage allocated to equity was used to demonstrate the impact on the choice of objectives on the risk-taking ability of the plan. In this chapter, we move to a graphical representation of portfolio composition and the success or failure of these portfolios in achieving strategic objectives.

Using the asset allocation to demonstrate the impact of changes in objectives is extremely useful. The graphical representation used in Figures 4.1 through 4.8 also demonstrates this impact, and is better at showing the relative performance of different strategies for the same objectives.

In Figure 4.1, the framework to compare different strategies is presented. The vertical axis is the risk of the plan and the horizontal axis is the average contribution rate. The outlined square in this plane represents a particular investment policy. The graph makes it clear that implementing this strategy implies a certain risk level for the plan (in this example the downside deviation is about 3 percent) and that the expected annual contribution rate for this strategy is a little below 0 percent. For example, if the expected funded ratio of outcomes below 100 percent (i.e., the expected value of the negative surplus) is 95 percent, a three-standard-deviation equivalent of the downside risk would

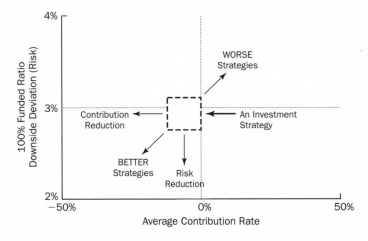

Figure 4.1   Framework for Strategy Comparisons

imply that when the funded ratio is below 100 percent, the corresponding confidence interval implies a funded ratio of 86 percent.

Further, we can discern from this figure that better strategies are those with either a lower risk level and/or a lower average contribution rate.

RESULTS

The following subsections each compare different investment strategies. The static investment strategy, described first, is used as a benchmark for comparison with each alternative strategy. Before the results are described, it must be noted that the outcomes and the conclusions thereafter are dependent on the assumptions that were made. Any modification in these assumptions will produce different results. In the next section the impact of such changes is evaluated.

Static Investment Policy Without Leverage and Without Derivatives

The results of this first strategy are used as a benchmark to compare the efficiency improvements of subsequent strategies. Figure 4.2 charts all efficient investment policies that achieve the objectives.

Figure 4.2 highlights a frontier that connects different investment policies. This frontier has been created using a hybrid simulation/optimization procedure, which has been described by Boender (1997). Each investment policy on

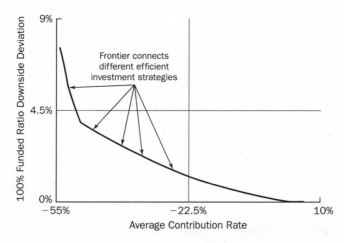

Figure 4.2   The Efficient ALM Frontier for Static Asset Allocation

this frontier is an efficient strategy; this means that given the average contribution level of this strategy, each policy has minimum risk. Alternatively, each policy has a minimum expected average contribution, given the risk imposed by this strategy.

Figure 4.2 demonstrates that the downside deviation risk of the plan ranges from nearly 0 percent to approximately 7.5 percent. The low-risk investment policies (i.e., in the figure, the policies with low downside deviation and high contribution rates) have hardly any allocation to equity, whereas the high-risk policies allocate the maximum allowable percentage to equity.[12] In addition, the figure shows that the average contribution level over the horizon decreases as the risk and expected returns of the plan increase, which intuitively is a reasonable result.

Static Investment Policy with Static Put Derivative Strategy (Without Leverage)

The foregoing exercise was conducted with the strategy of implementing a static put derivative position on the domestic equity portion of the portfolio. Figure 4.3 demonstrates two "efficient" frontiers. The first frontier is referred to as the basic frontier, described in the last section (i.e., static investment policy, without leverage and without derivatives). The second frontier connects the efficient investment policies with the derivative position.

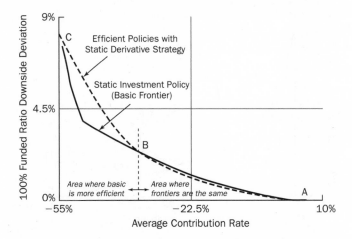

Figure 4.3   Comparing Static Derivatives Frontier with the Basic Frontier

Figure 4.3 highlights a distinction between two areas on the frontier. In the first area (A-B) the two frontiers are almost the same, whereas in the second (B-C), the optioned policies are less efficient than the basic investment strategy (i.e., for the same level of risk the basic investment strategy has a lower average contribution rate).

A comparison between a policy on both frontiers that has the same contribution rate and risk (i.e., in region A-B) suggests that the policy with the derivative strategy has a larger amount allocated to equity, especially to domestic equity, which is the investment class where the derivative strategy is being purchased. Hence, the extra return that has been generated by a larger allocation to equity is just enough to cover the costs of the derivative strategy.

The simple conclusion is that the static one-year derivative strategy is not more efficient than the policy without this derivative strategy, because the derivative strategy is applied blindly without regard to any ALM considerations. This strategy is expensive, as demonstrated by the B-C region.

Static Investment Policy with Dynamic Put Derivative Strategy (Without Leverage)

Figure 4.4 shows the results of the basic and the dynamic derivative strategy. It depicts two frontiers, and three areas can be broadly distinguished. In the first area (A-B) the frontiers overlap, which means that the strategies are similar to

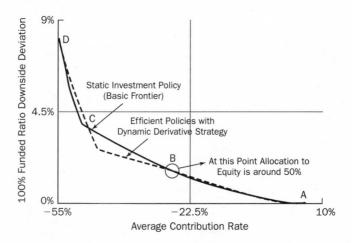

Figure 4.4 The Dynamic Derivatives Strategy

each other in performance. In the second region (B-C) the policy with the dynamic derivative strategy is more efficient than the basic strategy (i.e., for the same levels of risk the average contribution rate is lower for the policies with the derivative strategy). At the point where the derivative strategy becomes more efficient than the basic strategy, point B, the total allocation to equity is around 50 percent. This implies that once the total allocation to equity is higher than 50 percent, it would make sense to implement policies with dynamic option strategies. However, once the maximum allowable equity level has been reached, in this case 87 percent at point C, the basic investment strategy is slightly more efficient than the strategy with the derivatives (C-D).

Dynamic Investment Strategy

An advantage of analyzing investment strategies in a multiperiod framework is that plans can, and do, revise the asset allocation from one period to the other. Under a dynamic strategy, the periodic asset allocation is changed in accordance with the funded ratio or the financial status of the plan, which is captured by a rebalancing rule. Generally, a pension plan can experience efficiency gains by changing the asset allocation to a more risky portfolio when the funded ratio of the plan increases.[13] For example, a simple rebalancing rule would be of the form[14]

Percentage allocated to equities at time t

$= 15\% + 0.5 \times$ funded ratio at $t - 1$

Figure 4.5 allows for the comparison between a dynamic strategy and the basic investment policy. In this figure, two frontiers have been depicted. The frontier that represents the dynamic investment strategy connects policies where the rebalancing rule is optimized. The figure clearly shows that the ability to revise the asset allocation will result in significant efficiency gains (A-B). These efficiency gains are obvious for each risk level until a point where the maximum allowable allocation to equity has been reached (B).

Since the dynamic strategy increases its allocation to risk when the plan is most able to bear risk, and decreases risk when least able to bear it, risk-taking and hence efficiency is greater than in the case of a static investment strategy that may take risk when there is no risk-bearing capacity.

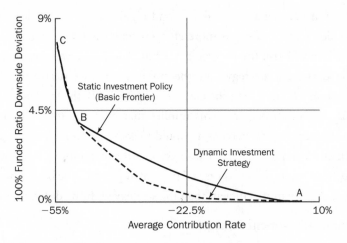

Figure 4.5 The Dynamic Asset Allocation Strategy

This brings us to our next investment truth: *A dynamic investment approach is better than a static investment approach.* A dynamic investment approach requires changing the asset allocation every year, based on the funded ratio of the plan. This involves increasing the equity allocation for any increase in the funded ratio. This strategy would result in higher expected terminal wealth and lower levels of risk than in a static investment approach. However, such rules need to be optimized using appropriate models.

Leveraged Portfolios

The next extension is to allow the plan to short any asset class with a compensating long position in another asset class. Figure 4.6 shows the results of this analysis; once again, we compare the basic frontier (i.e., investment strategy without leverage) with an efficient leveraged frontier.

This figure shows that the ability to have leveraged positions extends the range of investment opportunities and consequently results in a longer efficient frontier. Hence, it is now possible to determine the efficient strategy for higher levels of risk. Therefore, leveraging permits plans to satisfy utility functions that were previously not satisfied (i.e., those that were not tangential to the leverage-restricted efficient frontier). Further, the frontiers overlap each other until a certain point (B). From this point on, the leveraged investment

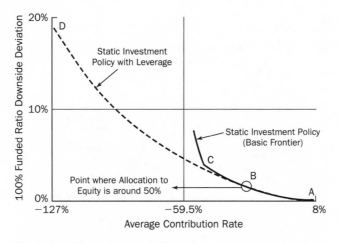

Figure 4.6 Evaluating Static Policies with Leverage

strategies are more efficient. At point B, the allocation to equity is approximately 50 percent. In addition, the picture shows that once the maximum allowable percentage of equity has been reached in the basic investment strategy (i.e., at point C where the basic frontier has an unusual bend), the efficiency gains of the leveraged strategy are significant.

Leveraging produces such results because a previous artificial constraint (i.e., no negative positions) has been lifted. This leads to greater exploitation of expected returns and a covariance matrix.

The last analysis was based on a static investment approach. The same analysis can be done using the ability to revise the investment policy periodically (i.e., using the dynamic investment approach). Figure 4.7 shows four different efficient frontiers. The four frontiers represent the static and the dynamic investment approach with and without the opportunity of leveraged positions. The critical result is that the dynamic investment approach with leverage is the most efficient of all the investment strategies.

Additional analyses on the policies with the leverage opportunities were done in the context of derivative strategies. However, it appeared that no additional efficiency gains were achieved if the leverage opportunity was combined with either the static or the dynamic derivative strategy. The latter result follows since the derivative strategy is implemented to cover only one asset class.

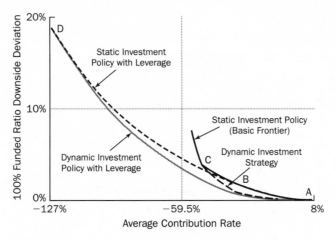

Figure 4.7 Four Efficient Frontiers

Consequently, the protection achieved is relatively small compared with the gains achieved from leveraging the entire asset portfolio. This result is not surprising, since by relaxing the nonnegative position constraint, the optimization is conducted in a less constrained environment.

In addition, dynamic leveraged strategies should outperform derivative strategies, as a derivative strategy is effectively a rebalancing and leveraging strategy. Dynamic leveraging outperforms the simple derivative strategy because it is applied on the entire portfolio rather than on a single asset class. Hence this result is consistent with the options theory, where the cost of an option on a portfolio must be less than that of a portfolio of options.

Comparison of All the Strategies

Figure 4.8 displays the efficient frontiers for all of the strategies. From their form, the following conclusions can be arrived at for a given funded status:

1. Imposition of a static one-year derivative strategy does not provide efficiency gains for the pension plan.
2. The dynamic derivative strategy could improve the performance of the pension plan when the total exposure to equity is larger than 50 percent (beyond B).

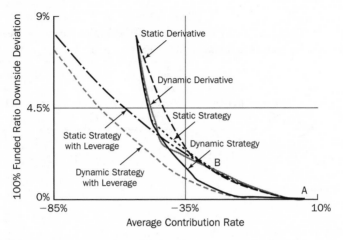

Figure 4.8   Comparing All Strategies

3. Although the dynamic derivative strategy can provide efficiency gains for the pension plan, the dynamic investment strategy, which allows the asset allocation to be revised from one year to the next, outperforms these derivative strategies.

4. Permitting leverage results in more investment opportunities and hence expands the efficient frontier. Consequently, investment strategies for more risky utility functions can be optimized (rather than having a constrained suboptimal allocation) by allowing leverage.

5. As the total allocation to equity exceeds 50 percent, the leveraged portfolios gain in efficiency. This is a function of the funded ratio and not a constraint imposed in the research.

6. The dynamic investment approach, with the ability to have short positions, offset by compensating long positions, is clearly the most efficient investment approach, regardless of the risk tolerance level of the plan.

Table 4.3 lists the optimal allocations for each of these investment strategies for a downside deviation of 2.0 percent.[15] This table also provides other statistics, such as the average funded ratio, contribution rate for these strategies, annualized returns, annualized standard deviations, and ALM risk

Table 4.3

Initial Asset Allocations Under Various Strategies Assuming Downside Deviation of 2.0% If Funded Ratio Falls Below 100%

	Static (%)	Static + Static Derivative (%)	Static + Dynamic Derivative (%)	Dynamic[a] (%)	Static + Leverage (%)	Dynamic[a] + Leverage (%)
U.S. equity	34	58	57	44	23	36
Non-U.S. equity (unhedged)	20	21	6	28	20	23
Emerging market equity	5	5	5	5	5	5
U.S. fixed income	0	0	3	0	38	33
Non-U.S. fixed income (hedged)	29	3	18	12	56	60
High-yield bonds	2	2	2	2	2	2
Real estate	7	7	7	7	7	7
Private equity	3	3	3	3	3	3
Cash	0	0	0	0	−53	−69
Avg. contribution rate (annual)	−32	−33	−35	−39	−34	−47
Avg. funded ratio (annual)	131	130	130	130	132	129
Std. dev. funded ratio (annual)	18	19	20	21	18	23
Avg. return (annual)	9.1	9.0	9.1	9.3	9.3	9.7
Std. dev. return (annual)	9.6	10.6	10.3	11.1	9.7	12.1
DsD (FR < 100)[b]	2.0	2.0	2.0	2.0	2.0	2.0
Prob (FR < 100)[c]	4.1	5.4	7.4	6.5	4.3	6.4
DsD (FR < 90)	0.8	0.8	0.5	0.6	0.8	0.6
Prob (FR < 90)	1.2	1.7	1.7	1.4	1.5	1.5
Prob (FR < 80)	0.4	0.4	0.2	0.1	0.3	0.1
DsD (FR < 80)	0.2	0.1	0.0	0.0	0.2	0.1

[a]Note that these strategies are dynamic investment policies. Hence the portfolios presented for these strategies are the initial asset allocations (i.e., the allocations at year 0).

[b]DsD (FR < 100%): The downside deviation in any year if the funded ratio falls below 100%.

[c]Prob (FR < 100%): The probability in any year that the funded ratio will fall below 100%.

measures. It is interesting to note that from the standard mean-variance perspective, the dynamic strategy with leverage has the worst risk-return trade-off. However, from an ALM perspective this strategy has the same downside risk of 2 percent as the other strategies and the average contribution rate is much lower. This would suggest that from an ALM perspective the greatest efficiency gain is from the dynamic strategy with leverage.

EXTENSIONS

Initial Funded Ratio

The results were developed assuming an initial funded status of 125 percent. These conclusions were also evaluated for initial funding ratios of 85 percent and 100 percent. The results appear to be relatively robust to the initial point, though the magnitude of the efficiency gain and the points of inflection (e.g., point B) may differ. An interesting point is that in the case of the initial funded ratio of 85 percent, the derivative strategies are ultimately too costly for the expected gains as the goal is to attempt to ensure a much higher target funded ratio (i.e., a 100 percent funded ratio).

Type of Derivative Strategy

For practical reasons, the derivative strategies that were evaluated have a maturity period of one year. In general, pension plans enter into derivative transactions with a one-year maturity. However, it appears from Boender, Oldenkamp, and Vos (1997) and Zwanenburg (1998) that the use of option strategies with a longer maturity period could lead to more efficiency gains. The result is not intuitively obvious, as one would expect a more rapid rebalancing to be more efficient. It is therefore likely that the results are derived from the assumptions on the term structure of volatility.

Further, we limit the use of derivatives to a long put position on the domestic equity allocation. An extension of this strategy to international equities could increase the (small) efficiency gains that have been detected with the dynamic derivative strategy. In addition, it could be preferable for pension plans to consider other types of derivatives (e.g., zero cost or exotic derivative strategies).[16] However, Zwanenburg (1998) suggests that the use of certain exotic derivative strategies will not lead to more efficiency gains than the simple derivative strategies that have been evaluated in this chapter (i.e., the long put derivative strategy).[17] Finally, the cap on total derivatives in the dynamic strategy could be raised above 10 percent, but this is not expected to significantly affect the results.

Importance of Correlation Assumptions

The strategies are largely driven by the correlation assumptions, and recent experience has shown that in times of market distress, correlations tend to unity. Hence, such strategies may be risky in the short term, but would be appropriate if the long-term correlation estimates are accurate.

Understanding Sources of Leverage Gains

A critical result is that permitting leverage expands the efficient frontier and makes it preferred to the unleveraged case. This happens for two reasons: permitting leverage allows for an increase in expected returns and a greater exploitation of the correlation matrix. Future research should focus on identifying what fraction of the gains can be attributed to these two aspects of the experiment.

SUMMARY

Two types of derivative strategies are evaluated in this chapter: a static derivative strategy and a dynamic derivative approach. The latter takes the financial status of the plan into account when the derivative is purchased. From a strategic point of view, it appears that the dynamic derivative strategy could be more efficient than a static investment strategy with or without derivatives. However, the dynamic investment strategy, which allows the asset allocation to change from one year to the next, outperforms the derivative strategies.

The most interesting results are derived by relaxing one of the simplest restrictions in determining the asset allocation, namely, the nonnegative constraint on portfolio positions. Permitting short and compensating long positions in asset classes increases the investment opportunity set substantially (i.e., the efficient frontier is extended significantly), and the dynamic investment strategy with leveraged positions outperforms the investment strategies with derivatives as well as the strategy without the leverage opportunity. This outperformance occurs because dynamic leveraging replicates, more cost effectively, any derivative strategy in an ALM context. More important, when asset-liability markets are incomplete, asset-liability strategies will outperform asset-only strategies.

Thus plan sponsors can add two more investment truths to the growing list, as shown in the accompanying box.

INVESTMENT TRUTHS

■ *Dynamic investment strategies outperform (or perform no worse than) static investment strategies.*

■ *Leveraged investment strategies outperform (or perform no worse than) unleveraged investment strategies from an asset-liability risk management perspective.*

1. See Peskin (1997) and Boender (1998).

2. Estimation under the closed group method means that the liability is the value of benefits expected to be paid, with both salaries and service projected to expected dates of termination or retirement, including the benefits in payments. This would be equivalent to valuation on a projected benefit obligation (PBO) basis, but it also incorporates expected future service of employees.

3. In some plans, as demonstrated in the next chapter, the present value of liabilities will be affected by changes in the real interest rate.

4. Given the expected returns and volatilities of these asset classes, there will be some rebalancing, but constraining these allocations bounds the problem to a more practical level.

5. This is not a buy-and-hold strategy; rebalancing to the same allocation will involve transaction costs. However, in the case of real estate and private equity, portfolios are marked-to-market infrequently and hence rebalancing is difficult. In high yield and emerging equity, rebalancings are affected by cost and delay in liquidating positions.

6. One could argue that contributions are not necessary for a high funded ratio. We make this assumption because we consider situations where the funded ratio is less than 100 percent and do not want to have to normalize for different contributions.

7. In the analysis we allow negative contribution rates, which is an assumption explained in more detail in the next section.

8. See Boender (1998) for a description and empirical results on this strategy.

9. See Vos (1997), pp. 28–32, for an elaborate discussion on this strategy. See also Boender, Oldenkamp, and Vos (1997) for results on this strategy for a pension plan. The impact of relaxing this constraint on the amount of the derivative overlay is evaluated later.

10. Modigliani and Modigliani (1997) and Muralidhar (2000) show that leveraging in a purely asset context may be appropriate to control for risk.

11. See also Philips (1997). The downside risk of the funded ratio declining below a threshold is analogous to the downside deviation of portfolio returns. See Sortino and Van der Meer (1991).

12. See Table 4.3.

13. See Boender (1998) and Krishnamurthi, Muralidhar, and Van der Wouden (1998b).

14. In a truly dynamic framework, the intercept and coefficient will be time-dependent. As an example, a linear relationship is given between the funded ratio and the amount of equity investments; however, these relationships can also be nonlinear or discrete.

15. A downside deviation of 2 percent if the funded ratio falls below 100 percent is a commonly used threshold in the Netherlands. It defines the maximum risk defined benefit plans are willing to take.

16. For instance, a pay-later derivative has the favorable characteristic that the premium payment and the payoff will take place simultaneously; this feature could be preferable to pension funds, since the cash flows will be conveniently arranged.

17. Zwanenburg (1998) evaluated pay-later, look-back, and barrier derivative strategies in an ALM context.

5

AN ASSET-LIABILITY ANALYSIS OF THE CURRENCY DECISION FOR PENSION PLANS

Arun S. Muralidhar, Ronald van der Wouden, and Robertus Prajogi

Existing research on the optimal currency hedge ratio for international equity or bond portfolios fails to recognize that an institutional investor has to match assets against liabilities. Therefore, previous recommendations on the optimal hedge ratio are incorrect and impractical for the average pension or insurance fund. This chapter shows how the asset-liability perspective differs from the asset-only perspective and demonstrates the implications for institutional investors. In addition, clients often determine their optimal asset allocation ignoring the currency question and optimize the currency hedge on international assets as a secondary decision. This chapter demonstrates that it is better to jointly optimize the asset allocation and hedge ratio simultaneously. Finally, using information on active currency management programs, this chapter demonstrates the benefit of these programs from an asset-liability perspective.

OVERVIEW

A wealth of research exists on the optimal currency hedge ratio applied to international equity or bond portfolios by institutional investors (Black 1989,

Adapted from Arun S. Muralidhar, Robertus Prajogi, and Ronald van der Wouden. "An Asset-Liability Analysis of the Currency Decision for Pension Plans." *Derivatives Quarterly,* Volume 7, Number 2, Winter 2000.

Nesbitt 1991, and Perold and Schulman 1988). However, these papers fail to recognize that the average institutional investor must match assets against liabilities, so they discuss issues from a purely asset perspective. Therefore, previous recommendations on the optimal hedge ratio are incorrect and impractical for the average pension or insurance fund. It has been recognized only recently that investors should select strategic hedge ratios on the basis of asset-liability studies (Hersey and Minnick 2000). In addition, a recent paper (Grinold and Meese 2000) declared that funds that conduct hedge ratio analyses in two stages (asset-liability and then a hedge-ratio analysis on international assets only) are likely to invest in fewer international assets and are less likely to be hedged than those that incorporate all decisions in an asset-liability study.

As demonstrated earlier, asset-only optimal portfolios can often be suboptimal in an asset-liability context. This chapter demonstrates the implications for institutional investors that have to select an optimal currency hedge ratio from an asset-liability management (ALM) perspective. In addition, often plan sponsors determine their optimal asset allocation while ignoring the currency question and then optimize the currency hedge on international assets as a secondary decision. This chapter will demonstrate why it is more optimal to jointly optimize the asset allocation and hedge ratio simultaneously.[1] In addition, using information on active management programs, the implications for allocation of risk to currency programs are evaluated and the analysis demonstrates the benefit of active currency management from an ALM perspective.

Outline

This chapter is structured as follows: the next section considers asset-liability objectives (and associated risks) for the case study and lists measures to evaluate the achievement of those objectives. The implications for passive currency hedging decisions by applying an asset-liability approach are then considered, followed by an evaluation of active currency programs and the allocation of risk to such programs. The chapter concludes with some suggestions for plan sponsors who are revisiting asset-allocation studies and are considering the currency hedging question or active currency management programs.

The case study considers a Canadian pension plan, as it raises two interesting issues: the fact that foreign content in 2001 is restricted to 30 percent of total assets from the former 25 percent;[2] and that foreign investments in equities (on a capitalization-weighted basis) from a Canadian perspective can be dichotomized into 50 percent U.S. and 50 percent other developed markets. The impact of these externally imposed constraints is evaluated. In addition, the chapter reviews implications for a uniform hedge ratio on all foreign assets as opposed to different hedge ratios for various currencies.

ASSET-LIABILITY OBJECTIVES AND RISK MEASURES

Pension plan sponsors should try to maximize wealth and pension income, while minimizing contributions. These objectives are in some sense opposed to each other, as highlighted in Table 5.1; however, in selecting the "right" investment strategy (both in terms of asset allocation and hedge ratio) an oversight committee must make trade-offs between these objectives.

Policy Issues

As highlighted earlier, these asset-liability objectives can be represented through simple questions:

- What asset allocation will maintain a fully funded status over a given time?

Table 5.1
Objectives, Target Levels, Risk Measures, and Weaknesses

Objective	Target Level	Risk Measure	Weaknesses
Asset perspective	Maximize return	Minimize volatility	Uncoupled assets and liabilities
Preserve funded status	Expected funded ratio	Mean of funded ratio in lowest quintile	Increased contributions help meet this goal
Minimize contributions	50th percentile of present value of contributions	Mean contribution in highest quintile	Funded status may deteriorate over time
Minimize income statement impact	Expected pension expense	Mean pension expense of highest quintile	Long-run return may be sacrificed

- What asset allocation will minimize the probability of making contributions over the same horizon?
- What asset allocation will maintain a pension income over the same horizon?

Table 5.1 transforms these questions into practical decisions by highlighting key objectives and mapping them directly into easily observed risk measures.[3] These measures are slightly different from those in previous chapters, demonstrating the many ways in which risk can be measured for the same objectives. The chosen parameters are somewhat arbitrary and each plan sponsor will need to decide what threshold of pain they can tolerate for these risk measures. The weaknesses of these approaches taken in isolation are presented in the table to highlight how these objectives may contradict one another.

Further, this chapter extends the graphical representation of portfolios and their achievement of objectives presented in Chapter 4. Figure 5.1 demonstrates the paradigm under which any asset allocation may be evaluated in an asset-only and an asset-liability context. The horizontal axis and the vertical

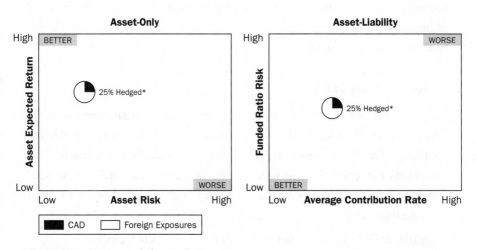

Figure 5.1 Framework for Analysis

Note: This is shown for illustrative purposes only and is not meant to illustrate the performance of any specific client account. Hedge ratio = [(hedged portfolio percentage of international assets)/(total percentage of international assets)] × 100%.

*Hedge ratios are applied equally to both U.S. and non-U.S. equities.

axis for the asset-only perspective represent the standard mean-variance objectives. In the asset-liability framework, the vertical axis represents the funded ratio risk (highlighted in Table 5.1) and the horizontal axis is the average contribution rate. The balls in the figure represent the performance of a particular investment strategy, with the black and white coding representing the currency composition of international assets. A portfolio where the international content is 25 percent hedged into Canadian dollars (CAD) is represented by balls three-quarters in foreign exposure (white) and one-quarter in Canadian dollars (shaded black). In the asset-only framework, moving to the northwest implies better portfolios, whereas in the asset-liability framework, moving to the southwest implies more efficient portfolios (that is, lower contributions and lower risk to the funded ratio).

IMPLICATIONS FOR ASSET ALLOCATION AND PASSIVE CURRENCY HEDGING

This section is composed of three subsections. The first provides the overall asset-liability framework and the details on the pension fund's liabilities; the second gives data on the asset market that underlies this study; and the third examines the performance of various asset allocations and currency hedge ratios vis-à-vis these objectives.

Asset-Liability Framework

The essence of any asset-liability study is to integrate the analysis of assets and liabilities over identical economic scenarios. The first step is to identify the liability profile after incorporating all the demographic data and actuarial assumptions. For simplicity, a generic liability structure for a Canadian defined-benefit pension fund has been chosen and the initial characteristics of the fund are described here:

Initial funded status: 109 percent (assuming a projected benefit obligation)

Initial contribution rate as percent of salary: 2.3 percent

Initial pension expense as percent of salary: 3.3 percent

Duration of liabilities: 23 years

Maturity of plan[4] (defined as present value of liabilities/salaries): 0.5

The analysis assumes that two key macroeconomic variables have an impact on the present value of liabilities: interest rates and inflation. In addition, these two variables also have an impact on asset valuations and hence influence the performance of any asset allocation strategy.

Forward-Looking Assumptions on Key Variables

To deal with the uncertainty and the impact of asset returns, different scenarios of the future economic environment are created (based on JP Morgan Fleming Asset Management's long-term economic projections). Each scenario represents the development of these returns over the chosen horizon of 5 years. This time period is more for convenience and could be extended to 9 years, as with the previous case study. A static investment policy will be evaluated for each scenario, and the impact of this particular investment policy will be captured by risk measures, which take into account the behavior of this policy to each different scenario.[5]

Each economic factor is assumed to follow a random walk: that is, the factors are not autocorrelated.[6] In addition, the statistical relationships among the economic factors are preserved in the simulations.[7] The assumptions for expected return, standard deviations, and correlations for the key asset classes are provided in Table 5.2. For simplicity, because foreign content is constrained, foreign bonds are not considered in the allocations, with the entire foreign content allocated to equities. Implicitly, it is assumed that investors wish to utilize the foreign content to capture the extra risk premium that equities provide. In addition, alternative assets are restricted to real estate.

Embedded in Table 5.2 are the assumptions of an expected real risk-free rate of 2.8 percent (that is, the difference between cash and expected inflation, which for Canada is assumed to be 2 percent), a real bond return (difference between fixed income and cash) of 1.7 percent, and an expected real equity risk premium of 3 percent (difference between the expected return on equity and fixed income). Unhedged U.S. equities are estimated to earn approximately the same as Canadian equities, and other international assets are

Table 5.2
Expected Return, Risk, and Correlation Assumptions (Passive Management)

	Expected Return (%)	Std. Dev. (%)	Correlation											
			1	2	3	4	5	6	7	8	9	10	11	12
Inflation	2.0	1.2	1.00											
Domestic cash	4.8	0.9	0.35	1.00										
Domestic bonds	6.5	6.0	0.08	0.12	1.00									
Domestic equity	9.6	14.2	0.03	−0.15	0.45	1.00								
Foreign bonds unhedged	6.7	7.5	0.00	0.01	0.09	−0.11	1.00							
Foreign bonds hedged	6.5	3.4	0.14	0.19	0.68	0.25	0.39	1.00						
Foreign equity ex-U.S. unhedged	10.6	17.3	−0.03	−0.18	0.10	0.44	0.32	0.17	1.00					
Foreign equity ex-U.S. hedged	10.3	16.8	0.03	−0.03	0.21	0.55	−0.12	0.18	0.81	1.00				
U.S. equity unhedged	9.2	12.7	0.00	−0.15	0.27	0.66	0.13	0.35	0.52	0.52	1.00			
U.S. equity hedged	9.1	12.0	0.12	0.33	0.41	0.65	−0.06	0.42	0.34	0.49	0.81	1.00		
EM[a] equity unhedged	14.5	22.8	0.04	−0.12	0.13	0.52	−0.14	−0.01	0.48	0.50	0.45	0.43	1.00	
Real estate	6.9	5.7	−0.21	−0.52	−0.24	−0.18	0.17	−0.16	0.03	−0.09	0.01	−0.38	−0.26	1.00

Note: These numbers are hypothetical examples shown for illustrative purposes only and are not meant to illustrate the performance or pension plan characteristics of any specific client's portfolio. The expected returns, standard deviations, and correlations are hypothetical estimates. There is also no assurance that any client account will perform in line with these estimates.

[a]EM = emerging markets.

expected to earn a slight premium (1 percent). Further, 10-year (monthly) historical data is used to create estimates of the correlations among these asset classes.

The return assumptions for the hedged and unhedged international assets are largely similar except that hedging the international and U.S. equity benchmarks will incur transactions costs of 30 and 10 basis points (bps) per year respectively. However, the hedged international equities normally have lower volatility than their unhedged equivalents and different correlations with other asset classes. It is interesting to note that the correlation of Canadian equities and unhedged foreign equities are largely similar to those of hedged equities.

In determining the hedge ratio for any asset allocation, the proportion of unhedged foreign assets should be compared to the total foreign allocation. For example, if the allocation to international assets is 30 percent with 5 percent in both hedged and unhedged foreign assets, this is a 50 percent hedge ratio.

Results

This section examine four cases, comparing asset-only conclusions with asset-liability conclusions:

1. Optimal hedge ratio when foreign content is capped at 30 percent and a uniform hedge ratio is applied to all foreign assets

2. A comparison between 30 percent foreign and 40 percent foreign content viewed from two perspectives: whether the 30 percent cap is beneficial or detrimental to Canadian investors, and what the implications are for the optimal hedge ratio

3. Whether international assets should be treated as a composite or decomposed into other foreign and U.S. assets (that is, are the hedge ratios the same from such an exercise?)

4. Whether a two-stage optimization is necessarily incorrect

Table 5.3 summarizes the different asset allocations that will be considered to answer these questions. Allocations to the different asset classes, expected return and standard deviation, unhedged foreign content, hedge ratio, and net of hedging currency exposure is provided for each policy mix.

Table 5.3
Information for Nine Portfolios (Passive Management)

	A	B	C	D	E	F	G	H	I
Domestic bonds (%)	31.00	31.00	31.00	31.00	31.00	31.00	31.00	31.00	31.00
Domestic equity (%)	35.00	35.00	35.00	25.00	25.00	25.00	25.00	25.00	25.00
Foreign equity ex-U.S. unhedged (%)	13.50	10.10	6.75	18.50	13.90	11.10	9.25	18.50	18.50
Foreign equity ex-U.S. hedged (%)	0.00	3.40	6.75	0.00	4.60	7.40	9.25	0.00	0.00
U.S. equity unhedged (%)	13.50	10.10	6.75	18.50	13.90	11.10	9.25	9.30	0.00
U.S. equity hedged (%)	0.00	3.40	6.75	0.00	4.60	7.40	9.25	9.20	18.50
EM[a] equity (%)	3.00	3.00	3.00	3.00	3.00	3.00	3.00	3.00	3.00
Real estate (%)	4.00	4.00	4.00	4.00	4.00	4.00	4.00	4.00	4.00
Expected return (%)	8.76	8.75	8.73	8.79	8.77	8.76	8.75	8.78	8.77
Standard deviation (%)	8.89	8.86	8.86	8.73	8.65	8.63	8.63	8.58	8.49
Sharpe ratio (%)	0.9854	0.9876	0.9853	1.0069	1.0139	1.0151	1.0139	1.0233	1.0330
Foreign content (%)	30%	30%	30%	40%	40%	40%	40%	40%	40%
Hedge ratio	Unh.	25%	50%	Unh.	25%	40%	50%	50%	100% H U.S.
Currency exposure (%)	30%	20.25%	13.5%	40%	27.75%	22.2%	18.5%	27.75%	18.5%

[a]EM = emerging markets.

Recommendations for Hedging Using an Asset-Liability Approach

Figure 5.2 demonstrates the first result. Although hedging (such as 25 percent hedging) is preferred in the asset-only framework for a 30 percent allocation to international assets, an unhedged benchmark is preferred for this client given the liability structure and objectives. In other words, even though portfolio B is preferred to both A and C on the basis of the Sharpe ratio (defined as expected return divided by the standard deviation),[8] A is preferred to B and C from an asset-liability perspective. The difference is not immense, as only 30 percent is allocated to international and this is a young plan, but the results are intriguing.[9] This result runs counter to the claim of Grinold and

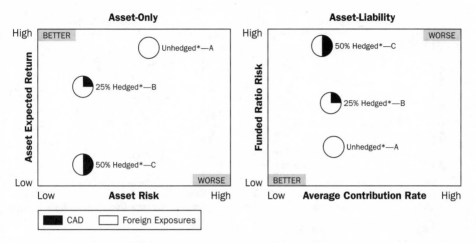

Figure 5.2   Comparing Asset-Only to Asset-Liability Analyses

Note: This is shown for illustrative purposes only and is not meant to illustrate the performance of any specific client account. Hedge ratio = [(hedged portfolio percentage of international assets)/(total percentage of international assets)] × 100%.

*Hedge ratios are applied equally to both U.S. and non-U.S. equities.

Meese (2000) that the one-stage asset-liability approach is likely to lead to greater hedging than the two-stage approach.

Note that the correlation between the Canadian equities and hedged assets are similar to those with unhedged assets. This analysis also suggests that unhedged international assets appear to be reasonably correlated with Canadian liabilities. Logically, it follows that Canadian interest rates and Canadian inflation influence Canadian liabilities. If Canadian dollars and foreign equities move in step with variables that influence Canadian liabilities, such a result will persist. For example, all else constant, if lower Canadian interest rates imply higher liabilities, a lower Canadian dollar and hence a higher international equity return, then this may explain why unhedged foreign equities provide a natural hedge against liabilities.

Impact of Constraints

Figure 5.3 proves a number of conclusions. First, a 30 percent cap on foreign content is detrimental to the plan on both an asset-only and an asset-liability

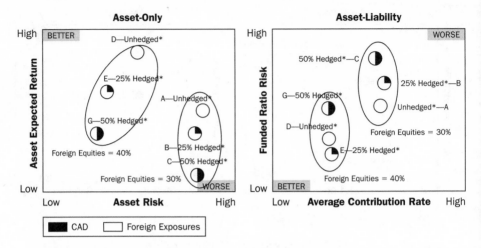

Figure 5.3 Investing More Than 30% Abroad Is Beneficial

Note: This is shown for illustrative purposes only and is not meant to illustrate the performance of any specific client account. Hedge ratio = [(hedged portfolio percentage of international assets)/(total percentage of international assets)] × 100%.

*Hedge ratios are applied equally to both U.S. and non-U.S. equities.

basis (comparing portfolios A, B, and C to D, E, and G, respectively). However, because some hedging is optimal in both situations (E is better than D in both cases), this Canadian investor would do well to access foreign markets through the use of derivatives, such as futures, which are collateralized with Canadian Treasury bills, to avoid exceeding the foreign content rule. The preference of the 25 percent hedge ratio to being unhedged in both situations is coincidental, but interesting. However, Table 5.3 highlights that a 40 percent hedge ratio has the highest Sharpe ratio (portfolio F), whereas a 25 percent hedge ratio is optimal from an ALM perspective.

Figure 5.4 demonstrates that splitting foreign content into U.S. equity and other developed markets can improve welfare and shows a greater bias to hedge U.S. assets than other international exposures.[10] Table 5.3 shows this by comparing portfolios E and G to H and I, respectively. This is most likely the result of two conditions: concentrated exposure to a single currency (the U.S. dollar) as opposed to a diversified basket of currencies (non-U.S. foreign), and the impact of the various correlations.[11] This result also depends on data

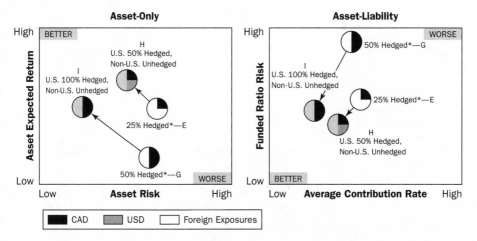

Figure 5.4 Useful to Distinguish Between U.S. and Other Foreign Exposures

Note: This is shown for illustrative purposes only and is not meant to illustrate the performance of any specific client account. Hedge ratio = [(hedged portfolio percentage of international assets)/(total percentage of international assets)] × 100%.

*Hedge ratios are applied equally to both U.S. and non-U.S. equities.

assumptions; as experience has shown, the result can be reversed for a different data set.

Two-Stage Optimizations Are Incorrect

Figure 5.2 also clarifies that using two-stage optimizations (such as an asset-liability analysis using unhedged assets and then an optimal hedge ratio on an asset-only basis) could mean choosing the wrong policy mix. This conclusion is consistent with Grinold and Meese (2000). For example, a plan sponsor is likely to choose a 25 percent hedge ratio when the unhedged alternative is still optimal and within regulatory requirements. The optimal foreign allocation is 30 percent international and the separate hedge ratio analysis would recommend 25 percent hedged. Alternatively, as shown in Figure 5.3, the two-stage method could exclude the possibility of investing more than 30 percent abroad provided postcurrency hedging foreign content is no greater than 30 percent. The practice of making decisions in two stages is common in many countries, including the United States and Canada, and is possibly a reflection of the influence of conventional research on this topic. These comparisons are summarized in Table 5.4.

Table 5.4

Summary Results of Asset-Only and Asset-Liability Comparisons

Issue	Asset-Only	Asset-Liability
30% foreign equity, optimal hedge ratio	25% hedged[a]	Unhedged[a]
40% vs. 30% foreign equity	40% foreign equity	40% foreign equity
40% foreign equity, optimal hedge ratio	40% hedged[a]	25% hedged[a]
40% foreign equity, hedge ratios for U.S. and non-U.S. equity	U.S. equity, 100% hedged; non-U.S. equity, unhedged	U.S. equity, 50% hedged; non-U.S. equity, unhedged

Note: The portfolio allocation is as follows: 31% domestic bond, 25% domestic equity, 37% foreign developed market equities (50% U.S. and 50% non-U.S. equities), 3% emerging markets equities, and 4% real estate.

[a]Hedge ratio = [(hedged portfolio percentage of international assets)/(total percentage of international assets)] × 100%.

IMPLICATIONS FOR ACTIVE CURRENCY MANAGEMENT PROGRAMS

The discussion so far has focused largely on passive strategic benchmark selection and did not examine whether the benchmark should be managed actively or passively. These studies assumed that interest rates determine future exchange rates so that there is no arbitrage possibility in the optimization process (that is, the forward exchange rate is an accurate predictor of the future spot exchange rate). However, an interesting aspect of currency markets is that forward exchange rates (determined by the interest rate differential between two countries) are poor predictors of future spot rates. In testing this assumption for a Canadian client versus a model that assumes the spot rate as the best predictor of the future (in a separate study), the results are not greatly changed, but some previously optimal portfolios may be dominated by others.[12]

Active Currency Management

This forward rate bias creates an interesting opportunity for active management of currency hedge ratios (Baz, Breedon, Naik, and Peress 1999). In addition, recent research has shown that naïve technical currency rules improve the performance of global equity returns from an asset-only perspective

(Reinert 2000). This section uses data from JP Morgan Fleming Asset Management's extensive experience in managing currency overlay and aggressive currency strategies to ask whether these programs add value from an asset-liability basis. This contrasts with a number of papers that highlight the benefits of currency overlay from an asset-only perspective (Hersey and Minnick 2000, Baldridge, Meath, and Myers 2000, Mehrzad and Muralidhar 2000).

Let us assume that the investor has 30 percent international exposure and an unhedged benchmark. Passive management of currency exposure, given an unhedged benchmark, would assume that nothing is done with the currency exposure. Active management, on the other hand, would permit the plan sponsor or a currency overlay manager to change the currency composition periodically by hedging some of the foreign exposure into Canadian dollars (or another currency) based on short-term tactical views. Therefore, active management of currencies changes the risk-return profile of the international exposure as well as its correlation to other assets and, hence, should be treated as a separate asset in such analyses.

Excess returns data from an active currency program, run against an unhedged benchmark with the Canadian dollar as the base currency, is used to represent such activities. Annualized excess return from this program was approximately 1.7 percent since inception in December 1994.[13] This strategy was also evaluated assuming no excess returns. Two new assets were created: unhedged U.S. equity with active currency management and other developed market equities (unhedged) with active currency management. Table 5.5 provides the returns, standard deviations, and correlations from the inclusion of these two assets (or alternatively, an active strategy). One can now easily distinguish between foreign currency exposures that are passively and actively managed. The critical question is whether the active strategy is selected from an ALM perspective, and if so, should the allocation to this strategy be equal to or less than 30 percent? Finally, is the active management strategy chosen because it controls the risk of the benchmark choice, adds return, or both?

Active management of currencies is implemented by buying and selling currency pairs using currency forwards (such as selling U.S. dollars for Canadian dollars if the U.S. dollar is expected to weaken). Because all currency forward

Table 5.5
Expected Return, Risk, and Correlation Assumptions (Active Management)

	Expected Return (%)	Std. Dev. (%)	Corre-lation	Correlation									
				1	2	3	4	5	6	7	8	9	10
Domestic bonds	6.48	6.0	1	1.00									
Domestic equity	9.60	14.2	2	0.45	1.00								
Foreign equity ex-U.S. (unh. pass.)	10.60	17.3	3	0.10	0.44	1.00							
Foreign equity ex-U.S. (hed. pass.)	10.30	16.8	4	0.21	0.55	0.81	1.00						
U.S. equity unhedged	9.20	12.7	5	0.27	0.66	0.52	0.52	1.00					
U.S. equity hedged	9.09	12.0	6	0.41	0.65	0.34	0.49	0.81	1.00				
EM[a] equity unhedged	14.50	22.8	7	0.13	0.52	0.48	0.50	0.45	0.43	1.00			
Real estate	6.89	5.7	8	−0.24	−0.18	0.03	−0.09	0.01	−0.38	−0.26	1.00		
Foreign equity ex-U.S. (unh. act.)	12.30	13.36	9	0.09	0.46	0.99	0.86	0.53	0.33	0.49	0.06	1.00	
Foreign equity ex-U.S. (hed. act.)	10.90	12.70	10	0.26	0.66	0.47	0.55	0.98	0.76	0.44	0.05	0.51	1.00

Note: These numbers are hypothetical examples shown for illustrative purposes only and are not meant to illustrate the performance or pension plan characteristics of any specific client's portfolio. The expected returns, standard deviations, and correlations are hypothetical estimates. There is also no assurance that any client account will perform in line with these estimates.

[a]EM = emerging markets.

trades are zero cost, no additional funding is required to implement active management, as these strategies are run as overlays on existing assets. Therefore, strategies can be implemented with or without leverage, depending on the desired objectives of the client.[14]

Implications for Active Management

Table 5.6 provides details of various portfolios highlighted in Figure 5.5. From an asset-only perspective, the Sharpe ratio increases with active management, as has been highlighted before (Reinert 2000; Baz, Breedon, Naik, and Peress 2000; Mehrzad and Muralidhar 2000). This is because the stream of excess returns from active management is largely uncorrelated with the returns of standard bond and equity returns. However, because active currency management has the additional property of lowering the standard deviation of returns, these active currency programs are valuable. As Figure 5.5 demonstrates, from an asset-liability perspective, the greater the proportion (or aggressiveness) of active management, the greater the efficiency of the pension plan. This contrasts with the evaluation in Muralidhar and Tsumagari (1999), where the active management choice was driven by the level of cash in the plan

Table 5.6
Asset Allocation with Active Management[a]

	Passive	5% Active	10% Active	15% Active	20% Active	25% Active	30% Active
Domestic bonds	31.00	31.00	31.00	31.00	31.00	31.00	31.00
Domestic equity	35.00	35.00	35.00	35.00	35.00	35.00	35.00
Foreign equity ex-U.S. unhedged	13.50	11.00	8.50	6.00	3.50	1.00	0.00
U.S. equity unhedged	13.50	11.00	8.50	6.00	3.50	1.00	0.00
EM[b] equity	3.00	3.00	3.00	3.00	3.00	3.00	3.00
Real estate	4.00	4.00	4.00	4.00	4.00	4.00	4.00
Foreign equity active	0.00	5.00	10.00	15.00	20.00	25.00	27.00
Expected return	8.74	8.82	8.91	8.99	9.08	9.16	9.20
Standard deviation	8.82	8.76	8.70	8.64	8.58	8.53	8.51
Return/risk ratio	0.990	1.007	1.024	1.041	1.058	1.074	1.081

[a]All seven portfolios have 30% foreign holdings and an unhedged benchmark.
[b]EM = emerging markets.

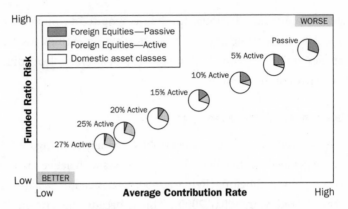

Figure 5.5 Active Management Is Beneficial

Note: This is shown for illustrative purposes only and is not meant to illustrate the performance of any specific client account. Passive investing is the naïve replication of a benchmark on a monthly or quarterly basis. Alternatively, an active strategy provides the manager with the discretion to deviate from the benchmark and there is no requirement to replicate the benchmark at any point in time. Portfolios shown have 30% allocation to foreign equity, including a 3% static emerging markets equity allocation. The active management proportions are shown relative to the total portfolio.

rather than the impact on the average contribution rate. Hence pension plans may improve their asset-liability profile with active currency management. With the removal of the 1.7 percent excess return, the average contribution rate is unchanged but there is a decline in the funded ratio and pension income volatility.

The proposition that active management improves asset-liability risk is very dependent on the type of active management and the asset class it is engaged in. Chapter 7 discusses this issue in the context of pension plan risk.

CAVEATS

The critical issue in any of these studies is the impact of data assumptions on results. This would be true in this case too, as the results are dependent on the assumed pension fund and the assumed future economic environment. However, data changes are likely to impact the magnitude of results rather than the results themselves.[15] In some cases, depending on the liability stream of the pension plan, results may differ from those of the study. The critical point is that the ALM perspective is correct and the fact that the results may not differ from an asset-only perspective is a chance occurrence and does not invalidate the results.

SUMMARY

This research highlights more "investment truths" and conclusions for currency hedging studies, namely those in the accompanying box.

INVESTMENT TRUTHS

- *Asset-liability studies provide recommendations that are no worse than those of asset-only studies.*

- *Constraining an asset class that has attractive diversification properties is always welfare reducing and potentially expensive for a pension plan.*

- *Each pension plan is unique and requires specific analysis rather than generic recommendations.*

- *Active management can reduce asset-liability risks beyond those embedded in the benchmark.*

The key conclusions for currency decisions are these:

1. An asset-liability perspective is preferred to an asset-only perspective for determining optimal currency hedge ratios.

2. It is important to identify and specify objectives and risk measures.

3. Recognize that passive hedging changes the risk profile of any asset allocation.

4. Therefore, a pension plan cannot first select an allocation and then a hedge ratio separately—these decisions must be simultaneously determined. In addition, plan sponsors should be wary of generic prescriptions about optimal hedge ratios and optimal proportions of international assets.

In the case of Canadian pension plans, it was also demonstrated that the 30 percent cap on foreign content could be detrimental, and further splitting of foreign content into other developed and U.S. assets provides additional recommendations about passive hedging. Finally, active currency programs, whether conservative or aggressive, have tended to be uncorrelated with the returns of standard asset class returns and, hence, improve the asset-liability characteristics of a pension fund. Inclusion of active currency management can benefit plan sponsors by lowering funded ratio risk and average contributions.

APPLICATION OF SIMILAR TECHNIQUES

TO CENTRAL BANKS

Central banks also can be modeled as having liabilities as pointed out in the appendix to Chapter 1. This section highlights potential errors that central banks could make by not taking a holistic look at currency decisions from an asset-only perspective. Today, a number of central banks are liquidating gold reserves and investing the proceeds in global fixed income assets. Traditionally, gold has been held unhedged.

A number of these central banks have been pondering the question of currency composition and currency-hedge ratio of fixed income assets. However, these simplistic analyses ignore the fact that gold sales will be gradual and hence the currency hedge ratio will evolve dynamically over time as more gold is sold and the portfolio gets more concentrated in fixed income assets. By implication, the hedge

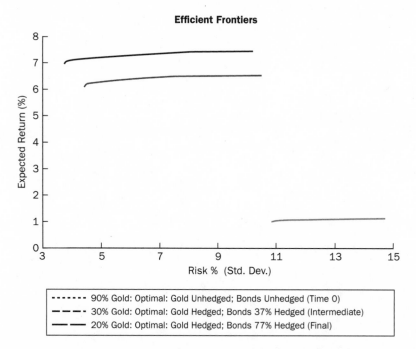

Figure A5.1.1 Optimal Strategy Dynamic Hedge Ratios for a Central Bank

ratio on gold will also evolve. Figure A5.1.1 demonstrates how a dynamic, holistic evaluation of the currency decision could provide different results from assuming that the gold and fixed income assets are different pools of assets.[16]

Assume a central bank holds 90 percent of its reserves in gold and the rest in a global mix of government bonds. Assume that the accounting currency is the base currency. The chart shows that the case for strategically hedging residual gold for this central bank rises as more gold is sold because of the trade-off between volatility reduction and the relative cost of hedging. When gold is the critical asset, the relative cost of hedging to the return of gold has an impact on the decision, and hence no hedging is optimal. However, as the allocation shifts to fixed income assets, the ratio of the cost of hedging to total portfolio return declines and the risk reduction benefit of hedging prevails. Had the central bank looked at these in isolation, gold may have been left unhedged and fixed income assets largely hedged.

1. This is a trivial result as any two-stage optimization can be no better than a one-stage optimization in a multiple objective optimization.

2. Plans are not restricted directly, but face tax issues if they exceed these limits. Moreover, foreign content is defined in terms of currency exposure and not total investments abroad. Hence, investments can exceed these limits through the use of derivatives or dual fund structures.

3. One shortcoming of all these model approaches is that they do not consider the cash flow implications of currency hedging. Currency forwards when they mature either provide inflows or need outflows and these can impact pension plans that want to minimize such flows. This may need to be considered on a qualitative basis.

4. This measure is important as it provides the impact on contributions from a 1 percent change in liabilities, all else held constant. This level suggests that the plan is very young.

5. In this chapter, for simplicity assume that the fund is rebalanced annually to a static asset allocation. A more optimal approach is to implement a dynamic strategy. However, such a strategy would complicate the exposition of optimal currency hedging as the optimal hedge ratio can change every year and is not easy to display visually.

6. One additional issue for currencies is that currency distributions have fat tails and are not normal. Few models can accommodate this issue and hence qualitative judgment is required as described in Mehrzad and Muralidhar (2000).

7. See Dert (1995) for a technical discussion of performing such analyses. These are standard simulation techniques.

8. See Sharpe (1994).

9. In an old plan, contribution policy is less critical than investment policy as mistakes in the investment policy can be devastating. In a young plan, mistakes in the investment policy can be corrected by future changes in the contribution policy, and hence have less impact.

10. Note that different shading is used to capture these currency exposures.

11. Because correlations influence these outcomes in a very complicated way, this is not covered in great detail here.

12. We would like to thank Towers Perrin, especially David Services, for their cooperation in this evaluation.

13. As of July 2000. Past performance is no guarantee of future results. Excess return is gross of fees for all Canadian accounts (two accounts) using this currency overlay strategy.

14. The way in which clients can adjust programs is the size of the mandate and the aggressiveness. These are linear and hence an unleveraged strategy could be equivalent to a twice-levered strategy on one-half the size.

15. The expected returns, standard deviations, correlations, and other data in the tables are estimates of hypothetical accounts. There is no assurance that any client account will perform in line with these estimates.

16. For the pension analogy see Mennis and Clark (1983).

RISK MANAGEMENT

6

A FRAMEWORK FOR

USING DERIVATIVES

Arun S. Muralidhar

In a 1995 survey of 200 pension funds, more than 30 percent used some form of derivative, and this proportion has most likely increased since then. This chapter assists oversight committees and pension fund staff in adopting derivative strategies. It highlights trade-offs and operational issues to be considered when implementing derivative strategies. It also helps evaluate how derivative strategies should be employed by pension funds for different objectives and time horizons.

OVERVIEW

Derivatives gained notoriety in the 1990s with many public examples of misuse through speculative trades or subversion of guidelines. Derivatives, like any other financial instrument, can be used to achieve good outcomes but are only publicized when put to perverse use. A 1995 survey of 200 pension funds, by Greenwich Associates, showed that 40 percent used equity index futures, 30 percent used options, and 11 percent used swaps. Hunter (1998), however, laments the slow growth in the use of derivatives among pension funds. Logue and Rader (1997) and Nakovick (1999) state that derivatives can be used for

Adapted from Arun S. Muralidhar and Masaki Tsumagari. "Derivative Strategies." Investment Management Department Working Paper Series, The World Bank, August 1998; adapted from Arun S. Muralidhar and Robert Weary. "Alternative International Equity Benchmarks." Investment Management Department Working Paper Series, The World Bank, 1998.

risk management (i.e., hedges) and return enhancement, and Burton (1996) provides an excellent discussion on the use of derivatives by pension funds. The last paper describes how the Virginia Retirement System used derivative strategies such as collars (buying a put and selling a call) and managed futures, and highlights their use in constructing index baskets, synthetic portfolio creation, and eliminating a defined risk.

This chapter assists oversight committees of pension funds in considering and adopting derivative strategies for a host of different objectives. Rather than highlighting specific transactions, it provides a framework within which to evaluate the use of derivatives. Chapters 4 and 5 demonstrated that derivatives, like put options on asset market indices or even forwards for currency hedging, could be used in a fund to achieve strategic objectives. The analysis is now extended to explore the various uses of derivatives from both a strategic and a tactical perspective.

Outline

This chapter highlights trade-offs and operational issues to be considered when implementing derivative strategies. It also helps evaluate how derivative strategies should be employed by pension funds for different time objectives and horizons. The chapter is organized as follows: First, it provides a framework for derivatives activities and allows oversight committees to identify strategies consistent with their goals. Second, it lists operational issues from such transactions that should guide overall portfolio management. The discussion is largely based on using derivatives as hedging instruments. This chapter concludes with a brief review of the possible extension of any derivatives strategy to different asset classes and examines market constraints. Appendix 6.1 provides examples of two specific innovative uses for derivatives that could help sponsors to establish better benchmarks and facilitate the dynamic asset allocation strategies proposed in Chapter 4.

TRANSACTIONS

The range of derivatives transactions that a pension fund might consider extends from simple futures, forwards, and options, to more exotic derivative transactions such as total return swaps. Forwards and futures are useful as they allow a fund to transform one exposure into another (e.g., a U.S. dollar exposure to a Japanese yen exposure, or a cash exposure to an equity exposure, respectively). However, within the realm of options, pension funds can purchase or sell either plain-vanilla puts or calls, or combinations of these instruments like collars or put-call spreads.[1] There are a wide variety of exchange-traded options that funds can enter into with minimal credit risk. In addition, market players are willing to offer over-the-counter derivatives (e.g., plain-vanilla or structured swaps) to provide the appropriate instrument to achieve the desired payoff profile.

For example, some funds may want an element of costless insurance. A fund may want to ensure it does not lose the first 15 percent decline in the S&P 500. However, because this transaction will cost money, it may be willing to lose beyond 15 percent and give up some of the upside, and hence it may consider a zero-cost put-call spread. This composite strategy is equivalent to buying a put struck at 100 percent of the current value of the S&P 500 index, and the premium required to purchase this put is financed by selling a put struck at 85 percent of the current value of the index and a call struck at 110 percent of the current value.[2] One reason for doing so is that the sponsor has made significant gains on the U.S. market and would like to protect some of the downside without necessarily paying for it. However, if the markets collapse the fund managers are comfortable performing as poorly as their peers. Figure 6.1 demonstrates the payoff pattern of the components and the entire strategy.

GOALS AND CORRESPONDING DERIVATIVES STRATEGIES

"Derivatives possess no fundamental return and risk characteristics beyond those of the underlying assets. Instead, a derivative security merely provides a means of altering, typically for a short time horizon, the return and risk characteristics of an asset. Since asset allocation policy is based on long-term investor objectives, the potential policy application of derivative securities is limited to techniques, such as portfolio insurance, that can use short-term instruments to achieve a long-run goal" (Ibbotson and Brinson 1993).

Keeping these features of derivatives in mind, this chapter examines the use of derivatives in pension investments. In general, selection of investment strategies, asset classes, and investment vehicles should be considered in light

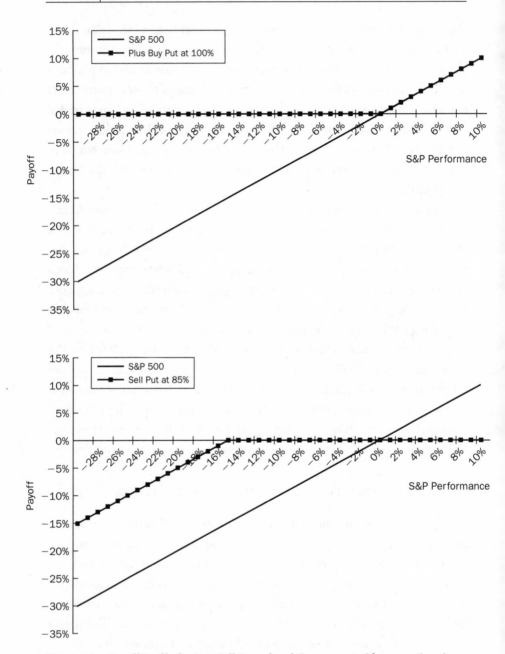

Figure 6.1   Payoff Profile for Put-Call Spread and Components (*figure continues*)

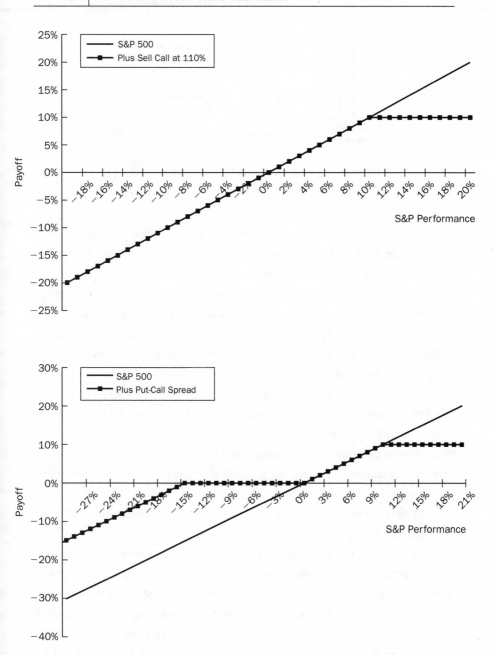

Figure 6.1   (*Continued*)

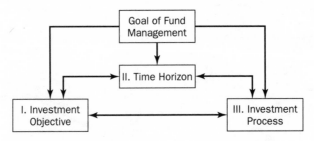

Figure 6.2 Linking Objectives to Time Horizon and Investment Process

of whether those investment decisions are consistent with the goal of fund management; in short, whether they are required to service liabilities (or reduce asset-liability risk) or lower the cost of achieving a target return.

Effectively, the goal of fund management is to generate a required return for a given risk preference, and to find the most cost-effective method to achieve that risk/return profile. For the oversight committee, these components are formalized along three dimensions: (1) investment objectives, (2) time horizon, and (3) the investment process.

As diagrammed in Figure 6.2, the investment objectives and process are intricately linked by the time horizon; namely, some investment processes are more directly tied to short-term horizons, and others are more credibly linked to long-term horizons. As a result, ownership of the process may be either with the committee (generally, longer-term objectives) or with the investment team (generally, shorter-term strategies).

With this perspective, use of derivatives in pension investment can be summarized through the matrix in Figure 6.3. This matrix gives a basic framework to check whether the decision on use of derivatives complies with the committee's objectives and decision horizon, and whether the appropriate authority makes the decision. Alternatively, as highlighted in Chapter 3, some committee members may be more comfortable evaluating in tandem asset strategies and objectives they satisfy, rather than specifying objectives first and then being asked to sign off on a particular strategy. Figure 6.3 can be used in this fashion as it allows one to imply objectives based on the selected transactions.

Time Horizon ⟶

			Long-Term Perspective	Short-Term Perspective
Objective	**ALM**	Protect Surplus	Dynamic asset allocation (Change policy asset mix)	Derivatives ("Floor" type options, portfolio insurance, collars, etc.)
		Delegated to: **Oversight committee**		
		Minimize Contribution	Dynamic asset allocation (Change policy asset mix)	Derivatives ("Floor" type options, portfolio insurance, collars, etc.)
		Delegated to: **Oversight committee**		
	Asset-Only	Active Strategy, e.g., TAA*	Derivatives (Index futures, options)	Derivatives (Index futures, options)
		Delegated to: **Investment team***		
		Select/Change External Managers	Block trading, derivatives—swaps, futures	Derivatives (index futures, options)
		Delegated to: **Investment team**		
		Enhance Return/ Secure Return*	Rebalancing actual portfolio	Derivatives (Exotic options, swaps)
		Delegated to: **External manager, Team**		

Investment Process

* These are based on asset-only views. Strict guidelines and monitoring are necessary.

Figure 6.3   Optimal Use of Instruments Based on Objective and Time Horizon

The matrix demonstrates the various types of trades that match different objectives and time horizons. It also identifies the group that should be responsible for the performance of these transactions. For cases where derivatives are suboptimal instruments, an alternative instrument/strategy is provided in the matrix.

Two broad categories of objectives should be delineated; namely, asset-liability objectives and asset-only objectives. Asset-liability objectives include protecting surpluses (i.e., funded ratios) and minimizing contributions. Asset-only objectives are directed toward generating returns from market or tactical views and/or minimizing the cost of achieving these returns.

All derivatives transactions are effectively trades on the volatility of the underlying security/index. For example, ignoring the specific reason for doing

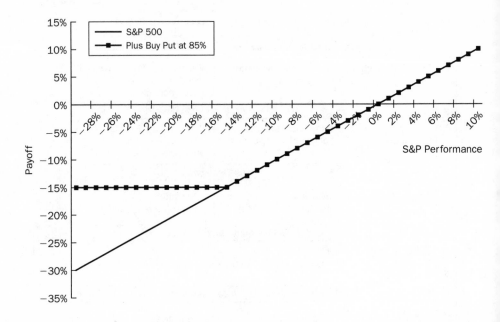

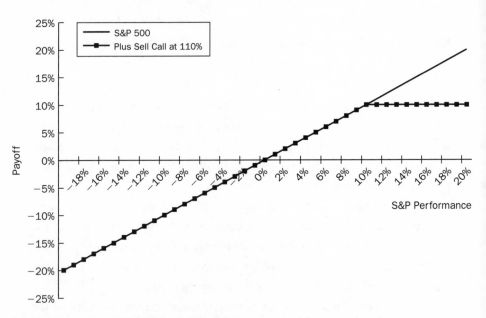

Figure 6.4 Payoff Profile for Collar and Components (*figure continues*)

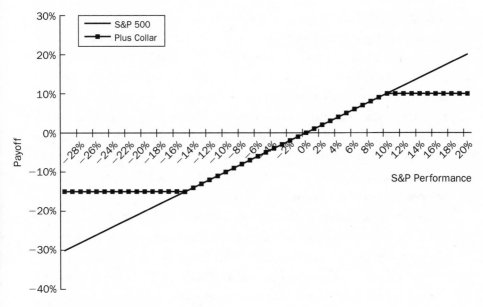

Figure 6.4   (*Continued*)

so, buying a collar on the S&P 500 (the payoff of the components and strategy are charted in Figure 6.4) implies that the pension fund has sold volatility on the index.[3] Therefore, it is critical for decision makers to clearly articulate their objectives prior to authorizing such transactions. In the absence of such clarity, trading derivatives is tantamount to taking a view on volatility.

Managing Strategic Risks

Figure 6.3 reinforces the conclusion of the earlier chapters. If the committee adopts a long-term horizon and focuses on asset-liability objectives, then the optimal method to achieve these objectives is through a dynamic investment and funding policy. But if the shorter-term horizon is adopted to counter the risk of underperformance, the use of insurance-type derivatives is recommended.

Use of Derivatives for Tactical Reasons

There is significant benefit to authorizing and delegating the use of derivatives to the investment team for tactical asset allocation shifts (e.g., overweighting a particular asset class relative to the benchmark), for managing transitions from one strategic asset allocation to another, or for manager liquidations and transitions. Derivatives such as options or futures contracts provide a quick and efficient mechanism to gain access to an entire market without having to purchase all the individual securities, which also makes for nimble implementation of tactical asset allocation decisions. Chapter 5 shows how derivatives can be used to circumvent regulatory constraints that lower asset-liability efficiency. However, changes in securities in a portfolio may be better achieved through block trades or the use of crossing networks. This may change with the introduction of futures on individual stocks.

The investment team itself should be allowed to authorize and delegate the use of derivatives to the actual portfolio managers, internal or external. Pension plans should take precautions to prevent the use of derivatives by active managers as a means to circumvent guidelines. For example, if a bond manager is permitted to purchase AAA bonds only, and would like to take a view on a lower grade of bond, one alternative would be to buy an AAA (structured) bond, with a coupon determined by the performance of the lower grade bond. Pension plans have to be very careful about the types of derivatives they permit external managers to use and must require clear and concise reporting on how the derivatives achieve the manager's objectives. In general, there is greater need for derivatives in a short time horizon, and they are of some use for hedging purposes in the long term.

Further, with special focus on currency hedging of non-U.S. investments (not covered in the matrix), the forward contract is the most liquid and commonly used instrument to convert foreign exposures back to domestic currency exposure. Increasingly, studies have shown that active currency management, in which the currency manager implements both the strategic and tactical position, is successful (Strange 1998, Baldridge, Meath, and Myers 2000, and Hersey and Minnick 2000). Hence, the use of such derivatives can provide significant benefit to the plan, as demonstrated in Chapter 5.

Operational Issues

Using derivatives to hedge risk is common. Plan sponsors need to closely monitor and manage operational issues such as market risk, credit risk, and pricing risk. There are two types of markets in which derivatives may be bought and sold—the exchange traded market (where there is limited credit and pricing risk) and the over-the-counter (OTC) market. The benefit of the OTC market is that transactions can be tailored to a plan sponsor's specific needs. However, specialization may not be adequately compensated by the higher credit risk and potentially, the opacity of pricing (in complex transactions).

Market/Basis Risk

Exchange-traded derivatives do not allow pension funds to hedge their surpluses directly as it is difficult to replicate liabilities with market instruments. Exchange-traded transactions focus on asset indices only. To hedge surplus risk, plan sponsors may utilize an OTC contract or hedge inefficiently using asset-only derivatives and rebalance this position periodically based on the surplus (see Chapter 4).

This creates the problem that any derivative transaction would have to be "rehedged" by the broker of the initial transaction. Transactions that involve market indices for which no futures contracts exist (e.g., Morgan Stanley Capital International's Europe Asia Far East index [MSCI EAFE] or the Lehman Aggregate Bond Index) are likely to be very expensive or the basis risk has to be borne by the pension plans. Basis risk is the risk between the security in which the derivative is written and the security with which the transaction is hedged. Transactions on an index such as the S&P 500 equity index are relatively common and incur low transactions cost due to the extremely liquid S&P 500 futures contract. It is interesting that within countries, the correlation across equity or bond indices covering the same market spectrum are extremely close to 1 (e.g., Nikkei/Topix and MSCI Japan, or MSCI Germany and DAX [Deutscher Aktienindex, a German stock exchange index]). On an ex-ante basis, if there are no significant expected return biases for a published index for every time horizon, and the correlations hold in the future, the investor/ broker should be indifferent to which market underlies the hedge for the benchmark of the portfolio. This is rarely ever true, and basis risk between the benchmark index to be hedged and the futures instrument used has to be monitored carefully.

For foreign portfolios, the problem that follows is to find an efficient way to reconstitute a multiple-country benchmark using derivatives. The classic approach is to find the five or six largest countries in the composite (usually consisting of 15–20 countries for developed markets) that explain a large fraction of the variations in the more exhaustive list. Alternatively, an optimal basket with the lowest historical tracking error to the underlying index is selected.[4] There is no guarantee that the history used to generate these numbers will repeat itself in the future and this generates basis risk. The appendix demonstrates the implications for benchmark creation and selection when basis risk in non-trivial.

An additional problem arises when investments are made in foreign currencies; namely, currency risk and the impact of translating local currency returns into dollar returns. For example, consider a portfolio with a currency benchmark for its non-U.S. equity portfolio, which is a 50 percent hedge of exposures. This is likely to lead to tricky transactions like "quantos"[5] that are difficult to price and expensive to purchase. Table 6.1 shows the decisions that the oversight committee and staff have to make to determine the optimal transaction in foreign bond or equity portfolios. Two sets of risk must be managed—market and currency risk. Single instrument hedging (i.e., equity or bond futures) may not be adequate and complex derivatives may be required.

Credit and Pricing Risk

When a plan sponsor enters into a derivatives contract in the OTC market it must select a counterpart with whom to do business. One major risk involved in transacting business in the OTC market is that if a plan sponsor buys a derivative from a counterpart and the counterpart defaults when the derivative is in-the-money, then the plan sponsor has to incur costs to reconstitute the hedge. This risk of default is termed credit risk. Credit risk is managed by

Table 6.1
Matrix of Decisions for International Portfolios

Market Index	Currency Return	
	Decline	Unchanged
Decline	Hedge both	Hedge market
Unchanged	Hedge currency	No transaction

selecting highly rated counterparts and distributing trades across a host of counterparts so that exposure is not concentrated with one entity.

Another issue with OTC contracts is they tend to be stylized, and pricing these transactions can be difficult for the average plan sponsor. The more difficult the transaction, the greater the difficulty in pricing the deal, and the plan sponsor may not know the true risk or value of its derivatives position. One way to mitigate this risk is to parcel the same trade to multiple counterparties and create multiple pricing sources. This may not be feasible for all types of transactions.

Feasibility of Extending Derivatives Strategies to Non-U.S. Equity and Fixed Income Asset Classes

Our analysis suggests that given the current market benchmarks implemented by pension funds in North America such as the MSCI EAFE or the Financial Times (FT)/Actuaries indices for non-U.S. equity or the corporate bond or high-yield markets for which no futures exist, derivatives transactions should not be undertaken unless the perceived benefit far outweighs the costs. Alternatively, the non-U.S. equity benchmark could be reconstituted to comprise all countries on which futures can be written, weighted by their market capitalization (Nakovick 1999). Only special pension plans can consider gaining exposure to all the foreign futures markets. Currently within the United States, pension plans are precluded by U.S. Commodity Futures Trading Commission (CFTC) regulation from participating in all markets in countries covered by the MSCI or FT indices. Appendix 6.1 provides a brief description of how clients may lower the cost of passive management and future transitions by creating benchmarks with an embedded instrument—a futures contract.

Further, in global fixed income where benchmarks are largely government bond indices, the underlying futures contracts on government bonds can be used to replicate the index.[6] These are fairly complicated procedures, as the underlying index is hedged by a multitude of futures contracts. However, there is a need to create a new instrument—a futures contract on bond indices—that will greatly facilitate portfolio management for pension plans. Currently, such instruments exist on municipal bond indices only, but Appendix 6.1 discusses possible approaches to this problem.

SUMMARY

It is critical for investment staff to seek guidance from the oversight committee about their objectives, time horizon, and delegation of any related responsibilities. If the objectives of the committee lean toward protecting surplus in the short term, then a derivatives strategy can be employed. If a longer-term perspective is taken, a dynamic asset allocation strategy is the preferred approach to achieve objectives. However, it may be difficult to implement dynamic asset allocation strategies if the benchmarks are difficult to replicate. Derivatives are also useful to effect manager and asset allocation transitions, and plan sponsors may consider modifying benchmarks to facilitate the use of derivatives for such purposes.[7] Derivatives can also be used for cost-effective implementation of tactical views on the market. Staff would have to develop appropriate reporting mechanisms to closely monitor the implementation (e.g., regular reporting on funded status, and returns from a tactical asset allocation strategy) and ensure that risk limits and credit limits do not exceed prespecified thresholds.

USING DERIVATIVES TO ESTABLISH

BETTER BENCHMARKS

The first section of this appendix proposes a new benchmark for non-U.S. equity portfolios, and the second section focuses on the need for futures instruments based on fixed income indices.

CREATING NEW NON-U.S. EQUITY BENCHMARKS FOR FUTURES TRADING

One problem investors face is that the most commonly used benchmark indices lack futures contracts. This section examines the ideal criteria necessary for a non-U.S. developed market benchmark, and applies them to the most widely available benchmarks. It introduces a synthetic benchmark that surpasses existing benchmarks in meeting the necessary criteria and has the advantage of being associated with existing futures contracts. This technique can be applied by an investor in any country vis-à-vis foreign investments.

To determine what benchmark to use in an asset-liability study and to measure an investment manager versus a benchmark for a non-U.S. developed market, the benchmark index should meet five criteria: (1) it must be representative of the market; (2) there must be ease in replication; (3) there must be significant trading volume; (4) it must be transparent; and (5) it must be possible to replicate the benchmark at relatively low cost.

Available Market Benchmarks

Based on the criteria listed, what benchmarks would be appropriate and how well do these benchmarks meet the criteria? The most commonly used benchmark for non-U.S. developed markets is the MSCI EAFE index, based on 21 developed countries in Europe, Asia, and the Far East, hence the name.[8] The other index used extensively appears to be the Financial Times Standard & Poors (FTSP) Europe and Far East index. A cursory analysis of the two indices demonstrates that over a 5-year period they are highly correlated at 99.6 percent with a tracking error of only 140 basis points. This suggests that most investors need not be too concerned about which benchmark to use in an asset-liability study or to measure a non-U.S. developed market investment manager against.

With regard to the five criteria mentioned above, both indices are fairly representative of developed non-U.S. markets, with the exception of Canada, which is not included in either index. Both indices can be managed in a passive manner. In the traditional sense, though, it is difficult to implement an "enhanced index" strategy as there are no futures markets for either index.[9] This strategy can be implemented only by taking substantial basis risk between the MSCI or FTSP local country indices and indices on which futures contracts are written. The MSCI and FTSP indices have significant trading volume and liquidity. There are no issues concerning transparency, as both indices present all relevant data on a monthly basis, that is, market capitalization weights of the countries used in each index, stocks listed by country, and so on. These indices can be replicated, but they are not as easily replicated as the S&P 500. An S&P 500 index fund would cost on average 6–10 basis points per annum, depending on the investment size to manage. In comparison, an MSCI EAFE or FTSP index fund would cost on average 12–20 basis points per annum. It is more expensive to replicate either index because of the number of countries involved and the absence of market instruments, such as futures, on the underlying country indices.

Alternative Benchmark Proposal

A new benchmark, similar to the MSCI and FTSP, with some improvements, is a synthetic index of the developed markets that includes 14 EAFE countries[10] *plus* Canada (see Table A6.1.1, row 4). These countries/indices have been selected because they have a relatively liquid futures market.[11] In simple terms, the benchmark is a composite of local indices on which futures are written, weighted by market capitalization for these markets, and are rebalanced monthly.

This new benchmark for asset-liability studies is proposed for several reasons. First, though this benchmark excludes some smaller countries, it is representative of the developed non-U.S. markets, and includes Canada. This benchmark would be very highly correlated with the MSCI EAFE or FTSP benchmarks, and would have similar correlations with other asset classes. Second, it is easily replicated by either cash instruments or futures and hence reduces costs. Third, the underlying country indices are the most actively traded, transparent, and liquid. Fourth, it tracks the MSCI EAFE Local Currency (LC) index fairly closely, and there are no systematic biases in returns vis-à-vis MSCI EAFE (LC) index.[12] Finally, it allows for easy tactical deviation and derivatives transactions, which neither of the other indices offers. This becomes critical when a pension plan makes a transition from one strategic asset allocation to another, as the cost of transition declines with the

Table A6.1.1
Performance of Synthetic Indices (January 1997 Through June 1998)

Row	Index	Coverage[a] (%)	Annual Return (%)	Tracking Error[b]
MSCI Market Weights				
1	11 EAFE countries	92.4	20.90	105 bps[c]
2	14 EAFE countries	95.1	21.28	96 bps
3	11 EAFE countries + Canada	97.4	20.67	93 bps
4	14 EAFE countries + Canada	100.1	21.05	82 bps
Local Stock Exchange Weights				
5	11 EAFE countries	NA	17.44	181 bps
6	14 EAFE countries	NA	17.84	170 bps
7	11 EAFE countries + Canada	NA	17.51	169 bps
8	14 EAFE countries + Canada	NA	17.90	157 bps
MSCI EAFE (LC) Index		NA	19.25	NA

[a]As a percentage of the total market capitalization of the MSCI EAFE index.
[b]Versus the MSCI EAFE Local Currency (LC) index. These values are largely the same even with the recent changes made by MSCI to their benchmarks.
[c]bps = basis points.

availability of more instruments. In such a situation, the pension plan bears limited risk relative to the benchmark as opposed to bearing up to 100 basis points of tracking error with the EAFE benchmark, as the transition manager uses these instruments for the less appealing benchmarks. Table A6.1.2 compares the non-U.S. developed market benchmarks using the required criteria.

Analysis

This analysis was motivated by the desire to create a benchmark that represents the asset class, can be easily replicated at low costs, and has sufficient turnover. The MSCI benchmark is often difficult to replicate, as there are no futures contracts on the respective indices. Eight different methods were adopted, using a combination of 15 countries/indices on which liquid, exchange-traded futures are available. It included Canada, which is excluded by the MSCI EAFE index. The MSCI EAFE (LC) index was replicated by taking the returns of local stock exchanges (for a list of the local stock exchanges, see Table A6.1.3, column 3) and a weighted return was calculated based on normalized MSCI market capitalization weights (see Table A6.1.1, rows 1–4). The same analysis was conducted using the local stock exchange market capitalization (see Table A6.1.1, rows 5–8). The ease with which

Table A6.1.2
Comparison of Non-U.S. Developed Market Benchmarks

Criterion	MSCI EAFE	FTSP	Synthetic Benchmark
Representative of the developed markets	Yes, but excludes Canada	Yes, but excludes Canada	Yes, but excludes Finland, Ireland, Norway, Portugal, Malaysia, New Zealand, and Singapore[a]
Ease of replication	No, cannot replicate in futures market without high basis risk	No, cannot replicate in futures market without high basis risk	Yes, very easy in either cash or futures
Significant trading volume	Yes	Yes	Yes, most actively traded
Transparent	Yes	Yes	Yes
Low cost of replication	No	No	Yes, primarily through futures market

[a]These seven countries account for just 4.5% of the MSCI EAFE index, while the inclusion of Canada on the basis of market capitalization is equal to 5.0% of the MSCI EAFE index.

the MSCI EAFE index is replicated is explained by the high correlation and low tracking error noted between the individual MSCI country indices and local indices (see Table A6.1.3).

From Tables A6.1.1–3, one can conclude that these are reasonable representations of non-U.S. equity developed markets. The conclusions are independent of returns, as over different time periods the perceived outperformance of any one method could be negated.

The benchmark should be constructed with 14 EAFE countries plus Canada (see Table A6.1.1, row 4), as that benchmark would carry most countries with the lowest tracking error vis-à-vis the MSCI EAFE (LC) index and have the greatest coverage. Alternatively, plan sponsors may use the 11 largest EAFE countries[13] plus Canada, as this model produces the second lowest tracking error (see Table A6.1.1, row 3).

Advantages of This Approach

There are multiple advantages to adopting this synthetic index as a non-U.S. developed market benchmark. First, on an ex-ante basis, there is no reason to believe that this benchmark will do worse than any other benchmark (such as the

Table A6.1.3
MSCI Country Indices Versus Local Indices

Row	Country	Local Index	Tracking Error (%)	Correlation (%)	MSCI Weight (%)	Index Weight[a] (%)	CFTC Approval[b]
1	Austria	ATX	7.2	92.8	0.4	0.4	No
2	Belgium	BEL	3.4	96.5	1.6	1.6	No
3	Denmark	KFX	2.4	98.3	1.0	1.0	No
4	France	CAC	1.7	99.7	9.3	9.3	Yes
5	Germany	DAX	2.0	98.6	11.2	11.1	Yes
6	Italy	MIB	2.6	99.3	5.0	4.9	Yes
7	Netherlands	EOE	4.3	97.0	6.1	6.1	No
8	Spain	IBEX	2.3	99.6	3.4	3.4	Yes
9	Sweden	OMX	1.5	99.5	3.3	3.3	Yes
10	Switzerland	SMI	1.4	99.6	8.1	8.1	No
11	UK	FTSE	1.5	99.5	20.9	20.8	Yes
12	Australia	All Ords	9.0	72.6	2.4	2.4	Yes
13	Hong Kong	Hang Seng	4.2	99.3	1.9	1.8	Yes
14	Japan	TOPIX	1.8	98.9	20.9	20.8	Yes
15	Canada	TSE	2.2	98.7	NA	5.0	Yes

[a]Weight in the recommended synthetic index (as of June 1998).

[b]The Commodities Futures Trading Commission (CFTC) approves investment in non-U.S. futures markets by U.S. institutions.

FTSP or MSCI EAFE). Second, benchmark/basis risk can be eliminated for passive management versus the synthetic index. As it is possible to buy futures in all the markets included in the index, the portfolio would closely track the benchmark, eliminating most of the trading risk. In most cases, the futures market is very liquid. The underlying notional amount that futures trade is half to three times the amount that stocks trade (see Table A6.1.4) and ensures ease of entry to and exit from the market.

Third, the costs incurred in gaining exposure to non-U.S. developed markets can be reduced. A recent study has shown that after accounting for all transactions, futures cost only 10–20 percent of the round-trip cost of owning the cash instrument (Hill 1998). Alternatively, it should be quite easy to gain exposure through the cash market. The choice of whether to replicate through cash or futures depends on many considerations, including tax issues, cash return, dividend yield, and treatment of domestic foreign investors.[14]

Finally, within the non-U.S. developed market sector, asset allocation decisions could be country driven, by overweighting or underweighting specific countries

Table A6.1.4
Ratio of Futures Volume to Stock Volume (December 31, 1997)

Country	Local Index	Futures/Stocks
France	CAC	3.39
Germany	DAX	1.77
Italy	MIB	2.73
Netherlands	EOE	0.81
Spain	IBEX	1.56
Sweden	OMX	0.36
Switzerland	SMI	1.54
United Kingdom	FTSE	0.85
Australia	All Ords	0.99
Hong Kong	Hang Seng	0.75
Japan	TOPIX	1.93
Canada	TSE	0.12

in the futures market. Furthermore, by managing the cash underlying the futures appropriately, a passive currency hedging strategy would be easier to implement.

Recommendations

Most U.S. pension funds may not find this synthetic benchmark an attractive alternative, as Commodities Futures Trading Commission (CFTC) approval is not available for all futures markets (see Table A6.1.3 for which countries are on the CFTC approval list).

A secondary issue is that someone would need to produce the index and provide the product. Considering the ease and transparency required to produce the synthetic benchmark, it would not be too difficult to find a provider (e.g., a custodian or an index provider) to maintain the benchmark.

Considering currency overlay, the strategies would be identical using either existing benchmarks or the proposed synthetic benchmark. With the ability to implement futures on the synthetic benchmark, it would be easier to implement a passive currency overlay strategy against the synthetic benchmark.

Finally, since this benchmark excludes a number of countries (Finland, Ireland, Norway, Portugal, Malaysia, New Zealand, and Singapore) from the MSCI EAFE index, the plan sponsor would need to decide how to treat these countries. Furthermore, it would have to decide how to treat the small cap market, as the proposed benchmark will be biased toward large capitalization stocks. Similarly, it would need to decide how to treat emerging market countries, in light of the existing emerging markets benchmarks. The excluded countries and capitalization sectors could be treated as tactical deviations.

In summary, one would expect pension funds and fund managers to adopt such a benchmark given the absence of ex-ante biases, and the fact that the benchmark can be constructed using the most monitored, actively traded indices, with the added advantage of having futures contracts on each of these indices.

THE NEED TO CREATE SPECIFIC INSTRUMENTS FOR FIXED INCOME FUTURES

This section presents a proposal for creating a futures contract for generic fixed income indices in different currencies. These could include indices on all maturity sectors of fixed income instruments (i.e., money market to long-term bonds), including indices for instruments linked to inflation indices. This proposal provides details on multiple contract specifications as there is a wide range of options. These futures contracts could be traded either on an exchange or OTC and either bought or sold by prospective traders. Currently, such futures contracts on entire indices exist in the equity market, but the sole example in the fixed income market is futures on municipal bond indices.

Background

In the fixed income area, institutional investors measure performance of their asset class and managers through specific indices. For bond indices, there are a number of index providers and different types of indices. For example, index providers include Merrill Lynch, Lehman Brothers, JP Morgan Chase, and Salomon Smith Barney, and the indices they offer include government 1- to 3-year indices and 3- to 5-year indices. These are the indices typically used by central banks for liquidity portfolios. In addition to government indices, many providers maintain money market indices and indices that are composites of government-, corporate-, and agency-issued securities. The Lehman Aggregate Bond Index is one of the most commonly used among institutional investors. Depending on the availability of instruments in different sectors and currencies, these indices may have any number of securities (e.g., the Merrill Lynch 1- to 3-year index may have as many as 61 securities).

As highlighted in the previous section on equity instruments, the choice of benchmark index to be included in an asset-liability study and to monitor managers against should meet five criteria: (1) it must be representative of the market; (2) there must be ease in replication; (3) there must be significant trading volume; (4) it must be transparent; and (5) it must be possible to replicate the benchmark at a relatively low cost. For fixed income indices, the second criterion is generally difficult to accomplish for the average pension plan; however, given the liquidity in major bond markets, the more commonly used indices can be passively replicated with a cost of 7–15 basis points.

Characteristics of Bond Indices

Indices are defined by some prespecified rules that are established by the index provider. For example, rules for inclusion could be based on fixed rate coupons, minimum maturity, minimum outstanding amount, minimum denomination, minimum quality (or issuer), redemption features, and whether embedded options are acceptable or not. Since bond indices are composed of a multitude of securities that fit these criteria, a bond index is likely to have an aggregate weighted maturity, duration (modified, Macaulay, or effective), convexity, yield to maturity, par weighted price, par weighted coupon, and market weighted coupon, among other features. In the case of the Merrill Lynch U.S. government 1- to 3-year and 3- to 5-year indices, these statistics are provided in Table A6.1.5.

One critical aspect of these indices is the rebalancing frequency and rules for reinvestment of cash flows received between two rebalancing dates. In many cases, coupons received between cash flow dates are assumed to be reinvested in the index (or treated as withdrawn from the portfolio, which has the same impact) or else reinvested in cash-like instruments until the next rebalancing date.

Table A6.1.5
Characteristics of Fixed Income Indices

Statistic	Merrill Lynch 1–3 Years	Merrill Lynch 3–5 Years
Maturity[a]	1.83 years	3.98 years
Duration (modified)	1.65 years	3.4 years
Effective convexity	0.04	0.14
Yield-to-maturity	5.9%	6.2%
Number of issues	60	36
Par weighted price	102.1	102.7
Par weighted coupon	6.4%	6.7%
Market weighted coupon	6.4%	6.78%

[a]Weighted average life.

Product Description

Ideally, a futures contract should exist for any fixed income index. For contract purposes, the rebalancing period and reinvestment rules will be identical to the underlying index. There can be multiple specifications of the futures contract for these indices depending on replication and settlement. Under replication, three subcategories can be distinguished, namely, exact replication, proxy replication, and single instrument replication. Under settlement, the contract can either be cash settled or with physical settlement. These are briefly discussed below.

Replication

Exact replication—This specification would require the securities underlying the valuation of the futures contract to be exactly identical to those in the index and in exactly the same proportion as of any previous rebalancing date. For example, if there are two securities in the benchmark, in a 50-50 proportion, the same composition would underlie the futures contract. This concept would be similar to the S&P 500 equity index.

Proxy replication—This specification requires a subset of securities (i.e., fewer securities than those in the original index) that closely track the performance of the underlying index. The proxy composition would be announced on the rebalancing date when the composition of the corresponding index is announced. This lowers the cost of replication, but increases the tracking error or basis risk. Proxy replication is less likely to be appealing than using the index itself if it has the appropriate properties.

Single security—Under this specification, a single security with the same remaining maturity, coupon, duration, and convexity as the underlying index is the reference for the futures contract (as provided, for example, in Table A6.1.5). This would be similar in principle to the specification of existing bond contracts on government securities. Since these numbers change on a daily basis, a prespecified set of parameters could be provided for each index as the equivalent underlying security.

Settlement

Physical securities—With physical settlement, the underlying replication strategy would determine what securities are delivered to the purchaser or seller of the contract. For example, under exact replication, the entire index basket would have to be purchased in the respective weights of the index. Alternatively, under the proxy arrangement, the proxy basket would need to be delivered. In the case of a single security, a list of cheapest-to-deliver securities would have to be estimated that could serve as the deliverable security to the purchaser of the contract. The final arrangement is identical to that of the U.S. Treasury contract.

Cash settled—In many futures contracts, cash settlement replaces physical delivery. Under this arrangement, the cash equivalent value of the securities underlying the contract is estimated and the contract is settled in cash. No securities exchange takes place between the buyer and seller, regardless of the method of replication.

Advantages of This Approach

There are many advantages to creating a futures contract on the respective fixed income index. First, benchmark risk could be eliminated for passive management versus the synthetic index. As it is possible to buy futures on the entire index, the portfolio would closely track the benchmark, eliminating most of the trading risk. Second, given the proportion of assets controlled by institutional investors referenced to these benchmarks, one would expect this would turn out to be a very liquid market (such as the futures contracts on bonds and notes) because there would be both buyers and sellers of this contract, ensuring ease of entry into and exit from the market. Third, it allows pension plans to manage passive portfolios in-house at extremely low cost, instead of delegating this decision to a passive manager or custodian. Fourth, the costs incurred in gaining exposure to the fixed income markets could be reduced. Therefore the global asset allocation decisions in the fixed income market could be country driven, by overweighting or underweighting specific country indices in the futures market. Furthermore, by managing the cash underlying the futures appropriately, a passive currency hedging strategy would be easier to implement. Finally, the transition from one strategic asset allocation to another is made more efficient and less expensive as benchmark risk is greatly reduced. This facilitates dynamic asset allocations.

Recommendations

Most U.S. pension funds are currently benchmarked to fixed income indices on which no futures contract exists. Complex optimization techniques have to be adopted to replicate these benchmarks through the futures market. This is inefficient and expensive for the average investor, who is likely to delegate the task to a passive manager. However, whenever the pension plan needs to make a transition to a new strategic asset allocation, it either bears the benchmark risk between the index and composite of the futures or is charged the cost of this risk by the transition manager.

In summary, given that institutional investors invest substantial amounts in the fixed income market (benchmarked to these indices), one would expect that at least one of the broker/dealers would be willing to create such a contract. The benefits to the institutional investor community are numerous and boil down to greater ease and efficiency in implementation.

NOTES

1. Some of these are described in greater detail in *The Chicago Board of Exchange Investor Series,* No. 4.

2. The specific level for the call will be set by the broker to ensure zero cost and will depend on market conditions at the time of the transaction.

3. These are also called risk-reversals and involve buying a put and selling a call to range the outcomes of a given index.

4. See Nakovick (1999).

5. This is a derivative on a currency index payable in another currency, for example, the DAX index payable in U.S. dollars.

6. See Dynkin, Hyman, and Wu (1997) for replication of government indices with futures.

7. See Krishnamurthi, Muralidhar, and van der Wouden (1998b).

8. These countries include Austria, Australia, Belgium, Denmark, Finland, France, Germany, Hong Kong, Ireland, Italy, Japan, Luxembourg, Netherlands, New Zealand, Norway, Portugal, Singapore, Spain, Sweden, Switzerland, and the United Kingdom.

9. An "enhanced index" strategy, in this case, is a strategy in which exposure to a market is achieved through the futures market, and the underlying cash assets are managed in a short-term fixed income portfolio.

10. See Table A6.1.3, rows 1–15, for a list of these countries and relevant local indices.

11. See also Nakovick (1999).

12. As the local markets are reported in local currency, and the synthetic benchmark is constructed with local market returns, the synthetic benchmark is compared to the MSCI EAFE Local Currency (LC) index.

13. See Table A6.1.3, rows 4–15, for a list of the 11 countries.

14. See Barclays Global Investors, *Investment Insights* (1998).

7

ASSET-LIABILITY
VALUE AT RISK

Arun S. Muralidhar and Kemal Asad-Syed

The three major risks faced by an investor are: asset-liability risk that the investment benchmark selected by the oversight committee does not hedge liabilities; tactical (and benchmark) risk taken by internal staff in an attempt to add value over the investment benchmark; and active risk taken by investment managers, who are overseen by internal staff, in an attempt to add value relative to indices to which they are measured. Most risk analyses focus on only the last two. This chapter demonstrates how a complete risk analysis should be conducted and explains how an incorrect implementation may lead to suboptimal asset-liability management.

OVERVIEW

Whereas the previous chapters highlighted asset-liability risks and indicated how they should be managed, the focus in this chapter is on the measurement of risks on an ongoing basis.[1]

The seminars on value-at-risk (VAR) are replete with discussions on whether the models implemented by investors should be based on the variance-covariance, Monte Carlo, historical simulation, or bootstrap methods.

Adapted from Kemal Asad-Syed and Arun S. Muralidhar. "An Asset Liability Approach to Value-at-Risk." Investment Management Department Working Paper 98-023, The World Bank, 1998.

Moreover, even the risk standards for such investors rely on numerous risks, such as interest rate risk, hedging risk, legal risk, and market-versus-credit risk.[2] For example, Logue and Rader (1997) suggest that funds should worry about investment risk, surplus risk, sponsor risk (that is, correlations of the cash flow of the sponsor and the fund are not unity), interest rate risk, currency risk, concentration risk, and inflation risk. In addition, most vendors providing such products concentrate on calculating either the absolute VAR of the portfolio or the relative VAR (that is, risk relative to the investment benchmark).[3]

In addition, Grinold (1990), in discussing a sponsor's view of risk, suggests that the risk to a sponsor is equal to the sum of target risk, misfit risk, and active risk, hence focusing largely on an asset-only perspective.[4] This chapter demonstrates that although these discussions are interesting and relevant, they could miss the most important aspect of risk management for institutional investors. In short, these debates are focused on the microscopic aspects of risk management but miss the big picture: whether the process applied captures the biggest risks faced by the investor. These issues have been highlighted in Gibson (1997), de Bever, Kozun, and Zvan (2000), de Marco and Petzel (2000), and Arnott and Bernstein (1990), but this chapter goes further to demonstrate the relative magnitude and interrelatedness of the risks.

THE PROBLEM

It is accepted today that the investment policy or the long-term asset allocation decision for an institutional investor accounts for 80–90 percent of the investment return, with active management capturing the balance (Brinson, Singer, and Beebower 1991). However, the true indication of a pension fund's (or any other institutional investor) performance is not return, but its solvency as represented by the ratio of assets to liabilities or whether the surplus (assets minus liabilities) is positive or negative. In the Netherlands, regulatory bodies increasingly require measures of asset-liability performance as an indicator of the competence of the oversight committee. Unfortunately, in the United States and the United Kingdom, incorrect peer comparator analyses are used to indicate whether or not a fund has performed well, without any adjustment for asset-liability or pure asset risk.[5]

A pension fund, by its very nature, gives rise to what is termed the principal-agent problem and as a result certain idiosyncratic risks. In this problem, the principal hires the agent to perform certain tasks and is not sure whether the agent is acting in the best interests of the principal or the agent. In essence, the agent may take risks that are not desirable for the principal. In respect of the pension fund, this problem may manifest itself in two specific layers: first, between the oversight committee and the investment team; and second, between the investment team and the external managers. In this complex scenario, the investment team is both agent (vis-à-vis the committee) and principal (vis-à-vis external managers). Hence, one needs to monitor the risks taken versus the benchmark and ensure that the performance derived from such deviations is consistent with the desired risk profile of the principal.

Risks for Pension Funds

The three major risks faced by a pension plan are: the asset-liability risk, or the risk incurred when the oversight committee selects a suboptimal benchmark to defease the liabilities; the tactical or benchmark risk taken by internal staff (such as over- or underweighting asset classes, countries, capitalization segments) in an attempt to add value over the investment benchmark; and the active risk taken by investment managers, who are overseen by internal staff, in an attempt to add value relative to the indices to which they are measured. Gibson (1997) combines the last two into one category and fails to recognize that different parties are taking, and different principals are bearing, the risk. These risks can be managed once they are monitored and measured (Figure 7.1). Most other risk analyses focus on only the last two of these risks, but the following sections demonstrate how a complete VAR analysis should be conducted and explains how an incorrect implementation of the risk evaluation system may lead to suboptimal asset-liability management.

The bias in measuring risks for pension funds tends to be towards relative risk measures, i.e., risk relative to benchmarks, rather than absolute risk measures. Each of these three risks can be measured relative to liabilities, strategic asset allocations, and individual market indices, respectively.

	Asset-Liability Risk	Tactical & Benchmark Risk	Manager/Active Risk
Responsibility	Oversight Committee	Internal Staff	Managers
Monitor	Annually	Monthly	Monthly
Manage	Funding/ Investment Policy	Tactical Allocations	Manager Allocations

Figure 7.1   Measuring, Monitoring, and Managing Pension Fund Risks

A CASE STUDY IN ASSET-LIABILITY VAR

Method and Models for Measuring Risk

For a hypothetical pension portfolio, a simple technique was developed to facilitate the VAR analysis. The value of the total portfolio was assumed to be $10 billion. The 99 percent confidence interval over a one-year horizon is the standard metric for VAR analyses (or the loss suffered once every 100 years). Alternative definitions of risk, such as tracking error, are discussed later in the book. Plan sponsors would ideally like to minimize the values for these metrics (risk). There are four elements that must be considered in any risk system: (1) liabilities; (2) strategic asset allocation or investment benchmark; (3) extended policy benchmark—which is the result of all decisions made by the investment team to tactically deviate from the strategic asset allocation by either overweighting asset classes or sectors within asset classes; and (4) the actual portfolio implemented by external managers. Chapter 8 explains how the plan sponsor can drill down further into the last three elements to establish the marginal contribution of allocations and bets to total risk.

An entirely new framework is proposed here, but the methodology used to calculate the VAR numbers is the same as that used in the Bankers Trust RAROC 2020 system. The results are independent of the model or vendor used; however, systems differ as to the level of aggregation that they assume. For example, the RAROC 2020 system evaluates risk based on every security held by the pension plan. Competing systems such as Pensionmetrics have incorporated liabilities as well, but evaluate risk at the level of individual managers. The benefit to the security level data is that there is an optimum degree of granularity; hence specific risks can be identified (such as interest rate, currency, inflation, a particular equity index) and risk evaluations are based on current holdings. The cons to such a system, which are overcome by manager-level data, are the degree of complexity and the slowness of evaluation. In the manager-level analysis, each manager is assumed to have a volatility and correlation to other managers, benchmarks, and liabilities. This can be based only on historical data and therefore may not capture the fact that a manager changed his or her style or portfolio composition. As these changes are likely to be gradual, the results should not be greatly influenced, but in choosing a vendor, plan sponsors should decide between greater granularity and effort versus lower cost and greater ease of implementation. In addition, some systems assume that the risk profile can be described by a simple bell-shaped curve (or a normal or Gaussian distribution). In such analyses the standard deviation measure then becomes the basis for risk calculations.[6] The implications from this assumption are discussed later.

Results

On an asset-only or absolute basis for this hypothetical variant, the VAR of the actual portfolio was approximately $1.7 billion or approximately 17 percent; however, relative to the investment policy (which sums risks [2] and [3]), the relative VAR is $192 million or 1.92 percent. The latter risk can be broken down into $128 million of VAR (or 1.28 percent) from internal staff tactically deviating from their benchmark or misfit risk and $168 million of VAR (or 1.68 percent) from active management by external managers (or active risk). The key statistic here, however, is the negative correlation between the two decisions, suggesting that external managers are negating decisions by internal staff. This detailed evaluation of these elements is what vendors have normally provided to plan sponsors by vendors. These results are illustrated in Figure 7.2.

A more interesting extension to standard VAR analyses is to establish the asset-liability VAR for the pension fund. There are major differences of opinion about how to model liabilities, especially how to replicate demographic risks in asset space (an option being to perform an econometric analyses where the

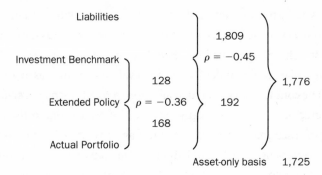

Figure 7.2 The Value-at-Risk Tree

Note: Numbers are in millions of dollars.

liabilities are regressed against all major asset indices), but for some simple assumptions that allow for the capture of the biggest risk to the pension plan's defined benefit liabilities (namely, unconditional indexation to inflation) novel asset-liability VAR results are derived.

The first critical result was that the VAR between the Liabilities and the - Long-term Investment Benchmark was $1.8 billion. This suggests that there is a 1 percent chance that the surplus of the fund could decline by $1.8 billion. Though the size is large, it is more important to consider the fact that it is approximately 10 times the active risk usually measured by risk systems or service providers. As is often the case, 90 percent of the effort is used to monitor 10 percent of the total risk; hence the earlier claim that most VAR analyses are measuring the wrong risk. This estimate of asset-liability VAR is somewhat consistent with the Brinson, Singer and Beebower (1991) result with regard to returns. The message from this statistic is that institutional investors should devote adequate resources to ensuring that the investment policy benchmark selected by them is not taken from some simple mean-variance framework, but rather established on the basis of an asset-liability study and developed in a manner that minimizes the most critical risk, namely, the risk that a surplus disappears.

But can the asset-liability VAR can be expressed in percentage terms? The critical factor here is that the liabilities and assets are not same size, which is not an issue for the other relative risk measures for asset decisions. For example, if a pension plan is overfunded with assets 1.5 times liabilities, a primary concern is whether the percentage calculation for risk should be of assets or liabilities.

Hence, it is more relevant to report asset-liability VAR in currency terms and relative asset VAR in currency and percentage terms. However, some pension plans may feel comfortable reporting all values as a percentage to assets, as this may be an indication of the cushion available with the existing level of assets.

An even more fascinating result of the VAR analyses was that when the actual portfolio was compared to the liabilities, the VAR was found to be lower than the VAR of the investment benchmark and the liabilities. This shows that active management actually reduced the asset-liability risk to the sponsor of the plan. This is not an unreasonable result, as the investment benchmark is composed of a limited set of broad asset indices, whereas the actual portfolio is allowed to span the entire global investment opportunity set. The greater freedom in active management need not necessarily lead to such a result, but is reassuring to a plan sponsor if it does. Interestingly, very few investment teams are measured for their impact on reducing asset-liability risk and are normally measured solely for outperforming their benchmarks. In this instance, the agents are acting intentionally or unintentionally, in the best interests of the principal. However, as demonstrated in Chapter 5, active currency management has the potential to reduce asset-liability risk, and investment teams who are delegated the responsibility of managing the assets should be rewarded for lowering the asset-liability risk even if they do not outperform their benchmarks. If this is not monitored carefully, one could experience the opposite result. Agents who are monitored solely on performance may take risks that increase the overall risks to the plan sponsor.

ALTERNATIVE DEFINITIONS OF RISK: ABSOLUTE DOWNSIDE OR DRAWDOWN

Although from a theoretical perspective it may be appropriate to look at the 99 percent confidence interval for relative risk, a number of sponsors would argue that the true risk to a pension fund or to a staff member is not negative return *relative* to a benchmark, but negative *absolute* performance of a manager or the portfolio. There is an implicit assumption in relative risk calculations that it is not important to worry about the absolute loss as long as the relative portfolio outperforms. Therefore, in a relative analysis, if a portfolio outperforms a benchmark with a return of −15 percent versus the benchmark performance of -20 percent, then this is acceptable. The nature of the principal-agent situation is such that committees may choose to express displeasure when the absolute performance of the portfolio or manager turns negative, as this leads to reductions in the size of the overall fund. In such a situation, one needs to look at measures of absolute drawdown risk (that is, performance worse than zero). This is another variant of the downside risk measure, because it provides an indication to the individual running the risk report of how bad things can get when performance is below some fixed threshold (as opposed to a variable threshold in the relative analysis).

ALTERNATIVE METHODS TO MEASURE RISK:
THE EFFECT OF NON-NORMALITY

A number of commentators have remarked that normal distributions or bell-shaped curves do not appropriately describe financial market variables. Some would argue that these return series have "fat tails"—that is, more observations at the extremes than the normal distribution. Hence, in such situations, using a normal distribution assumption for returns of portfolios may greatly underestimate the risk to a plan sponsor, as it will understate the magnitude of the shock when something bad happens. The cautionary note to plan sponsors is that they are ultimately responsible for the assumptions embedded in any risk system they use, so it is important to know the shortcoming of their models.

A Case Study in Downside Risk Management

Assume that a plan sponsor has to hire an equity manager who is to be measured relative to the S&P 500 Index. This person must choose between Fund A and Fund B, both with historical average returns of approximately 24 percent versus the annualized return of 16 percent for the S&P 500. The annualized return profiles of these two funds and the S&P 500 are provided in Figure 7.3. One obvious observation is that the returns of Fund A are not bell-shaped and so risk will be misestimated using the standard deviation measure. In addition, if the investor is worried about negative returns from these funds (and the S&P 500), one can see from Figure 7.4 that the average expected drawdown is -26 percent for the S&P 500, -14 percent for Fund A, and -8 percent for

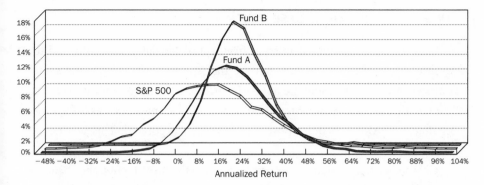

Figure 7.3 Return Distributions

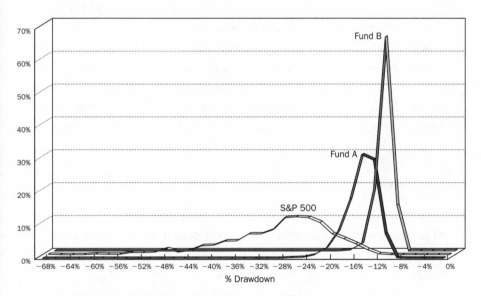

Figure 7.4 Drawdown Distributions

SOURCE: We thank Samir Varma and Sanjay Santhanam for their simulations for both Figures 7.3 and 7.4.

Fund B. Therefore, if the investment professional was worried about how poor performance could be relative to a zero benchmark (or even the S&P 500), Fund B is more appealing. Drawdown risk was not considered in the late 1990s as plan sponsors benefited from the bull market in equities. However, with the recent downturn in markets, committees are not happy with positive excess returns when the total returns of the fund are negative.

AREAS OF ADDITIONAL RESEARCH

Clearly, the specification (or misspecification) of the liabilities could lead to misleading results. This would indicate that sponsors should use the same framework for determining the optimal benchmark in asset-liability space (as the liabilities are extensively modeled in the ALM framework), and for estimating the VAR if portfolio positions can be incorporated. This is a not a trivial exercise.

Chapter 4 explains that permitting leverage in the investment policy benchmark (even for small amounts) leads to significant reductions in asset-liability risk. Hence, for sponsors looking to minimize the asset-liability risk, leverage should be allowed either in the investment benchmark or by active managers. This is consistent and complementary to the propositions in Modigliani and Modigliani (1997) and Muralidhar (2000) that leverage in tactical decisions can actually reduce risk. However, these results, like those underlying the VAR analyses, rely to a significant extent on the quality and integrity of the data. This can be fatal if our recent experience (such as the Long Term Capital Management collapse) with correlations increasing in times of market crises continues to persist.

SUMMARY

This chapter demonstrates that simple VAR analyses offered by vendors may not provide a plan sponsor with an accurate representation of the largest risk. The "truths" shown in the accompanying box can thus be derived from this chapter.

INVESTMENT TRUTHS

- *Often, the risk between assets (either investment benchmark or actual portfolio positions) and liabilities is substantially higher than the asset-only risk that is monitored by most plan sponsors.*

- *Active strategies can be designed to reduce risk from an asset-liability context.*

The results discussed suggest that plan sponsors and oversight committees should devote more attention to doing asset-liability analyses either for VAR or in selecting the optimal investment benchmark, rather than relying on traditional asset-only VAR analyses, simple mean-variance methods to select optimal benchmarks, or peer comparison as a measure of good performance. In addition, investment teams that effectively lower asset-liability risk with or without outperforming their pension benchmarks should be favorably compensated by sponsoring organizations for this value-added activity. Further, the investment team should measure risk regularly, and have its own performance measured by these criteria. Finally, team members should understand the assumptions (and should exercise due diligence) underlying any analyses so that they can recognize how they are modeling risks and thereby the possible over- or underestimation of risk. Ultimately, the biggest mistake in risk analyses is measuring the least important aspect of risk and underestimating the potential impact on performance.

NOTES

1. Thanks to Neil Paragiri, Joseph Slunt, Michelle McCarthy, Ken Penningtion, and others at Bankers Trust for their comments and assistance.

2. See *Risk Standards for Institutional Investment Managers and Institutional Investors.*

3. Pensionmetrics is one of the few software products that is targeted specifically to pension funds and evaluates the risks highlighted in this chapter.

4. Winkelman (2000), in a discussion on budgeting active risk at the total fund level, ignores the importance of linking active risk to liabilities.

5. See Muralidhar and U (1997).

6. The author thanks Samir Varma and Sanjay Santhanam for discussions on this topic.

8

DECOMPOSING AND

UNDERSTANDING RISK

Arun S. Muralidhar, Kemal Asad-Syed,
and Paolo Pasquariello

Portfolio managers may take many bets to outperform a benchmark. This chapter provides two simple methodologies to calculate the contribution of a specific bet to total risk, whether the risk measure is an absolute or a relative one, and demonstrates how investors can develop simple in-house models to measure such risk. In addition, it demonstrates how other measures that are not derived from finance theory, but are used as first approximations, are incorrect. These simple tools allow investors to measure and monitor the risks in their portfolios and thereby manage them more effectively.

OVERVIEW

The issue of risk management and risk budgeting is becoming more important for institutional investors, especially pension funds, and a number of working groups have been formed to evaluate the risk standards that should be adopted by oversight committees for the management of such plans. However, a current shortcoming in the industry is that no uniform model has been adopted to measure risks, which would allow pension funds to manage them. In addition, many software providers have focused only on the absolute risk of

Adapted from Kemal Asad-Syed, Arun S. Muralidhar, and Paulo Pasquariello. "Understanding Risk—Estimating the Contribution to Total Risk of Individual Bets." Unpublished working paper, 2000.

a portfolio in measuring the value-at-risk (VAR) of a portfolio. Most risk systems have often not captured the largest risk that most pension plans are exposed to, namely, asset-liability risk. This was highlighted in Chapter 7.

Further, when the performance of an institutional investor is measured relative to a passive benchmark, it is imperative to measure not only the absolute risk of the benchmark and the actual portfolio, but also the risk relative to a benchmark (Ambarish and Seigel 1996). Chapter 7 provided high-level measures of risk relative to different benchmarks such as (1) liabilities, (2) strategic asset allocation, (3) tactical asset allocation, and (4) specific market indices. Even those software packages that have focused on relative risk have not adequately captured the contribution to total risk of any specific bet taken by portfolio managers, which is termed marginal risk. This measure is important because it provides the plan sponsor with an indication of the concentration of risk and relatedness of bets in the portfolio.

Litterman (1996) highlights the usefulness of this measure and gives an indication of how it may be computed; however, the article does not provide the methodology for the calculation. In addition, Gibson (1997) suggests that pension funds should monitor the contribution to risk of positions, that is, correlated risks attributable to a position vis-à-vis either liabilities or some asset benchmark. When such adjustments are made, the contribution can be termed the marginal contribution, and the sum of all marginals should equal total risk. The appendices to this chapter provide two simple methodologies to calculate the contribution of a specific bet to total risk, whether the risk measure is an absolute or a relative one, and demonstrates how plan sponsors can develop simple in-house models to measure plan risk.

The first approach develops the mathematical technique suggested by Litterman (1996); the second provides a more intuitive approach, which is derived from the basic theory of asset pricing. In addition, this chapter demonstrates how other measures that are not derived from finance theory, but used as first approximations, are incorrect.[1] This approach also provides valuable insight into the correlation of bets with the entire portfolio of bets, thereby enhancing the evaluation of risk-taking activities. These simple tools can allow sponsors to measure and monitor the risks in their portfolios and thereby manage them more effectively. In addition, the measurement of risk can be done at any level—across asset classes, across managers within an asset class, and across securities in a specific portfolio. In this chapter the analysis is conducted at the highest level of a pension fund—across asset classes—but the extensions are trivial.

This chapter provides the math for the calculations in the chapter appendices, but the nontechnical reader can skip the technical sections to gain key insights without loss of continuity. The chapter also considers the feasibility of using such statistics for the allocation of risk capital. The discussion is developed in the context of a pension plan, but the concepts and conclusions apply more generally to any investor, whether a portfolio manager or an institutional investor with investment advisers.

PENSION PLAN RISKS

Prior to discussing the contribution to risk of a specific bet, the different risks that a plan is exposed to are briefly recapitulated. Risk is generated in pension plans at different levels. At the highest level, selecting a benchmark for the asset portfolio creates the possibility for risks from asset-liability mismatches (or asset-liability risk). Alternatively, selecting an asset benchmark for purely asset reasons implies targeting an absolute risk point or a target variability of returns. At the next level, once target asset-class allocations and benchmarks have been determined, a plan sponsor may create additional risk by investing tactically in the actual portfolio away from these target levels (or tactical risk) (Mashayekhi-Beschloss and Muralidhar 1996). At the simplest level, tactical risk is created by underweighting or overweighting individual asset classes.

In this chapter, the focus is only on (1) the absolute risk of the benchmark portfolio; (2) the absolute risk of the actual portfolio on any given day (which, if tactical bets are permitted, could be quite different from that of the benchmark); and (3) the relative risk implied by the actual portfolio vis-à-vis the benchmark or tactical risk. Thereafter, it is possible to demonstrate the contribution to the total risk or variability of returns of each asset class in which the plan has made either a target allocation or a tactical deviation.[2] The concept of the "marginal" is very well developed in economics in determining optimal consumption, pricing, and so on, and in an analogous fashion this chapter attempts to demonstrate whether the marginal risk measure can be used in the optimal utilization of a risk budget.

DEFINITION OF TERMS

For convenience, two portfolios are defined, namely the benchmark and the actual portfolio, and three risk measures identified: the absolute risk of the benchmark, the absolute risk of the actual portfolio, and the relative risk of the actual portfolio.

> *Benchmark portfolio:* This is the strategic long-term asset allocation of the plan that is described by listing the various asset classes in which the plan is invested and the long-term target allocations. A hypothetical benchmark portfolio is provided in Table 8.1.

> *Actual portfolio:* This is the investor's portfolio on any measurement day. As a consequence of portfolio managers overweighting or underweighting asset classes, the live portfolio can and will differ from the benchmark. For illustrative purposes, a hypothetical actual portfolio is provided in Table 8.1, which is relative to the benchmark. The last column gives the percentage deviation of each asset class from its benchmark; the sum of these deviations is zero.[3]

> *Absolute risk of benchmark:* In asset space, the variance or standard deviation of the expected returns of this portfolio describes the risk of the benchmark portfolio.[4] Mathematically, the absolute risk is

Table 8.1
Benchmark, Actual, and Relative Portfolios: Weighting of Assets

Asset Classes	Benchmark Portfolio (%) (v)	Actual Portfolio (%) (w)	Relative Portfolio (%) (z)
U.S. equities	30.0	32.0	2.0
Non-U.S. equities	35.0	29.0	−6.0
Emerging equities	5.0	8.0	3.0
U.S. fixed income	7.0	9.0	2.0
Non-U.S. fixed income	10.0	8.0	−2.0
High-yield bonds	2.0	4.0	2.0
Private equities	10.0	8.0	−2.0
Cash	1.0	2.0	1.0
Total	100.0	100.0	0.0
Standard deviation	11.69%	11.37%	1.24%

estimated by taking the benchmark or target weights and multiplying them through a variance-covariance matrix:

$$\sigma^2(\text{benchmark}) = (v^T\Gamma v) \qquad (8.1)$$

where v = matrix of benchmark asset class weights (v^T is the transpose of v), Γ is the assumed variance-covariance matrix, and v_i is the target weight of the ith asset class. The square root, or the standard deviation, is also a risk measure, as it captures the dispersion of the portfolio return around its mean. Using the hypothetical benchmark portfolio in Table 8.1 and the assumed variance-covariance matrix in the appendix (Table A8.3.1), the standard deviation (i.e., risk) of this portfolio is provided in Table 8.1.[5]

Absolute risk of the actual portfolio: The variance of the actual portfolio is calculated in a fashion identical to that of the benchmark:

$$\sigma^2(\text{actual}) = (w^T\Gamma w) \qquad (8.2)$$

where w = matrix of actual asset class weights, and w_i is the actual weight of the ith asset class. The square root or standard deviation is an alternative expression of this risk measure and is provided in Table 8.1.

Relative risk of the actual portfolio: This is the risk engendered by off-benchmark positions. Ambarish and Seigel (1996) demonstrate why this measure should be used when a portfolio is measured relative to a benchmark. The relative risk or variance of the active portfolio is calculated in a fashion identical to those above:

$$\sigma^2(\text{relative}) = (z^T\Gamma z) \qquad (8.3)$$

where z = matrix of the differences between the actual and target asset class weights, and z_i is the deviation from benchmark in the ith asset class. Any component of the z matrix can be positive or negative, as the investment team could have chosen to underweight or overweight a particular asset class. The square root of $\sigma^2(\text{relative})$ per unit of time is referred to as the tracking error of a portfolio. Mathematically,

$$\text{Tracking error} = \sqrt{z^T\Gamma z} = \frac{z^T\Gamma z}{\sqrt{z^T\Gamma z}} \qquad (8.4)$$

The tracking error measures the amount by which the performance of the actual portfolio can deviate from the benchmark and is provided in Table 8.1.

The mathematical details for the calculation of marginal risk and correlation of bets are provided in the chapter appendices for the more technical reader. In the next few sections the specific benchmark and actual portfolio are examined to decompose the risks of the portfolio.

A CASE STUDY IN MARGINAL RISK ANALYSIS

Table 8.1 gives a benchmark portfolio and a tactical portfolio that is maintained relative to the benchmark. This hypothetical "actual" portfolio is overweight U.S. equities, U.S. fixed income, and high yield by 2 percent, underweight non-U.S. equities by 6 percent, overweight emerging equities by 3 percent, underweight non-U.S. fixed income and private equities by 2 percent, and overweight cash by 1 percent. This causes a tracking error versus the benchmark of 1.24 percent. Tables 8.2 and 8.3 provide the marginal contribution to total risk (in percentage points) and percentage contribution to total risk, respectively, for the portfolios in Table 8.1. These diagnostics provide a number of useful insights. It is apparent from the tables that the risk is

Table 8.2
Contribution to the Standard Deviation of the Three Portfolios

Asset Classes	Absolute Risk		Relative Portfolio (%)
	Benchmark (%)	Actual (%)	
U.S. equities	3.8	4.1	−0.045
Non-U.S. equities	5.8	4.9	0.783
Emerging equities	0.5	0.8	0.241
U.S. fixed income	0.1	0.2	0.019
Non-U.S. fixed income	0.2	0.2	0.001
High-yield bonds	0.1	0.1	0.040
Private equities	1.2	1.0	0.203
Cash	0.0	0.0	0.000
Total standard deviation	11.69%	11.37%	1.24%

Table 8.3

Percentage Contribution to the Standard Deviation of the Three Portfolios

Asset Classes	Absolute Risk		Relative Portfolio (% of Total)
	Benchmark (% of Total)	Actual (% of Total)	
U.S. equities	32.2	36.2	−3.7
Non-U.S. equities	49.7	43.4	63.1
Emerging equities	4.4	7.4	19.4
U.S. fixed income	1.1	1.5	1.5
Non-U.S. fixed income	1.6	1.3	0.1
High-yield bonds	0.6	1.3	3.3
Private equities	10.5	8.8	16.4
Cash	0.0	0.0	0.0
Total standard deviation	100.0	100.0	100.0

Table 8.4

Implied Correlation of Asset Class Bet to Portfolio of Bets

Asset Classes	Relative Portfolio
U.S. equities	−0.152
Non-U.S. equities	−0.670
Emerging equities	0.343
U.S. fixed income	0.179
Non-U.S. fixed income	−0.009
High-yield bonds	0.206
Private equities	−0.376
Cash	0.000

additive, thereby validating the "marginal" label. Hence this measure allows for a decomposition of risk (standard deviation) of all asset classes/bets while capturing the correlation with other asset classes/bets.

First, it is relevant to observe that although the actual portfolio in Table 8.1 is overweight U.S. equities, overweighting this asset class reduces the tracking error, as this bet is negatively correlated with other bets in the portfolio (Table 8.4), thereby lowering the total relative risk (Tables 8.2 and 8.3). This is evident by the negative coefficient on U.S. equities in the Relative Portfolio column.

Second, the absolute or relative size of a bet may mask the actual contribution to the total risk. For example, although the 2 percent overweight in U.S. equities actually lowers the tracking error, the same absolute bet in high-yield bonds (+2 percent) contributes positively to the relative risk (3.3 percent in Table 8.3).[6] In addition, the 2 percent underweight in non-U.S. fixed income has a negligible impact on the tracking error, whereas the same absolute and relative deviation in private equities contributes 16 percent of the total tracking error. Although private equities are more volatile, there is a more complex relationship at work, which includes the relationship with other bets in the portfolio.[7]

Third, in evaluating the correlation of bets with the overall portfolio of bets as in Table 8.4, it is relevant to notice that the bets in U.S. equities, non-U.S. equities, non-U.S. fixed income, and private equities are all negatively correlated with the portfolio of bets. One could ask if all these are therefore risk reducing by offsetting other bets in the portfolio. However, where the portfolio is long in respect of the benchmark and is negatively correlated, the contribution to the tracking error is negative (as in U.S. equities). On the other hand, where the portfolio is short in respect of the benchmark (non-U.S. equities, non-U.S. fixed income, and private equities), the negative correlation, in conjunction with the short position, contributes positively to the tracking error.

USEFULNESS OF THIS MEASURE

Any ability to drill down into a total risk measure and attribute the value to its components is useful for portfolio managers. As highlighted in the results, when the marginal contribution is negative, all else being equal, a marginal unit increase in the direction of the current bet lowers the total tracking error.[8] Only the U.S. equity bet changes the risk posture by effectively being risk reducing. Therefore, this breakdown can be used to size bets more effectively and capture the maximum alpha for a given risk tolerance.[9] In addition, the portfolio manager determines whether the bets are all correlated and is able to disaggregate how diversified their bets may be. For example, in Table 8.1 there are eight asset class bets; however, the three bets in non-U.S. equity, emerging markets, and private equity contribute 99 percent of the risk exposure. If the marginal contribution is concentrated in a few bets, even the implementation of a large number of bets suggests that risks are not diversified. Similarly, a negative correlation in isolation is insufficient information for ascertaining whether bets are risk increasing or risk reducing, as demonstrated above.

The marginal contribution is dependent on current allocations; hence a slight change to a position implies very different results. For example, by shifting 2 percent more to U.S. equities from non-U.S. fixed income (i.e., extending the previous bet), the contribution from U.S. equities to the tracking error turns positive, and the correlation of U.S. equities and non-U.S. fixed income to other bets in the portfolio is now positive. However, now the contribution to the tracking error from non-U.S. fixed income turns mildly negative as the correlation has shifted sign. Therefore, the sensitivity of the marginal risk analysis to the portfolio changes would make it very difficult to allocate risk capital on this basis, for it would require a constant fine-tuning, and each asset class manager would need to be cognizant not only of his or her view on that specific market, but also its impact on other views.

This technique has also been adopted by investment managers to manage the risk of their portfolios. For example, this can easily be used for equity, bond, or currency management, where instead of having asset classes one can list the securities or currencies and thereby decompose the risk relative to the passive benchmark. In addition, Muralidhar and Pasquariello (2001) extend this analysis to imply the currency views of various positions implemented by currency overlay managers for a client. They are able to demonstrate some seeming inconsistencies in positions and views in a fashion similar to some seeming inconsistencies highlighted above. This method effectively allows for a clearer understanding of the concentration of bets and which bets can lower tracking error for optimal risk utilization.

COMPARISON WITH OTHER METHODOLOGIES

This section covers other methodologies that are applied in standard risk-management software and explains the deficiencies of each. The content is based on the experience in evaluating a number of risk-management software programs for implementation in the World Bank's pension fund portfolio.

Table 8.5
Comparing Methods of Estimating Contribution to Benchmark Risk Percentage

Asset Classes	Assuming Independence (% Contribution)	Marginal Not Rebalanced (% Contribution)	Marginal Rebalanced (% Contribution)	Proposed Method (% Contribution)
U.S. equities	71.5	40.67	−61.2	32.2
Non-U.S. equities	21.5	37.7	−70.5	49.7
Emerging equities	1.6	5.9	4.2	4.4
U.S. fixed income	1.8	2.7	92.7	1.1
Non-U.S. fixed income	0.1	2.1	70.8	1.6
High-yield bonds	0.5	2.4	27.8	0.6
Private equities	3.0	8.5	8.8	10.5
Cash	0.0	0.0	27.4	0.0
Total	100.0	100.0	100.0	100.0
Total variance of portfolio	0.60%	1.66%	−0.26%	1.37%
Standard deviation	7.73%	12.90%	N/A	11.69%

Table 8.6
Comparing Methods of Estimating Contribution to Relative Risk Percentage

Asset Classes	Marginal Not Rebalanced (% Contribution)	Proposed Method (% Contribution)
U.S. equities	45.3	−3.7
Non-U.S. equities	−34.6	63.1
Emerging equities	35.3	19.4
U.S. fixed income	−3.3	1.5
Non-U.S. fixed income	−1.0	0.1
High-yield bonds	6.4	3.3
Private equities	51.9	16.4
Cash	0.0	0.0
Total	100.0	100.0
Total tracking error	1.06%	1.24%

In Tables 8.5 and 8.6, the contribution to the total risk is compared using the method proposed above and the following three methods, which appear to be most commonly used by vendors to provide an estimate of the magnitude of the error of not capturing the diversification benefits of an asset class.

- *Contribution assuming an identity correlation matrix:* Under this method, it is assumed that diagonal elements are unity, and off-diagonal elements in the correlation matrix are zero. This is done to simplify the calculation. Therefore, the assumption of independence between assets would provide a variance estimate whereby adding the weighted variance of each asset class equals the portfolio variance. The problem in assuming that off-diagonal elements are zero is that the true benefits of diversification are never captured in such analyses. In addition, as Table 8.5 demonstrates, the total risk of the benchmark portfolio is wrongly estimated, thereby rendering this approach incorrect (7.73 percent versus 11.69 percent).

- *"Marginal contribution" (with and without rebalancing):* Under this methodology, which is embedded in the most commonly available software, the user calculates the variance using all the assets and then extracts one asset class at a time from the portfolio and recomputes the variance or standard deviation. In fact, Rahl (2000) describes marginal VAR as "the difference between overall portfolio VAR and VAR excluding certain accounts, risk factors or positions." This new standard deviation (excluding a particular asset class) is compared to the full portfolio risk to give an estimate of the "contribution" of that particular asset class. The most critical problem is that the contribution to risk for a total portfolio is to be computed when portfolios are complete (i.e., with all asset classes, including the one whose contribution is being estimated) and not by using subsets of portfolios. Therefore, even if correct, the sum of all "marginal estimates" should equal the true variance of the portfolio (in the case of the benchmark portfolio, 11.69 percent). As is evident from Table 8.5, this is not the case, and the marginal method overestimates the total risk of the portfolio (12.9 percent). There are actually two ways to perform this calculation: not to rebalance the remaining asset class weights (i.e., so that the sum of the assets need not total 100 percent) and to rebalance the remaining assets.[10] The rebalancing method is clearly incorrect as it excludes the possibility of the asset class ever being in the portfolio. As indicated in Table 8.5, it gives a negative variance, which is an infeasible result for an asset portfolio.

- *Tracking error of each bet in isolation:* Under this method the bet being evaluated is assumed to be the only bet in the portfolio and its risk is considered in isolation. This assumes that the bets are independent and is identical to the first method (identity correlation matrix).

Clearly, the marginal method assuming rebalancing and the method assuming independence of assets are incorrect in estimating either the total variance or the percentage contribution of an asset class or an asset class bet. Similarly, it can be shown numerically that these alternative methods are inadequate for estimating the percentage contribution to relative risk. For completeness, Table 8.6 includes the results of the marginal, no rebalancing calculation vis-à-vis the proposed method for the tracking error calculation. Not only are the resultant totals wrong, but also the magnitude, and often the signs too, are incorrect for the portfolio bets, providing the user with incorrect statistics on the contribution of bets to the risk of the overall portfolio.

CAVEATS

In the case of the two absolute measures of benchmark risk and actual risk, the implied correlations are meaningful. However, the implied correlations of the asset class bet to the portfolio of bets are based on the assumption that the variance-covariance matrix for asset classes is applicable also for asset class bets (which need not always be true). However, this is an acceptable first approximation and assumes no bias in the bets away from the respective benchmarks. This can be easily corrected by using a revised variance-covariance matrix should the plan sponsor so decide.

SUMMARY

This chapter set out to demonstrate simple methods by which the contribution of an asset class allocation or an asset class bet to the total absolute or relative risk of the portfolio could be determined. Such an evaluation is useful for a plan sponsor not only to measure risk but also to effectively manage risk by decomposing it into its constituent parts. Four key investment truths, highlighted in the accompanying box, emerge from this discussion.

INVESTMENT TRUTHS

- *The size of bet need not be a good indicator of the contribution to total risk.*

- *The direction of a bet need not be a good indicator of the contribution to total risk.*

- *It is difficult to allocate risk capital on the basis of marginal risk measures.*

- *One can determine if risk is concentrated in a few bets and correct for this through better portfolio construction.*

In addition, this methodology is superior to other methodologies that are available to institutional investors for implementation by risk management software companies. However, a plan sponsor can easily implement these tools using spreadsheet-type computer programs. Finally, this chapter has demonstrated only how contributions of asset class allocations to total risk are determined; the extensions to estimate the contribution of a selection of a benchmark of a manager or an individual manager's security selection (in either equities, bonds, or currencies) to an entire portfolio is a simple extension of this methodology.

THE MATHEMATICAL SOLUTION FOR

MARGINAL CONTRIBUTION

The marginal contribution to total risk from an individual bet is nothing but a function of the first derivative of the risk measure vis-à-vis the bet under consideration. Litterman (1996) defines it loosely as "the marginal rate of change in risk per unit change in the position (at the current position size) times the position size itself, can be thought of as the rate of change in risk with respect to a small percentage change in the size of the position." For simplicity, the tracking error is used for this estimation.

Marginal contribution of the bet in the ith asset class (z_i) to tracking error

$$= z_i \frac{\partial(\text{tracking error})}{\partial z_i} \qquad (A8.1.1)$$

(such that $\sum_i z_i \dfrac{\partial(\text{tracking error})}{\partial z_i} = \text{total tracking error})^{[11]}$

$$= z_i \frac{\partial \sqrt{z^T \Gamma z}}{\partial z_i}$$

$$= z_i \frac{z^T \Gamma}{\sqrt{z^T \Gamma z}} \qquad (A8.1.1')$$

where $\left(\dfrac{z^T \Gamma}{\sqrt{z^T \Gamma z}} \right)$ is a $1 \times N$ matrix measuring the marginal risk per unit of deviation.

Notice that the denominator in the second term is nothing but the tracking error, thereby normalizing the calculation.

The same approach can be followed to measure the marginal contribution of each individual position to the total absolute risk of the portfolio. In this case, the marginal contribution of the position in the ith asset class to the portfolio's risk is given by

$$w_i \times \frac{\partial(\text{std dev})}{\partial w_i} \qquad (A8.1.2)$$

which equals

$$w_i \frac{w^T\Gamma}{\sqrt{w^T\Gamma w}} \qquad (A8.1.2')$$

where $(w^T\Gamma)/\sqrt{w^T\Gamma w}$ is a $1 \times N$ matrix measuring the marginal risk per unit of the positions.

Finally, the marginal contribution of the position in the ith asset class to the benchmark's risk is given by

$$= v_i \times \frac{\partial(\text{std dev})}{\partial v_i} \qquad (A8.1.3)$$

$$= v_i \frac{v^T\Gamma}{\sqrt{v^T\Gamma v}} \qquad (A8.1.3')$$

where $(v^T\Gamma)/\sqrt{v^T\Gamma v}$ is a $1 \times N$ matrix measuring the marginal risk per unit of the positions.

THE INTUITIVE APPROACH

There is another approach to estimating the contribution of an allocation to total risk that is derived from asset pricing theory. For simplicity, this is called the intuitive approach. Define the contribution of a stock I to the total risk of a portfolio of N stocks (P) as r_i. Define the contribution of an asset class I to the total risk of a portfolio of N asset classes (P) as c_i. From the basics in finance, the contribution to total risk of a stock I to a total portfolio of N stocks (P) or r_i is equal to

$$r_i = s_i \times \text{covariance}(I, P) \qquad (A8.2.1)$$

where s_i is the weight of stock i in portfolio P. Mathematically, this is equivalent to

$$r_i = s_i \times \sigma(I, P) = s_i \times \rho_{I,P} \times \sigma(I) \times \sigma(P) \qquad (A8.2.2)$$

where $\rho_{I,P}$ is the correlation between I and P, $\sigma(I, P)$ is the covariance between I and P, and $\sigma(P)$ and $\sigma(I)$ represent the standard deviations of P and I respectively. Usually, the correlation among stocks is known and stable, whereas that of an individual stock to a specific portfolio is uncertain. Where the correlation factor is unknown ex-ante, the contribution to risk can be calculated by the following:

$$r_i = s_i \times \sum s_j \times \sigma(i, j) \qquad (A8.2.3)$$

where $\sum$ is the summation operator for $j = 1$ through N stocks and $\sigma(i, j)$ is the covariance of stocks i and j. The sum of all r_i in the portfolio must equal $\sigma^2(P)$. Hence in percentage terms, the contribution of stock I to the variance of portfolio P would be $r_i/\sigma^2(P)$.

In an analogous fashion to equations (A8.2.1–3), the contribution to the total risk of an asset class for either absolute or relative risk can be defined as above. However, in the case of asset class structuring, the correlation between that of a specific asset class and the total portfolio (or those of asset class bets with the portfolio of bets) is difficult to determine ex-ante and probably changes as the portfolio composition changes. The correlation between two asset classes is easier to estimate. Hence an adaptation of equation (A8.2.3) is applied to estimate the contribution of an asset class to portfolio risk. Thus, in the case of the actual risk of the portfolio:

$$c_i(\text{actual}) = w_i \times \sum w_j \times \sigma(i, j) \qquad (A8.2.4)$$

where $\sigma(i, j)$ is the covariance between the ith and the jth asset class and $\sum$ is the summation operator for $j = 1$ through N asset classes. For the absolute risk of the benchmark portfolio, define

$$c_i(\text{benchmark}) = v_i \times \sum v_j \times \sigma(i, j) \qquad (A8.2.5)$$

In the case of the relative risk calculations, the correlation of a tactical bet in an asset class with the portfolio of tactical bets can be determined as

$$c_i(\text{tactical deviation}) = z_i \times \sum z_j \times \sigma(i, j) \qquad (A8.2.6)$$

It is clear that the c_i are calculated using variance as a measure of risk. To normalize for the standard deviation being the measure of risk and using equation (8.4), define

$$c_i'(\text{actual}) = \frac{c_i(\text{absolute})}{\sqrt{w^T \Gamma w}} = \frac{w_i \times \sum w_j \times \sigma(i, j)}{\sqrt{w^T \Gamma w}} \qquad (A8.2.7)$$

$$c_i'(\text{benchmark}) = \frac{c_i(\text{benchmark})}{\sqrt{v^T \Gamma v}} = \frac{v_i \times \sum v_j \times \sigma(i, j)}{\sqrt{v^T \Gamma v}} \qquad (A8.2.8)$$

$$c_i'(\text{tactical}) = \frac{c_i(\text{tactical})}{\sqrt{z^T \Gamma z}} = \frac{z_i \times \sum z_j \times \sigma(i, j)}{\sqrt{z^T \Gamma z}} \qquad (A8.2.9)$$

Note that the last equation describes the marginal risk of a single bet to the total tracking error. For the portfolios in Table 8.1 (benchmark, actual, and deviation), Tables 8.2 and 8.3 provide the marginal contribution to the total risk (in percentage points) and the *percentage contribution* of each asset class or asset class bet to the total risk, respectively.

CORRELATIONS OF ASSET ALLOCATIONS

TO PORTFOLIO ALLOCATIONS

An interesting statistic that can be derived from the above is the correlation of an asset class allocation to the overall allocation (as differentiated from the asset class correlations in Table A8.3.1) or a specific asset class bet to a portfolio of bets. This section develops the analytical solutions for estimating these correlations. This statistic is useful as it allows the portfolio managers to determine whether bets are positively correlated, negatively correlated or uncorrelated with other bets—something that is not obvious at the time of constructing portfolios.

Measures of correlation of a single position with the total portfolio and of a single bet with the total portfolio of bets can be explicitly obtained from the following definitions. First, for the absolute portfolio:

$$\mathrm{cov}(w_i y_i, y_P) = \mathrm{cov}\left(w_i y_i, \sum_{j=1}^{N} w_j y_j\right) = w_i^2 \, \mathrm{var}(y_i) + \sum_{\substack{j=1 \\ j \neq i}}^{N} w_i w_j \, \mathrm{cov}(y_i, y_j)$$

$$= \sum_{j=1}^{N} w_i w_j \, \mathrm{cov}(y_i, y_j) \qquad\qquad (A8.3.1)$$

$$\rho_{iP} = \frac{\mathrm{cov}(w_i y_i, y_P)}{\sigma_{w_i y_i} \sigma_P} = \frac{\displaystyle\sum_{j=1}^{N} w_i w_j \, \mathrm{cov}(y_i, y_j)}{w_i \sigma_i \sqrt{w^T \Gamma w}} = \frac{c_i(\text{actual})}{w_i \sigma_i \sqrt{w^T \Gamma w}}$$

where y_i is the return from the ith asset class.

Then, for the correlation of an individual bet with the portfolio of bets:

$$\mathrm{cov}(y_{Zi}, y_{Zp}) = \mathrm{cov}\left(z_i y_i, \sum_{j=1}^{N} z_j y_j\right) = z_i^2 \, \mathrm{var}(y_i) + \sum_{\substack{j=1 \\ j \neq i}}^{N} z_i z_j \, \mathrm{cov}(y_i, y_j)$$

$$= \sum_{j=1}^{N} z_i z_j \, \mathrm{cov}(y_i, y_j) \qquad\qquad (A8.3.2)$$

$$\rho_{ZiZP} = \frac{\mathrm{cov}(y_{Zi}, y_{ZP})}{\sigma_{Zi} \sigma_{ZP}} = \frac{\displaystyle\sum_{j=1}^{N} z_i z_j \, \mathrm{cov}(y_i, y_j)}{z_i \sigma_i \sqrt{z^T \Gamma z}} = \frac{c_i'(\text{tactical})}{z_i \sigma_i}$$

where y_{zi} is the spread expected return from the ith asset class.

Alternatively, using the intuitive approach, since the correlation between an asset class and the portfolio is unknown ex-ante, from equations (A8.3.1–2) and (A8.2.2), the following can also imply the correlation coefficient of each asset class to the benchmark portfolio:

$$\rho_{i,B} = \frac{c_i(\text{benchmark})}{\sigma(P) \times \sigma(I) \times v_i} \qquad (A8.3.3)$$

The correlation coefficient of each asset class to the actual portfolio (or $\rho_{p,P}$)

$$= \frac{c_i(\text{actual})}{\sigma(\text{actual}) \times \sigma(I) \times w_i} \qquad (A8.3.4)$$

or the correlation of the bet in asset class I to the portfolio of bets ($\rho_{Zi,ZP}$)

$$= \frac{c_i(\text{tactical})}{\sigma(TE) \times \sigma(I) \times z_i} \qquad (A8.3.5)$$

where TE is the tracking error.

Table 8.4 provides the implied correlation coefficient of each asset class bet to portfolio of bets based on their respective allocations.[12] This table shows that the bets in four asset classes are negatively correlated with the portfolio of bets, at the current position.

Table A8.3.1
Data on Asset Classes

Asset Classes	Standard Deviation (%)	USEQ	NUSEQ	EMEQ	USFI	NUSFI	HY	PE	Cash
U.S. equities	15.0%	1.0	0.5	0.3	0.4	0.4	0.5	0.4	−0.08
Non-U.S. equities	19.5%	0.5	1.0	0.3	0.2	0.3	0.2	0.1	−0.13
Emerging equities	23.3%	0.3	0.3	1.0	0.3	0.3	0.2	0.1	−0.10
U.S. fixed income	5.2%	0.4	0.2	0.3	1.0	0.4	0.3	0.0	−0.02
Non-U.S. fixed income	4.5%	0.4	0.3	0.3	0.4	1.0	0.3	0.0	−0.05
High-yield bonds	9.8%	0.5	0.2	0.2	0.3	0.3	1.0	0.0	−0.07
Private equities	27.0%	0.4	0.1	0.1	0.0	0.0	0.0	1.0	0.00
Cash	1.0%	−0.08	−0.13	−0.10	−0.02	−0.05	−0.07	0.00	1.00

NOTES

1. Litterman (1996) makes a similar point in a footnote for one of these methods.

2. For the purpose of this analysis it is demonstrated how asset class allocations at a target or tactical level can be used to determine contribution to risk. The extension of determining the contribution of any deviation from a benchmark (e.g., security, country, or currency selection) is trivial.

3. We are assuming unleveraged deviations from the benchmark, but the results would be unaffected if leverage is appropriately captured.

4. See, for example, Markowitz (1959).

5. Since numerical simulations are provided to illuminate the key points in this chapter, we provide a variance-covariance matrix of the various asset classes in Table A.8.3.1. Every institutional investor can select his or her own matrix; these values were based on estimates from historical data.

6. This point has been made elsewhere, more specifically with respect to managing the risks of currency overlays. See Mashayekhi-Beschloss and Muralidhar (1996).

7. Litterman (1996), who makes a similar observation, terms the point where risk contribution is zero as a candidate for a "best hedge."

8. Up to a point. If the bet size increases, this becomes the dominant bet in the portfolio and will contribute positively to the tracking error.

9. A cautionary note: any risk analysis depends on the correlations and variances remaining stable over time, and a violation of this assumption would put any risk analysis in doubt. Also, once the positions are changed, the statistics need to be recalculated for the new portfolio.

10. I would like to thank Mr. P.S. Srinivas for pointing this out.

11. See also Litterman (1996).

12. As the allocation weights change, the total risk of a portfolio and hence the implied correlation will also change.

IV

IMPLEMENTATION OF

ASSET ALLOCATION

9

PERFORMANCE ATTRIBUTION AND RISK-ADJUSTED PERFORMANCE

Arun S. Muralidhar

This chapter examines performance attribution methodologies for a pension plan and other investment portfolios, and recommends a more expansive method. These suggestions are based on the experience of attributing performance to the multiple decisions made in pension plan management. The chapter also presents and compares various risk-adjusted performance measures. It demonstrates that only one measure is consistent with an evaluation of the confidence in the skill of a manager.

OVERVIEW

Previous chapters demonstrated how benchmarks must be established and how risks should be monitored and decomposed. This section attempts to do much the same with performance to facilitate decision making. Whereas risk management is a largely forward-looking exercise, performance evaluation can largely be a backward-looking exercise. The key aspect of performance attribution is to ensure that the value added by each decision in the investment

Adapted from Arturo Balana and Robert Weary. "A Decision-Based Approach to Performance Attribution." Investment Management Department Working Paper Series, The World Bank, 1998; adapted from Arun S. Muralidhar. "Risk-Adjusted Performance—The Correlation Correction." *Financial Analysts Journal,* Volume 56, Number 5, September/October 2000. Copyright 2000, Association for Investment Management and Research. Reproduced and republished from *Financial Analysts Journal* with permission from the Association for Investment Management and Research. All Rights Reserved.

process is captured so that these decisions can either be enhanced if profitable or reduced if unprofitable. In doing so, performance attribution is made into a forward-looking activity. In addition, this chapter demonstrates how performance can be adjusted for the risk taken to generate such performance and compares various methodologies. This focuses on the evaluation of an investment decision, and facilitates future decision making. These decisions could either be the overall asset allocation or the allocation of assets to a manager vis-à-vis their peers or the selection of securities by investment managers. This chapter also examines conclusions that can be drawn from such data on the skill (as opposed to luck) inherent in these decisions.

PERFORMANCE ATTRIBUTION

This section begins with an overview of the conventional methodology and also suggests a new methodology for expanding performance attribution for a pension plan.[1] Specifically, it adjusts the standard methodology used by most plans to deal with benchmark risk and the contribution from selecting a roster of managers. Appendix 9.1 provides an innovative way to account for performance of currency overlay portfolios (a portfolio with performance, but little or no "market value"). The methodology adopted herein focuses on decisions rather than investment factors such as market capitalization and price to earnings (P/E) ratios for the equity market, and duration convexity and others for the fixed income market.[2] Although factor-driven decisions are not dismissed wholesale, factor-based performance attribution is found to be more relevant for decision making at the micro or asset level. At the macro or total plan level, decision-based performance attribution captures the decisions of investment staff in favoring one asset class over another, one manager over another, or the assignation of benchmarks to managers.[3]

Attribution needs to be conducted at several levels to mirror the levels of accountability in the plan.

The Standard Attribution Methodology

There are various ways to divide the total return of a pension plan. The basic equation in the attribution methodology, applied by most pension plans, states that total return is the sum of contributions from the investment policy, plan sponsor, and managers. For example, Surz (1997) suggests that detailed performance attribution should examine the value added from three sources: (1) from sponsors on policy and timing; (2) from sponsors and managers on timing and selectivity (i.e., in choosing managers); and (3) from managers in their timing and selectivity. The goal of this exercise is to decompose total return. Traditionally, the following method has been adopted:

Total plan return = policy return

+ contribution from the plan sponsor

+ contribution from the managers   (9.1)

Figure 9.1 presents a schematic of this methodology. The notations are at the asset class level: w_A = actual weight, w_P = policy weight, r_A = actual return, r_P = policy return, r_B = aggregate benchmarks' return.

The contribution from policy is the return from the policy benchmark of the asset class. Its contribution to total return is calculated by multiplying policy weight w_P by policy return r_P.

The contribution from tactical asset allocation (TAA) comes from the plan sponsor's skill in *timing*, that is, selection of asset classes to underweight or overweight relative to policy. Its contribution is equal to the amount of deviation of the asset class weight from policy weight, $w_A - w_P$, multiplied by the policy return, r_P.

The contribution from benchmark risk (also called misfit risk) measures the mismatch between the (aggregate) styles of the managers and asset class benchmark. It is calculated as the deviation of the return of the aggregate

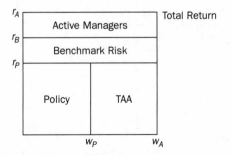

Figure 9.1   Traditional Performance Attribution Methodologies

managers' benchmarks from the return of the asset class policy, $r_B - r_P$, multiplied by the actual weight, w_A. For example, if the non-U.S. equity benchmark is 50 percent United Kingdom and 50 percent Japan, but a Japanese equity manager has been allocated 60 percent and a UK equity manager 40 percent of the portfolio, benchmark risk is caused by the weights being different from the benchmark. However, this is much too expansive as demonstrated later as it includes TAA in benchmark risk. The TAA and benchmark risk components are the plan sponsor's contribution to total plan return.[4] In the discussion of asset-liability risk in Chapter 7, the sum of TAA risk and benchmark risk is termed *extended investment policy.*

The value added by active managers is a catchall that covers everything else—from skill in selection of managers to skill in security, country, and currency selection. It is calculated by multiplying the actual weight of assets under active managers, w_A, with the excess return of managers over benchmark, $r_A - r_B$.

The drawback of the last measure is it lumps together the portion of return arising from the plan sponsor's skill in selecting managers and the value added by the active managers' skill in security selection and so on. This is addressed and corrected in the proposed methodology.

The Proposed Attribution Methodology

Figure 9.2 illustrates the proposed methodology that addresses the weakness of the current procedure and focuses more on all decisions made by a plan

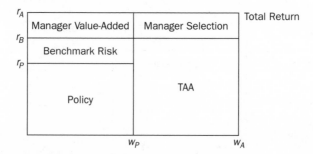

Figure 9.2 Proposed Performance Attribution Methodology

sponsor. The framework uses a three-layered structure, by defining precisely the asset class policy proxies/styles and manager benchmarks.

Since the plan sponsor is responsible, among other things, for selecting managers and determining their benchmarks, this methodology further breaks down the plan sponsor contribution into three parts:

Tactical asset allocation (TAA), which measures the timing skill of the sponsor to move into and out of asset classes

Manager selection, which measures the ability of the sponsor to choose superior managers

Benchmark risk, which measures the value added by the sponsor in choosing a set of styles for managers, intentional or not, away from policy benchmark

The following equation completes the attribution methodology:

Policy	$w_P r_P$
$+$	
TAA	$(w_A - w_P) r_B$
$+$	
Benchmark risk	$w_P (r_B - r_P)$
$+$	
Manager selection	$(w_A - w_P)(r_A - r_B)$
$+$	
Value added by manager	$w_P (r_A - r_B)$
$=$	
Total return:	$w_A r_A$

(9.2)

Note that r_B is a weighted average of all manager benchmark returns, $r_B = \sum r_M w_M$, where r_M is the manager benchmark return and w_M is the manager weight.

Figure 9.3 illustrates the results of a hypothetical fund using this performance attribution methodology.[5] The graph illustrates a number of positive changes that occurred to the total plan over the 3-year period. The methodology does a better job of demarcating benchmark risk from TAA and manager selection from manager value added. Note that in 1995 the plan

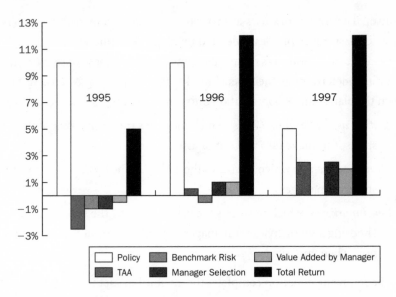

Figure 9.3 Hypothetical Total Fund Performance Attribution

underperformed its benchmark by 500 basis points. By 1997, the plan outperformed its benchmark by 200 basis points. What was responsible for the turnaround? According to the performance attribution chart, the biggest factor was improvement in TAA. Instead of subtracting 250 basis points of value (as in 1995), TAA added 250 basis points of value in 1997. This indicates that the investment staff correctly identified which asset classes to underweight or overweight vis-à-vis the policy weights. Furthermore, benchmark risk declined by 100 basis points over these 3 years. Again, this demonstrates improved selection of managers and individual benchmarks vis-à-vis the asset class benchmark, on the part of the plan's investment staff. In addition, benchmark risk was perceived as unintentional in 1995 and hence ineffectively monitored. As a consequence, the reduction of benchmark risk to zero in 1997 made risk taking more efficient and focused.

LUCK VERSUS SKILL

Outperformance over a benchmark unfortunately does not tell the plan sponsor whether the decision maker (internal staff or external manager) is skillful. It does not provide the plan sponsor with a measure of confidence that the alpha is generated by skill-based processes. Critical factors involved in answering the luck versus skill question include time, desired degree of confidence, investment returns of the portfolio and benchmark, standard deviation of the portfolio and the benchmark, and the degree of correlation between the two. The problem is there can be a lot of noise in performance data, and the more volatile the portfolio and the excess return series of a manager, the greater the noise and, hence, greater the time needed to resolve this question. Ambarish and Seigel (1996) demonstrate that the minimum number of data points or time horizon T should be large enough for skill to emerge from the noise or, equivalently,

$$T > \frac{K^2(\sigma_1^2 - 2\rho\sigma_1\sigma_B + \sigma_B^2)}{\left[\left(r(1) - \frac{\sigma_1^2}{2}\right) - \left(r(B) - \frac{\sigma_B^2}{2}\right)\right]^2} \qquad (9.3)$$

where 1 is the investment manager/mutual fund, B is the benchmark, r denotes the return, σ denotes the standard deviation, ρ is the correlation of returns between the active fund and the benchmark, and K is the number of standard deviations for a given confidence level. Appendix 9.2 provides a more detailed evaluation of the Ambarish and Seigel (1996) technique. One can see that it is theoretically more appropriate and simpler than statistical process control alternatives such as Philips and Yashchin (1999).[6]

If the tracking error of portfolio 1 versus the benchmark is defined as the standard deviation of excess returns, it is trivial to define $TE(1)$ as follows:

$$TE(1) = \sqrt{(\sigma_1^2 - 2\rho\sigma_1\sigma_B + \sigma_B^2)} \qquad (9.4)$$

Note: the second term in the numerator of the confidence in skill calculation or equation (9.3) is the same as the square of the tracking error of portfolio 1 versus the benchmark.

This suggests that even a 300-basis-point outperformance may require 175 years of data to claim with 84 percent confidence that the manager is skillful.[7] Muralidhar and U (1997) and Muralidhar (1999a) recognize that T is often given by the performance history of a manager and solve for the degree of confidence, K, instead.

Equation (9.3) makes it clear that the confidence in skill is intricately linked to the information ratio (IR). The annualized information ratio is equal to the annualized excess return divided by the annualized tracking error or, alternatively,

$$IR(1) = [r(1) - r(B)]/TE(1) \qquad (9.5)$$

As a result, equation (9.4) can be rewritten in terms of K, where K is a function of IR.

$$K < \sqrt{T}\left[IR(1) - \frac{\sigma_i - \sigma_B}{2TE(1)}\right] \qquad (9.6)$$

The confidence in skill is derived from converting K to percentage terms for a normal distribution. When the second term in equation (9.6), or $[(\sigma_i - \sigma_B)/2TE(1)]$, is generally small or insignificant, the IR and length of data history will largely determine the confidence in skill. This is the case when tracking error is substantial and driven largely by a low correlation between the portfolio and the benchmark (i.e., $\sigma_i \cong \sigma_b$). This luck or skill evaluation can be applied to any of the decisions highlighted earlier that contribute to total performance.

RISK-ADJUSTED PERFORMANCE

Practitioners and academics recognize that performance unadjusted for risk is not very meaningful. Various risk measures are used to adjust performance. The two most commonly used measures of risk adjustment are the Sharpe ratio and the information ratio (also known as the differential Sharpe ratio).[8] Newer measures have been proposed that are variations on these measures.

The Sharpe Ratio and the Information Ratio

The Sharpe ratio effectively adjusts performance above the risk-free rate by the volatility of the asset class, and the information ratio, demonstrated above, adjusts excess of benchmark performance by the volatility of the excess return series. Logue and Rader (1997) suggest that the Sharpe ratio is the best way to adjust for risk. The information ratio (described above) is a variation of the Sharpe and is based on excess returns and volatility of excess returns. Very simply, a higher ratio is preferred as it suggests a better payoff per unit of risk. Some practitioners have difficulty using these ratios as they do not express risk-adjusted performance in percent and practitioners are not sure what the implications are for portfolio construction if, for example, the ratio is 0.3.

The M² Methodology

Modigliani and Modigliani (1997) make an important contribution by showing that the portfolio and the benchmark must have the same risk (defined as standard deviations of returns) to compare them in terms of *basis points of risk-adjusted performance*. They propose that the portfolio be leveraged or deleveraged using the risk-free asset. If B is the benchmark being compared to portfolio 1, the leverage factor, d, is defined as follows:

$$d = \sigma_B/\sigma_1 \tag{9.7}$$

Figure 9.4 demonstrates this transformation. It creates a new portfolio, called the risk-adjusted portfolio (RAP), whose return $r(RAP)$ is equal to the leverage factor multiplied by the original return plus 1 minus the leverage factor multiplied by the risk-free rate. Then, if portfolio F is the riskless asset with zero standard deviation and is uncorrelated with other portfolios, the risk-adjusted return is calculated as follows:

$$r(RAP) = dr(\text{actual portfolio}) + (1 - d)r(F) \tag{9.8}$$

where

$$\sigma_{RAP} = \sigma_B \tag{9.9}$$

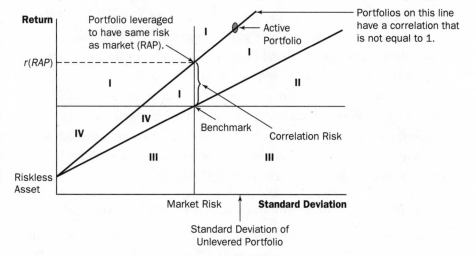

Figure 9.4   An Evaluation of the M² Measure

The correlation of the original portfolio to the benchmark is identical to the correlation of the RAP to the benchmark, as "leverage or deleverage" using the risk-free rate does not change the correlation characteristics. The correlation is normally less than unity. If the correlation is 1, it could lead to a riskless arbitrage.

Figure 9.4 demonstrates four regions using the M^2 measure:

I. Portfolio outperformance on an absolute and a risk-adjusted basis

II. Portfolio outperformance on an absolute basis and underperformance on a risk-adjusted basis

III. Portfolio underperformance on an absolute and a risk-adjusted basis

IV. Portfolio underperformance on an absolute basis and outperformance on a risk-adjusted basis

Modigliani and Modigliani (1997) suggest that this M^2 adjustment allows for a comparison of "apples to apples," namely, returns from the benchmark and the RAP have the same volatility. It shows that peer rankings of mutual funds or managers can be reversed by making this adjustment.[9] The rankings are shown to be identical using the Sharpe ratio measure as the principle is similar. The M^2 measure, however, was preferred as it expressed risk-adjusted performance in terms of basis points of outperformance and provides guidance on how much should be invested in the active fund and the risk-free asset. The paper also discards the use of the information ratio as it could lead to incorrect decisions. For example, portfolios in region IV would have a negative information ratio, but would have a risk-adjusted performance greater than the benchmark. Graham and Harvey (1997) propose a variation of this method, assuming the riskless asset need not be an asset uncorrelated with other assets. This only leads to different allocations across funds rather than suggesting a new approach. The problem with the M^2 measure is that RAPs for different funds imply very different tracking errors because of differences in correlations with the benchmark (Tables 9.1 and 9.2).

The M^3 Methodology—Adjusting for Differences in Correlation

An investor must rely on available data to make projections for the future about the variability of future returns of a fund around a benchmark. The tracking error statistic provides such guidance. Differences in tracking error imply different variability in performance and, all else equal, plan sponsors would prefer less tracking error. Most plan sponsors would not want managers to take unlimited tracking error as it would hamper an evaluation of skill and cause too much variability.[10]

Assuming historical distributions are preserved in the future, the three-dimensional problem of a comparison of return, standard deviations, and correlations has to be synthesized into a simple two-dimensional space of return and risk.[11] In mean-variance space, the riskless asset is portfolio F (with returns $r(F)$) and it can be used to leverage or deleverage the desired mutual fund/manager. In tracking error space, the only portfolio with zero tracking error is the benchmark portfolio as it is perfectly correlated with itself (where $\rho = 1$, $TE = 0$, as $\sigma_B = \sigma_1$). Therefore, combining active mutual funds/managers with passive benchmarks and the riskless asset can be used to alter the overall portfolio's standard deviation and its correlation with the benchmark.

To create measures of correlation-adjusted performance, the investor needs to invest in the mutual fund, the riskless asset, and benchmark to ensure (1) the volatility of this composite is equal to that of the benchmark (Modigliani and Modigliani 1997); and (2) the tracking error of this composite is equal to a target tracking error.[12] The M^2 adjustment made the comparison in terms of basis points of outperformance by ensuring all portfolios had the same variance as the benchmark. This section highlights a new measure, the M^3 measure, which recognizes that in three-dimensional space, the investor has to consider basis points of risk-adjusted performance after ensuring that *correlations of various funds versus the benchmark are also equal (i.e., tracking errors are equalized in a very specific way).*

The M^3 Model as Applied to a Defined Contributions Plan Investor

Although the principle is identical for any investor hiring an external manager, this section assumes that an investor is invested in a DC pension plan and must evaluate several mutual funds. Hammond (1997) states that to establish performance-related thresholds for managers, the investor must set a target tracking error and compare funds to the target. Assume that the investor is willing to tolerate a certain target annualized tracking error around the benchmark, say 3 percent; this is TE(target).[13] The investor essentially wants to earn the highest risk-adjusted excess return for given tracking error and variance of the portfolio. Now define a, b, and $(1 - a - b)$ as the proportions invested in the mutual fund, the benchmark, and the riskless asset. Let CAP be the correlation-adjusted portfolio. The returns of a CAP are

$$r(CAP) = ar(\text{mutual fund}) + br(B) + (1 - a - b)r(F) \qquad (9.10)$$

Further, the investor must hold appropriate proportions of each to ensure the final portfolio has the target tracking error and the standard deviation of the benchmark. For a specific mutual fund, say mutual fund 1, with a risk-adjusted return $r(CAP - 1)$, equation (9.10) can be rewritten as

$$r(CAP - 1) = ar(1) + (1 - a - b)r(F) + br(B) \qquad (9.10')$$

where the coefficients of each portfolio represent the optimal weight of that specific portfolio to ensure complete risk adjustment.[14] In addition, from the constraint on tracking error, there is a unique target correlation between the CAP and benchmark B. This target correlation of the portfolio with that of the benchmark $(\rho_{T,B})$ is given by the equation for tracking error when $\sigma_B = \sigma_1$; namely,

$$\rho_{T,B} = 1 - \frac{TE(\text{target})^2}{2\sigma_B^2} \qquad (9.11)$$

The detailed solution for a, b, and $(1 - a - b)$, given the constraints on variance and tracking error, is provided in Appendix 9.3. In summary, for mutual fund 1,

$$a = +\sqrt{\frac{\sigma_B^2(1 - \rho_{T,B}^2)}{\sigma_1^2(1 - \rho_{1,B}^2)}} = \frac{\sigma_B}{\sigma_1}\sqrt{\frac{(1 - \rho_{T,B}^2)}{(1 - \rho_{1,B}^2)}} \qquad (9.12)$$

$$b = \rho_{T,B} - a\frac{\sigma_1}{\sigma_B}\rho_{1,B} \qquad (9.13)$$

If you substitute for a in equation (9.13), the allocation to the benchmark is independent of variances and is only a function of the correlation terms. Although b and $(1 - a - b)$ may be greater than or less than zero (negative coefficients being equivalent to shorting the futures contract relating to the benchmark and borrowing at the risk-free rate), a is constrained to being positive as it is not possible to short mutual funds.[15] Notice also that if the correlations were not important, then a equals σ_B/σ_1, which is the RAP leverage measure, and b is 0. Further, allocations to the mutual fund under the M^3 will be larger than those under the M^2 only if

$$\sqrt{\frac{(1 - \rho_{T,B}^2)}{(1 - \rho_{1,B}^2)}} > 1$$

Ranking Mutual Funds and Managers Using These Methods

Monthly data on 10 mutual funds and the S&P 500 equity index were obtained for the period September 1989 through August 1999. Table 9.1 lists these funds based on their unadjusted return. Relevant details for calculation of the RAP and CAP portfolios are also provided assuming a 3 percent target tracking error ($\rho_{T,B} = 0.93$). Table 9.2 calculates $r(CAP)$ for a 7 percent tracking error ($\rho_{T,B} = 0.86$) since these funds engender significant tracking error. Table 9.3 provides a simple ranking of the funds using the methods discussed earlier. The following conclusions are drawn from these three tables:

- The unadjusted returns for the mutual funds range from an annualized 33.24 percent to 20.56 percent, all of which are greater than the annualized return of the benchmark over the period.

- The standard deviations of all mutual fund returns are greater than that of the benchmark. These would be type I and II portfolios in Figure 9.4.

- The correlations of the mutual funds with the benchmark range from a low of 0.59 to a high of 0.92. For target tracking error less than or equal to an annualized 5.2 percent, this would imply that $\rho_{T,B} > \rho_{i,B}$.

- Given the substantial excess returns over either portfolio F or B, unadjusted returns are higher than $r(RAP)$ or $r(CAP)$.

- RAP leverage is between 50 percent and 100 percent (i.e., $d < 1$), and on a RAP basis, funds 2, 3, 4, 5, and 8 underperform the benchmark.

Table 9.1
Performance of Mutual Funds Assuming a 3% Target Tracking Error

Fund (1)	Return (%) (2)	Standard Deviation (%) (3)	ρ (4)	d (5)	r(RAP) (%) (6)	TE(basic) (%) (7)	TE(RAP) (%) (8)	a (9)	b (10)	(1 − a − b) (11)	r(CAP) (%) (12)	Excess over r(RAP) (%) (13)
F	5.50	0.00	0.00									
B	17.09	13.27	1.00	1.00	17.09							
1	33.24	27.57	0.71	0.48	18.85	20.45	10.14	0.15	0.75	0.10	18.43	−0.42
2	25.63	24.93	0.77	0.53	16.21	17.02	9.04	0.19	0.71	0.11	17.43	1.22
3	25.04	25.02	0.73	0.53	15.86	17.74	9.68	0.18	0.73	0.09	17.41	1.55
4	24.08	21.33	0.80	0.62	17.06	13.34	8.38	0.23	0.67	0.09	17.65	0.59
5	21.95	21.75	0.59	0.61	15.53	17.52	11.97	0.17	0.81	0.02	17.68	2.14
6	21.90	13.84	0.84	0.96	21.21	7.76	7.57	0.39	0.63	−0.02	19.26	−1.95
7	21.61	14.37	0.83	0.92	20.37	8.13	7.74	0.37	0.64	−0.01	18.91	−1.46
8	20.89	23.06	0.79	0.58	14.36	15.07	8.69	0.21	0.69	0.10	16.70	2.35
9	20.77	14.00	0.89	0.95	19.97	6.53	6.32	0.46	0.54	0.00	18.83	−1.14
10	20.56	14.79	0.92	0.90	19.00	5.74	5.24	0.52	0.44	0.04	18.43	−0.57

Note: Data for September 1989 through August 1999.

Table 9.2
Performance of Mutual Funds Assuming a 7% Target Tracking Error

Fund (1)	Return (%) (2)	Standard Deviation (%) (3)	ρ (4)	d (5)	r(RAP) (%) (6)	TE(basic) (%) (7)	TE(RAP) (%) (8)	a (9)	b (10)	(1 − a − b) (11)	r(CAP) (%) (12)	Excess over r(RAP) (%) (13)
F	5.50	0.00	0.00	1.00								
B	17.09	13.27	1.00		17.09							
1	33.24	27.57	0.71	0.48	18.85	20.45	10.14	0.35	0.35	0.30	19.18	0.33
2	25.63	24.93	0.77	0.53	16.21	17.02	9.04	0.42	0.25	0.33	16.92	0.71
3	25.04	25.02	0.73	0.53	15.86	17.74	9.68	0.40	0.31	0.29	16.86	1.00
4	24.08	21.33	0.80	0.62	17.06	13.34	8.38	0.53	0.18	0.29	17.41	0.35
5	21.95	21.75	0.59	0.61	15.53	17.52	11.97	0.39	0.49	0.13	17.47	1.94
6	21.90	13.84	0.84	0.96	21.21	7.76	7.57	0.89	0.08	0.03	21.07	−0.14
7	21.61	14.37	0.83	0.92	20.37	8.13	7.74	0.84	0.10	0.05	20.27	−0.10
8	20.89	23.06	0.79	0.58	14.36	15.07	8.69	0.47	0.22	0.31	15.27	0.92
9	20.77	14.00	0.89	0.95	19.97	6.53	6.32	1.04	−0.12	0.07	20.09	0.12
10	20.56	14.79	0.92	0.90	19.00	5.74	5.24	1.18	−0.35	0.17	19.18	0.18

Note: Data for September 1989 through August 1999.

Table 9.3
Ranking Funds Using Different Methods

Ranking (1)	Unadjusted (2)	Skill Using Raw Returns (3)	RAP or Sharpe (4)	Skill Using r(RAP) (5)	CAP (6)	Skill Using r(CAP) (7)	Information Ratio (8)
First	1	6	6	6	6	6	1
Second	2	9	7	9	7	7	6
Third	3	7	9	7	9	9	10
Fourth	4	10	10	10	1	1	9
Fifth	5	1	1	1	10	10	7
Sixth	6	4	4	4	5	5	4
Seventh	7	2	2	2	4	4	2
Eighth	8	3	3	3	2	2	3
Ninth	9	5	5	5	3	3	5
Tenth	10	8	8	8	8	8	8

- The CAP ranking is independent of the target tracking error, but allocations to the risk-free asset, the benchmark, and the mutual funds are affected. With a 3 percent tracking error target, there is limited borrowing (i.e., less than 2 percent for funds 6 and 7 in Table 9.3).

- On a CAP basis, only mutual fund 8 underperforms the benchmark for a target tracking error of 3 percent, and mutual funds 2, 3, and 8 underperform for a target tracking error of 7 percent. Therefore, for a target tracking error of 3 percent, the allocation to B or indexing actually improves overall performance. For higher tracking error targets, shorting the benchmark and "leveraging" mutual funds (e.g., funds 9 and 10 in Table 9.2) are optimal.

- On a CAP basis, the ranking is changed vis-à-vis the RAP ranking (Table 9.3), but there is no clear dominance between $r(RAP)$ and $r(CAP)$—column 13 in Tables 9.1 and 9.2.

- Table 9.3 shows that the analysis of luck versus skill also favors the CAP measure. Since the only difference across funds to compare confidence in skill is the $r(CAP) - r(B)$, as demonstrated earlier, this measure is preferred. All other methods have rankings that are inconsistent with rankings based on skill, because excess returns have to be normalized for tracking error.

In summary, as pointed out in Modigliani and Modigliani (1997), the information ratio by itself is not a useful measure of outperformance or for ranking portfolios. It is only valid when leverage is not permitted. However, the M^2/Sharpe measure is appropriate only for reviewing historical performance and fails the test on a forward-looking basis (as it ignores tracking error) or where adding the benchmark can improve the RAP. The M^3 measure provides the most accurate measure of risk-adjusted performance by correcting for differences in standard deviation and in correlation. It also ratifies the conclusion of Modigliani and Modigliani (1997) that leverage may not always be bad. The M^3 measure is able to demonstrate how portfolios should be structured across active and passive funds to achieve a target tracking error, which the information ratio or Sharpe ratio cannot do.

Risk-Adjusted Performance and Luck or Skill

Several defined contribution (DC) plan investors in the United States use Morningstar ratings to decide which funds to invest in. Figure 9.5 plots the simple annualized excess return over the S&P 500 from August 1989–1999 against the confidence level that this outperformance is derived from skill for a number of five-star rated (Morningstar rating) funds. The confidence in skill

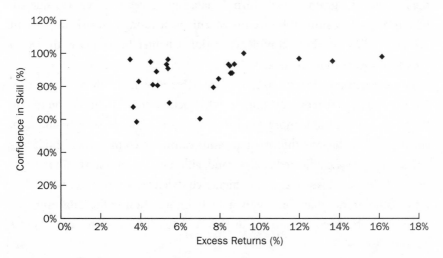

Figure 9.5 Comparing Annualized Absolute Outperformance (Versus S&P 500) and Confidence That Outperformance Is from Skill (Data from August 1989–1999)

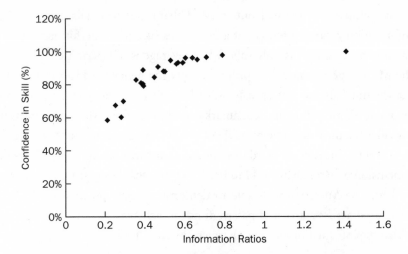

Figure 9.6 Comparing Annualized Information Ratios (Versus S&P 500) and Confidence That Outperformance Is from Skill (Data from August 1989–1999)

is derived from equation (9.6). Figure 9.5 demonstrates that there are managers in whose skill one can have high confidence and others who rate low on confidence. Any rational investor would be biased toward funds managed by the former for a given excess return. If data since inception were considered, the profile is very similar. Hence the Morningstar rating and risk adjustment gives no indication about confidence in skill. Chapter 10 compares the M^3 to the Morningstar in more detail.

Some investors believe funds can be ranked based on their information ratios. It is hypothesized that by adjusting for risk (tracking error) in the denominator, the information ratio is more consistent with confidence in skill. In addition, equation (9.6) suggests information ratios can drive confidence in skill. Figure 9.6 provides an adjusted analysis and, although the profile is more attractive, it is clear an investor can have higher confidence in a manager with a low information ratio than one with a high information ratio. However, the relationship between confidence in skill and the information ratio appears reasonably close.

In principle, investors should prefer a more "linear" shaped pattern, as in Figure 9.7, where there is no ambiguity that outperformance is skill based and that underperformance can be attributed to a lack of skill. Here the

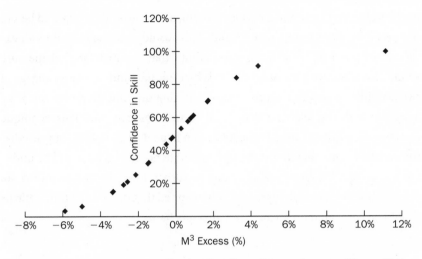

Figure 9.7 Comparing Annualized Risk-Adjusted Excess Returns (Versus S&P 500) and Confidence That Outperformance Is from Skill (Data from August 1989–1999)

risk-adjusted excess returns applying the M^3 method are used and compared to the confidence that the risk-adjusted performance is based on skill. Neither the Sharpe nor M^2 measures can provide such an attractive profile. Table 9.3 demonstrates that only the M^3 rankings are consistent with those based on skill (columns 6 and 7). All other risk-adjusted measures provide rankings that are either entirely different from skill (unadjusted returns and the information ratio) or marginally so (Sharpe and M^2).

Caveats

In the analysis for the correlation-adjusted performance measure, the returns, volatilities, and correlations were estimated using a relatively long data series.[16] This technique assumes that there is stability in the distributional characteristics of mutual funds on a forward-looking basis (either based on history or some ability to predict the future). It will also be interesting to see how such techniques, when applied on an ex-ante basis, perform on an ex-post basis. If it is difficult to accurately forecast the distribution of either the benchmark or mutual fund returns, or to forecast the correlation between the portfolio and the benchmark, techniques will need to be developed that account for this degree of uncertainty. This could create problems as these correlations may not be stable over time and a reasonably long history would be required before one could be comfortable with a fund. This would potentially lead to an exclusion of relatively new funds—something that the luck or skill measure would also advocate. One other caveat is that mutual fund managers engage in two activities to generate excess returns—timing the allocation between risky assets and cash and selecting an optimal portfolio of securities. This technique does not decouple the two. This could be an issue if such analyses suggest that the manager is not talented at the former and hence the investor will be undoing the same with an M^3 rebalancing, in turn raising the cost of doing so. Finally, though not explicitly stated, it is assumed that the mutual fund returns should be compared on an after-fee, after-tax basis.

SUMMARY

Decision-based performance attribution serves as another tool to aid investment professionals in the management of pension plans. Focusing on a decision-based methodology, rather than a factor-based methodology, permits a clearer picture at the macro level of added value that is attributable to the investment staff versus value added by external managers.

This chapter also demonstrated how previously used measures of risk-adjusted performance such as the Sharpe ratio, the information ratio, or the M^2 measure are insufficient for assisting investors in making decisions on how to rank mutual funds and managers or structure portfolios. The critical point is that it is important not only to adjust for differences in standard deviation between a portfolio and a benchmark, but also to adjust for the fact that different correlations imply different relative risk and possibly insufficient return for such risk. A new measure is reviewed that takes into consideration differences in correlation and the fact that investors have a target relative risk. Correlations are important for two reasons—as a measure of covariance with other assets for optimal portfolio selection and as a forward-looking risk measure. By focussing on the latter role, this chapter demonstrates the M^3 adjusts for standard deviations and correlations to provide rankings of portfolios that are different from other techniques. The importance of correlations in the former role is exploited in subsequent chapters.

Additional conclusions are derived to help investors manage portfolios, namely, those in the box of investment truths.

Further, the M^3 technique facilitates portfolio construction to achieve investor objectives by combining an optimal fraction of the risk-free asset, the benchmark, and the risky mutual funds. Not only is this a different paradigm and a form of three-fund separation, but it also gives investors optimal mixes of active and passive management based on market information and their target tracking error, rather than biases that investors may have on market efficiency.

INVESTMENT TRUTHS

■ *Absolute performance may provide little information about the skill of a manager.*

■ *The information ratio by itself is not a useful measure of out-performance or for ranking the portfolio and is only valid when leverage is not permitted.*

■ *Leverage can be useful for achieving high risk-adjusted performance from tactical decisions.*

■ *The M^2/Sharpe measure is appropriate only for reviewing historical performance and fails the test on a forward-looking basis or where adding the benchmark can improve risk-adjusted performance. It does not adequately capture the risk of hiring an agent to manage a portfolio.*

■ *The M^3 measure provides the accurate measure of risk-adjusted performance by correcting for differences in standard deviation and for differences in correlation/tracking error.*

■ *The M^3 measure is the only measure that provides rankings that are consistent with confidence in skill.*

ATTRIBUTING PERFORMANCE TO

CURRENCY OVERLAY AND LONG-SHORT PORTFOLIOS

Balana and Weary (1998) provide a very appealing way to deal with attribution analyses for currency overlay and certain types of long-short portfolios. Laubscher, Muralidhar, and Reynolds (2001) evaluate other performance issues with overlay programs. Conceptually, it can be difficult to measure and attribute performance on portfolios with no "real" investment assets, such as currency overlay portfolios or long-short portfolios. At the total plan level, there are two methods for capturing the effects of a currency overlay strategy in performance attribution. The first method is simply to use the actual and benchmark hedged returns, where applicable, for calculating performance attribution. At the asset class level, the hedged returns incorporate the profit or loss of the currency overlay strategy. Although it is a fairly accurate method for capturing the overall effect of a currency overlay strategy, this method does not delineate a separate currency overlay program from the performance of the underlying asset class that generates these exposures. Therefore, the skill of any particular currency overlay manager is lost among the returns of the particular hedged asset class, and the hedged total returns of that asset class do not necessarily reflect the actual aggregate returns of the managers in that asset class.

They address this problem by looking at the currency overlay managers as an asset class unto themselves, and their "assets" as being the notional size of their respective currency overlay strategy. Their return is therefore calculated as simply the manager's profit or loss divided by the notional size of the currency overlay strategy. At the total plan level the returns of the currency overlay managers are then incorporated as a separate asset class. This method accurately captures the returns of the currency overlay strategy by using the notional size of the underlying assets, but in doing so it increases the total plan market value by an amount equal to the notional size of these assets. They correct for this by creating an imaginary portfolio with a negative market value exactly equal to the notional size of the currency overlay strategy, and assign this portfolio a return of zero, thereby returning the total plan to its correct market value.

Table A9.1.1 demonstrates this with an example of a $1 billion fund with an overlay account.

Table A9.1.1

Example of Fund with Overlay Account

Asset Class	Notional Size	Performance
U.S. equity	$500 million	10%
Non-U.S. equity	$500 million	10%
Currency overlay	$500 million	2%
Adjustment	−$500 million	0%
Total	$1,000 million	11%

THE LUCK OR SKILL TECHNIQUE

Assume that one wants to determine how a fund has performed relative to a benchmark using a data series that extends over many periods of time. In order to establish luck from skill, Ambarish and Seigel (1996) assume that one is evaluating a portfolio (P) versus a benchmark (B). One would expect that a measure of relative risk (per unit of time) would be the variance per unit of time of $(dp/P - dB/B)$ or variance per unit of time of $[r(P) - r(B)]$. Assume that P and B follow a generalized Weiner process, so that

$$\frac{dP}{P} = \mu_p\, dt + \sigma_P\, dz_p$$

$$\frac{dB}{B} = \mu_B\, dt + \sigma_B\, dz_B$$

(A9.2.1)

where (μ_p, σ_P) and (μ_B, σ_B) and are instantaneous mean and volatility parameters of the portfolio and benchmark, respectively. The parameter dt is the change with respect to time and $dz_i = \varepsilon(t)(dt)^{1/2}$ is the increment on standard Brownian motion for i. $\varepsilon(t)$ has zero mean and unit standard deviation. $E[dz_i] = 0$ and $E[(dz_i)^2] = dt$.

If $\rho_{P,B}$ is the coefficient of correlation between P and B, then the dynamics of $R(t) = [P(t)/B(t)]$ can be discovered by applying Ito's lemma such that

$$\frac{dR}{R} = (\mu_P - \mu_B + \sigma_B^2 - \sigma_B\sigma_P\rho_{P,B})dt + \sigma_P\, dz_p - \sigma_B\, dz_B \quad (A9.2.2)$$

Now define the stochastic variable dw such that

$$\sigma_R\, dw = \sigma_P\, dz_p - \sigma_B\, dz_B \qquad (A9.2.3)^{[17]}$$

where

$$\sigma_R^2 = \sigma_B^2 + \sigma_P^2 - 2\sigma_P\sigma_B\rho_{P,B} \qquad (A9.2.4)$$

which is the square of the tracking error, $TE(P)$, of portfolio P versus the benchmark, B.

Then, as in any simple Brownian motion, $R(t)$ can be defined in the following way:

$$R(t) = R(0)\exp[\sigma_R \varepsilon \sqrt{t}]\exp\left[\left\{\left(\mu_P - \frac{\sigma_P^2}{2}\right) - \left(\mu_B - \frac{\sigma_B^2}{2}\right)\right\}t\right] \quad (A9.2.5)$$

where ε is the standard normal variable, and exp[] stands for exponential. The first exponential term in (A9.2.5) is the noise (or luck) and the second exponential term is the signal (or skill). Therefore, for skill embedded in managing portfolio P to dominate noise associated with returns from luck, it must be the case that the history of the fund (or number of data observations), T, satisfies the following equation; namely that

$$T > \frac{K^2(\sigma_P^2 - 2\rho_{P,B}\sigma_P\sigma_B + \sigma_B^2)}{\left[\left(\mu(P) - \frac{\sigma_P^2}{2}\right) - \left(\mu(B) - \frac{\sigma_B^2}{2}\right)\right]^2} \quad (A9.2.6)$$

where K is the number of standard deviations for a given confidence level.

DETERMINING a AND b

IN THE CAP EQUATION

Consider $r(CAP)$ for mutual fund 1:

$$r(CAP - 1) = ar(1) + (1 - a - b)r(F) + br(B) \qquad (A9.3.1)$$

The investors wants to select a and b such that

$$\sigma^2_{CAP-1} = \sigma^2_B \qquad (A9.3.2)$$

and

$$TE(CAP) = TE(target) \qquad (A9.3.3)$$

which can be rewritten as

$$\rho_{CAP-1,B} = \rho_{T,B} \qquad (A9.3.4)$$

Expanding on (A9.3.2),

$$\sigma^2_{CAP-1} = \sigma^2_B = a^2\sigma^2_1 + b^2\sigma^2_B + 2ab\sigma_1\sigma_B\rho_{1,B} \qquad (A9.3.5)$$

Also, the covariance of $r(CAP - 1)$ and the benchmark B is

$$\rho_{CAP-1,B}\sigma_{CAP-1}\sigma_B = a\sigma_1\sigma_B\rho_{1,B} + b\sigma^2_B \qquad (A9.3.6)$$

Using (A9.3.2) and (A9.3.4), equation (A9.3.6) can be rewritten as

$$\rho_{T,B}\sigma^2_B = a\sigma_1\sigma_B\rho_{1,B} + b\sigma^2_B \qquad (A9.3.7)$$

$$b = \rho_{T,B} - a\frac{\sigma_1}{\sigma_B}\rho_{1,B} \qquad (A9.3.8)$$

Substituting (A9.3.8) in (A9.3.5),

$$a^2\sigma^2_1 + \left(\rho_{T,B} - a\frac{\sigma_1}{\sigma_B}\rho_{1,B}\right)^2\sigma^2_B$$

$$+ 2a\left(\rho_{T,B} - a\frac{\sigma_1}{\sigma_B}\rho_{1,B}\right)\sigma_1\sigma_B\rho_{1,B} = \sigma^2_B \qquad (A9.3.9)$$

Solving for a,

$$a = +\sqrt{\frac{\sigma_B^2(1 - \rho_{T,B}^2)}{\sigma_1^2(1 - \rho_{1,B}^2)}} \qquad (A9.3.10)$$

Substituting for a in A9.3.8,

$$b = \rho_{T,B} - \rho_{1,B}\sqrt{\frac{(1 - \rho_{T,B}^2)}{(1 - \rho_{1,B}^2)}} \qquad (A9.3.11)$$

Assume that $a > 0$ as one cannot short the mutual fund; however, it is possible that $b < 0$ (e.g., sell the benchmark short through a futures contract) and $(1 - a - b) < 0$, which would involve borrowing money to invest in the benchmark and/or the mutual fund.

NOTES

1. This section is adapted from Balana and Weary (1998); see the footnote at the beginning of the chapter.

2. See for example Wilshire Associates Attribution Methodology.

3. ORTEC Consultants currently offers a decision-based performance attribution system.

4. See Muralidhar and Mashayekhi-Beschloss (1996).

5. Although performance attribution can be performed over any time horizon down to a monthly period, it is not until one is able to look at consecutive quarterly and yearly data that one can begin to divine the skill from the noise. See for example Ambarish and Seigel (1996).

6. One of the problems of Philips and Yashchin (1999) is that the user is required to specify an information ratio above which funds would be rated good. In the technique employed here, no such classification is required.

7. This result is from outperformance engendered through 13.2 percent basis points of tracking error, where the benchmark standard deviation = 15 percent, the actual standard deviation = 25 percent, and the correlation between the two was 0.9.

8. See Sharpe (1994).

9. One counterintuitive result of this approach is that if the RAP outperforms the benchmark (with the same standard deviation as the benchmark) and has a correlation less than one, then if the benchmark is the market portfolio, one has a portfolio with a beta less than one outperforming the benchmark. Roll (1992) had posed such a problem, but could not explain the outcome. Counterintuitive results are also derived when the benchmark has negative returns as in the case of currencies—see Muralidhar (1999b). However, a capital asset pricing model (CAPM) purist will conclude that you obtain such a result as the benchmark is not the market portfolio and hence makes no comment on market efficiency.

10. This section is adapted from Muralidhar 2000; see the footnote at the beginning of Chapter 9.

11. These are heroic assumptions to say the least. Some forecast needs to be made on expected outperformance, variability of performance to achieve this outperformance, and correlations between portfolio and benchmark returns.

Historical performance is one way of making forecasts, but the M^3 measure is independent of the forecasting technique. In addition, to conduct such analyses one must believe that markets are inefficient.

12. A somewhat similar, though less sophisticated, approach to portfolio construction was provided in Muralidhar and Tsumagari (1999).

13. This measure is independent of the level of tracking error and hence is applicable across all tracking error targets.

14. This is a form of two-fund separation, except that since the benchmark is a numeraire and tracking error is a constraint, three-fund separation follows. See Brennan (1993) and Muralidhar (1999b).

15. In some cases it may be difficult to short the benchmark as well and then b must be constrained to being greater than or equal to zero.

16. We essentially assume that static allocations can be made to these mutual funds and benchmarks, when in reality the expected returns, volatilities, and correlations are evolving daily. Therefore, an annual frequency for rebalancing would seem appropriate.

17. Notice that this is exactly what was desired for the relative risk measure.

FUND SELECTION:

THE IMPORTANCE OF SKILL

Arun S. Muralidhar and Shaila Muralidhar

Investors require assistance in selecting investment managers or funds that meet their objectives. Mutual fund rating schemes adjust returns for risk and provide percentile rankings of funds for a given time horizon, within peer groups. These schemes are neither intuitive nor transparent. This chapter proposes a rating system that simultaneously evaluates funds over multiple time horizons "(based on performance over the short and long term)," and rates confidence in the skill of the manager vis-à-vis a passive alternative (or peer group). This method is more user-friendly than existing schemes, as investors can specify their own parameters based on individual objectives. It explicitly incorporates managers' skill and ranks multiple mutual fund portfolios. This method can also be used by investors working for defined benefit plans to rate and rank investment managers.

OVERVIEW

Social security systems worldwide are undergoing reform from government-sponsored defined benefit (DB) schemes to privatized defined contribution (DC) systems. Several private companies are also transforming their pension

Adapted from Arun S. Muralidhar and Shaila Muralidhar. "A Better Approach to Rating Mutual Funds—The Importance of Skill." Unpublished working paper, 2001.

plans from company-sponsored defined benefit plans to defined contribution or cash-balance schemes. Both trends put the onus of managing pension assets on the individual, who may or may not have the financial sophistication or resources to evaluate investment options. This chapter attempts to satisfy the growing need for simple tools to help individual investors make decisions on mutual fund selection to achieve their desired objectives. Mutual fund selection by DC investors is no different from selection of investment managers for DB plans by investment teams. Kehrer (1991) highlights the fact that smaller plans may consider investing in mutual funds. Hence this technique can be applied broadly across all types of plans.

In the United States, the mutual fund industry experienced spectacular asset growth between 1981 and 1998—assets under management grew more than 20 times, from $241 billion to $5.5 trillion, and the number of funds rose from 665 to 7,314 (*Mutual Fund Fact Book* 1999). This increased use of third parties to manage funds, in turn, created the need to measure performance of these vendors relative to the benchmark and to their peers. DB plans have traditionally used consultants or their own metrics to evaluate managers. Morningstar is a popular fund rater, but a recent prize-winning article (Sharpe 1998) demonstrates the shortcomings in the Morningstar method of ranking funds. This is particularly troubling, as research has shown that as much as 90 percent of fund flows in 1995 went to funds rated four or five star by Morningstar (Damato 1996).

Technical limitations aside, the Morningstar rating system is not intuitive to the average investor, as the "stars" assigned to a particular fund are based on risk adjustment of returns and comparison relative to some peer group that is not transparent to the investor. Moreover, to understand the performance of a fund over different time horizons, one has to review multiple ratings over these horizons (and few funds report these in their newspaper ads). Other service providers, such as Lipper and Standard and Poor's, provide simple alphabetic ratings or numerical ratings that do not provide investors with adequate information about the fund. None of these rating schemes provide the investor with information about the degree of skill of the mutual fund manager. One is expected to glean this from percentile rankings.

In the real world, investors invariably manage a portfolio of investments and rarely select a single fund. This points to another shortcoming of the

Morningstar rating—it does not rate multiple mutual fund portfolios. A more useful tool for investors would be one that allows an evaluation of the performance of a specific fund, both individually and as part of a portfolio of assets.

The goal of every investor in selecting mutual funds is to identify the best-performing fund(s) of the many available for any asset class. Each investor has a stylized utility function, so the definition of "best" may differ among investors. For example, some prefer the highest absolute return (or even excess returns relative to the benchmark), others may want the highest risk-adjusted return, and a third group may want to hire a manager with a high degree of skill in outperforming either the benchmark or peers. In addition, whether participants are in the accumulation or decumulation phase of investment may influence their choice of fund.[1] Once again, there is a need to tailor the evaluation and ranking tool to the individual utility function.

This chapter provides a methodology to rank the performance of a fund regardless of objectives. It demonstrates how these rankings can be adjusted to account for risk, specification of the benchmark (passive index alternative), and comparison across peers. Most important, it explicitly evaluates whether mutual fund managers have been skillful or merely lucky in managing portfolios, and assigns a grade based on this measure. In short, this chapter attempts to provide an intuitive, user-friendly, and skill-based fund rating and ranking system that allows investors to construct multiple mutual fund portfolios consistent with their objectives. This can also be applied to a DB fund.

THE PROBLEM

To begin, let us assume investors know their desired asset allocation among different asset classes and seek a single mutual fund in each asset class with an attractive track record relative to a passive index fund (implicitly, also to peers). These are the two choices open to investors once they know their allocation to an asset class—low-fee benchmark performance (passive management) or higher fees to managers who will attempt to outperform these benchmarks on an after-fees basis (active management).

The major mutual fund rating companies include Morningstar, Lipper, and Standard and Poor's. Morningstar appears to be the most popular and most commonly discussed in research (Blume 1998, Simons 1998, and Sharpe 1998). Morningstar currently maintains an elaborate method of ranking funds (a five-star rating being the highest), in which the overall rating is a combination of ratings over 3, 5, and 10 years. Funds with a history of less than 3 years are not rated and data beyond 10 years appear to be ignored. The rating for each period is determined by calculating the following:

- Raw rating for each fund equals Morningstar return minus Morning-star risk
- Morningstar return equals load-adjusted fund excess over 90-day T-bill divided by the average excess return for the asset class
- Morningstar risk equals the fund's average underperformance divided by the average underperformance of its asset class.

Stars are then assigned based on the percentile ranking of a fund relative to its peers (top 10 percent equals five stars, next 22.5 percent equals four stars).

This is an elaborate procedure, but the overall rating is not intuitive and does not tell investors about:

- How the performance of a fund has evolved over time without individually examining 3-year, 5-year, and 10-year ratings[2]
- How a fund has performed if it has less than a 3-year history (a constraint on many new technology funds)
- How mutual funds have performed relative to the standard benchmarks, regardless of percentile, for their respective asset classes (such as S&P 500 returns for U.S. equity mutual funds rather than comparing the latter to 90-day T-bills)
- How skillful a mutual fund manager has been over the history of the fund or any interim period in outperforming passive alternatives
- How skillful a mutual fund manager has been in outperforming peers

As Sharpe (1998) has noted, these ratings are applicable to a unique objective function. What is interesting is discussions of individual investors in chat rooms on Morningstar.com are biased much more toward absolute returns than risk-adjusted returns. Yet, when it comes to selecting mutual funds, investors tend to be biased to moving monies based on a rating that adjusts for risks based on the Morningstar method. It would seem that the rating is at odds with the behavior of individual investors. However, institutional investors who budget for risk are more likely to look at risk-adjusted returns and the need for ratings on this basis.

THE SOLUTION

This chapter proposes a simple three-alphabet rating scheme for all funds. The first two alphabets rate performance relative to a benchmark over short- and long-term horizons, and the third provides a rating based on the confidence that performance is based on the skill of the manager. Potentially, additional alphabets can be added to compare a mutual fund with peers and the confidence that the fund manager is skillful in outperforming the average peer performance (to align it with the Morningstar rating). However, this should be redundant, as the three-alphabet rating would provide adequate information about performance and skill to rank funds appropriately.

The Simplest Case

Take the case of a plan sponsor who evaluates U.S. equity funds with a large capitalization bias and adopts the S&P 500 as the relevant benchmark.[3] The choice of benchmark is usually made in the context of an asset-liability study, as demonstrated in Chapter 3. However, even if the benchmark for comparing funds is poorly selected (for example, NASDAQ instead of the S&P 500), from Chapter 9 it is clear that any seemingly higher excess returns are conditioned by the fact that there is low confidence in skill because of the higher tracking error.

In the simplest version, designed for a certain class of individual investor, performance based on raw returns (unadjusted for risk) is examined. This objective may be inconsistent with finance theory that requires investors to trade off return for risk, but no assumptions are made about the financial training of the investors or their desired objectives. This preference for high returns is accommodated without comment on its desirability. Risk adjustment is considered in the next section. The ratings to be adopted in the simplest version are outlined in Table 10.1.

Table 10.1
Proposed Grading Scheme for the Simplest Case

Grade	Column I *3-year history of annualized outperformance relative to benchmark*	Column II *Since inception, annualized outperformance relative to benchmark*	Column III *Confidence that manager is skillful relative to benchmark (since inception)*
A	>4 percent	>4 percent	>90 percent
B	>3 percent and ≤4 percent	>3 percent and ≤4 percent	>80 percent and ≤90 percent
C	>2 percent and ≤3 percent	>2 percent and ≤3 percent	>70 percent and ≤80 percent
D	>1 percent and ≤2 percent	>1 percent and ≤2 percent	>60 percent and ≤70 percent
E	>0 percent and ≤1 percent	>0 percent and ≤1 percent	>50 percent and ≤60 percent
F	Underperform	Underperform	≤50 percent
N	Not available	Not available	

In this scheme, assume F denotes very low confidence in skill or lack of skill. As the technique is flexible, in the case of underperformance of a fund, the plan sponsor can estimate the confidence that underperformance is due to lack of skill. These could be identified by alphabets with brackets around them—for example, (B) for 80–90 percent confidence that underperformance is due to a lack of skill. Finally, when the time horizons for columns II and III are the same, an F in column II implies a lack of skill. Note that column II could be selected to be 5- or 10-year performance if "since inception" is irrelevant because of manager changes.

Using this as our starting point, let us examine a few ratings. An AAA-rated fund has consistently outperformed the benchmark over the short (column I) and long (column II) time horizons, and one can have a high degree of confidence (in excess of 90 percent) that the mutual fund manager is skillful in outperforming the benchmark (column III) since inception. A fund manager with a 2-year track record of skillfulness could have an NAA-rating, and funds that underperform consistently would be FFF-rated. A fund that has done well recently, but whose manager has not been skillful over a long period, could have an ACD rating, whereas a good fund with recent management changes and hence weak recent performance could have an FAA rating.

Testing This Approach

To make this more practical, data from 15 U.S. equity funds was examined. Fund selection was based on chat board lists created by users, as funds with strong performance; recommendations from investment newsletters; and recommendations from investment advisors. Most were rated five-star by Morningstar (one had a four-star rating). The list includes a mix of large and small capitalization funds. Data ending August 1999 is used and the funds have a high 10-year return. Data was collected for these funds since their inception or from September 1979 (or 20 years of data), whichever was earlier.

We call this scheme FirstRate. Table 10.2 provides the basic data on the respective funds, including annualized returns and standard deviation of returns for time horizons of 3 years, 5 years, 10 years, and since inception. Similar data is also provided for the S&P 500 benchmark. The table also includes the correlation of the mutual fund returns with those of the benchmark.

Using the technique for evaluating confidence in skill and optimal risk adjustment in Chapter 9, this section provides detailed scores on various parameters for different horizons in Table 10.3, to demonstrate the variability in results.[4] Fund 12 is the only four-star rated fund. The funds in Table 10.3 are ranked by annualized 10-year excess returns, followed by 5-year and 3-year excess returns respectively.

Table 10.4a ranks funds using the FirstRate scores for 3-year and since inception raw returns followed by a since-inception evaluation of skill. In Table 10.4b, the ranking is modified to begin with skill and then performance, and it is evident that the rankings are quite different.

The conclusions:

- Of the six funds with a high confidence in skill since inception (grades of A or B), four underperformed the S&P 500 in the short-term horizon (funds 10, 11, 12, and 15), and one just barely outperformed the S&P 500 (fund 8). For nine funds with outstanding 3-year outperformance, confidence in skill since inception is very low, with one F, three Es, and two Ds. Therefore, outperformance need not correlate highly with skill, and vice versa, when the outperformance evaluation period is short.

Table 10.2

Data for U.S. Equity Mutual Funds over Different Time Horizons

| | | Unadjusted Performance | | | | | | | | | | |
| | | 3-Year | | | 5-Year | | | 10-Year | | | Since Inception | | |
Fund No.	Inception	Return	Std. Dev.	Correlation	Return	Std. Dev.	Correlation	Return	Std. Dev.	Correlation	Return	Std. Dev.	Correlation
1	Aug 85	49.45%	36.25%	0.74	43.63%	31.82%	0.69	33.24%	27.57%	0.71	20.33%	28.78%	0.71
2	Aug 85	49.80%	33.38%	0.68	39.62%	29.40%	0.64	30.75%	27.05%	0.68	22.63%	28.44%	0.72
3	Aug 85	49.75%	31.29%	0.78	36.33%	27.56%	0.74	29.09%	24.66%	0.76	19.82%	26.98%	0.77
4	Mar 82	33.83%	29.52%	0.77	33.21%	26.17%	0.71	25.04%	25.02%	0.73	22.35%	27.46%	0.76
5	Mar 85	43.25%	23.08%	0.83	33.71%	19.33%	0.83	22.40%	18.73%	0.86	20.97%	18.98%	0.86
6	Sep 79	32.75%	23.24%	0.88	31.70%	21.55%	0.80	24.08%	34.10%	0.80	21.93%	22.09%	0.83
7	Aug 85	32.50%	29.13%	0.76	30.96%	24.92%	0.71	25.72%	24.42%	0.72	21.55%	25.30%	0.75
8	Oct 87	29.10%	30.45%	0.81	31.50%	26.23%	0.75	25.63%	24.93%	0.77	23.43%	25.36%	0.79
9	Dec 87	38.96%	31.48%	0.73	28.60%	27.82%	0.69	22.54%	25.50%	0.71	25.16%	25.55%	0.70
10	Jun 84	27.63%	13.68%	0.87	27.60%	12.09%	0.83	21.90%	13.84%	0.84	22.46%	15.61%	0.86
11	Aug 81	26.47%	15.71%	0.78	26.31%	14.05%	0.73	22.47%	16.84%	0.73	22.04%	19.61%	0.82
12	Mar 88	23.51%	15.85%	0.98	20.14%	13.26%	0.97	21.61%	14.37%	0.83	21.34%	13.71%	0.83
13	Feb 84	45.39%	25.24%	0.80	32.09%	20.91%	0.79	21.00%	17.28%	0.77	21.39%	15.98%	0.74
14	Sep 79	34.00%	29.56%	0.79	30.17%	25.76%	0.75	20.72%	22.14%	0.78	17.11%	21.17%	0.86
15	Jan 88	26.91%	17.08%	0.98	21.94%	14.87%	0.93	20.56%	14.79%	0.92	20.76%	14.69%	0.92
S&P 500	Sep 79	28.59%	16.55%	1.00	25.11%	13.85%	1.00	17.09%	13.27%	1.00	18.60%	13.11%	1.00

Table 10.3
FirstRate Ratings for Different Time Horizons and Objectives

Fund No.	Inception	Unadjusted Returns				M³ Returns				Confidence in Skill: Raw Returns					Confidence in Skill: M³ Returns			
		3-Yr.	5-Yr.	10-Yr.	Since Inc.	3-Yr.	5-Yr.	10-Yr.	Since Inc.	3-Yr.	5-Yr.	10-Yr.	Since Inc.	Equally Wtd.	3-Yr.	5-Yr.	10-Yr.	Since Inc.
1	Aug 85	A	A	A	C	F	F	C	F	B	A	A	E	B	F	F	B	F
2	Aug 85	A	A	A	A	D	E	D	F	B	B	A	D	B	D	E	C	F
3	Aug 85	A	A	A	C	D	F	D	F	A	B	A	E	B	D	F	C	F
4	Mar 82	A	A	A	B	F	F	E	F	E	C	B	E	C	F	F	E	F
5	Mar 85	A	A	A	C	A	E	E	F	A	A	A	C	D	B	E	E	F
6	Sep 79	A	A	A	A	F	F	F	F	D	B	D	B	D	F	F	F	F
7	Aug 85	B	A	A	B	F	F	E	F	E	D	B	D	C	F	F	D	F
8	Oct 87	E	A	A	A	F	F	E	E	E	D	B	B	D	F	F	E	D
9	Dec 87	A	B	A	A	F	F	F	F	D	E	D	C	C	F	F	F	F
10	Jun 84	F	C	A	B	A	A	B	C	F	D	B	A	A	B	A	A	A
11	Aug 81	F	D	A	A	E	D	D	E	F	D	A	A	E	E	C	B	C
12	Mar 88	F	F	A	B	F	F	C	C	F	F	A	A	B	F	F	A	A
13	Feb 84	A	A	B	D	B	F	E	D	A	B	B	D	F	C	C	D	C
14	Sep 79	A	A	B	F	F	F	F	F	E	D	D	F	E	F	F	F	C
15	Jan 88	F	F	B	C	F	F	C	E	F	F	A	B	E	F	F	B	E

Table 10.4a
FirstRate Rankings First by Absolute Returns and Then by Confidence in Skill

Fund No.	Inception	Performance		Luck vs. Skill
		3-Year	Since Inception	Since Inception
6	Sep 79	A	A	B
9	Dec 87	A	A	C
2	Aug 85	A	A	D
4	Mar 82	A	B	E
5	Mar 85	A	C	C
1	Aug 85	A	C	E
3	Aug 85	A	C	E
13	Feb 84	A	D	D
14	Sep 79	A	F	F
7	Aug 85	B	B	D
8	Oct 87	E	A	B
11	Aug 81	F	A	A
12	Mar 88	F	B	A
10	Jun 84	F	B	A
15	Jan 88	F	C	B

Table 10.4b
FirstRate Rankings First by Confidence in Skill and Then by Absolute Returns

Fund No.	Inception	Performance		Luck vs. Skill
		3-Year	Since Inception	Since Inception
11	Aug 81	F	A	A
12	Mar 88	F	B	A
10	Jun 84	F	B	A
6	Sep 79	A	A	B
8	Oct 87	E	A	B
15	Jan 88	F	C	B
9	Dec 87	A	A	C
5	Mar 85	A	C	C
2	Aug 85	A	A	D
13	Feb 84	A	D	D
7	Aug 85	B	B	D
4	Mar 82	A	B	E
1	Aug 85	A	C	E
3	Aug 85	A	C	E
14	Sep 79	A	F	F

- Performance of the funds is inconsistent over time. Most funds have a good 10-year track record by virtue of the selection procedure, but with the inclusion of 1987 in the analysis, a number of funds begin to look less attractive. This shows that excluding data beyond 10 years may not be entirely appropriate.

- Only five funds have grades of B or higher for all the performance horizons in Table 10.3. In the luck-or-skill comparison, not a single fund meets this criterion, even with 20 years of data. If Cs are included in the luck-or-skill evaluation, only one fund (fund 5) qualifies. Shockingly, 10 of these funds have at least one E or F in the luck-or-skill evaluation over the four horizons in Table 10.3. This suggests that these managers have significant periods over which they are barely skillful, if not merely lucky.

- The rank correlation between ranks in Table 10.4a and 10.4b is negative at -0.36.

- In a number of cases, confidence in skill over 3 years is greater than that since inception. This implies that even funds with short horizons need to be evaluated and not ignored, as they could generate skill-based excess returns. This result is contrary to that in Ambarish and Seigel (1996), which suggests the time required to have a high confidence in skill could be as many as 175 years.

As these tables demonstrate, investors need to be careful about making judgments based on short-term performance, as it may say nothing about confidence in skill. The Morningstar rating does not enhance such evaluations because it does not provide the investor with adequate information on the performance and skill of the mutual fund manager. In addition, the lack of flexibility to adjust for either different periods of measurement (especially where personnel changes have taken place at the mutual fund company) or benchmarks limits the scope of the ratings. Further, the proposed scheme provides greater color on consistency of performance.

EXTENSIONS

One could criticize the proposed scheme for being naïve, as outperformance is not adjusted for risk. Alternatively, some sponsors may want to evaluate multiple fund structures. This section examines a number of extensions.

Risk-Adjusted Ratings

This claim has little merit, as the luck-versus-skill evaluation appropriately adjusts for risk. It would be interesting, however, to see how the same scheme would rate funds if performance were adjusted for risk. The question is, how can risk-adjusted performance be measured? Chapter 9 highlights the advantages of the M^3 measure, and we use it here.

Results

Table 10.5a provides the FirstRate rankings using the M^3 measure of risk-adjusted performance, assuming investors are willing to tolerate an annualized tracking error of approximately 6 to 7 percent over all horizons. The choice of

Table 10.5a
FirstRate Scores First by M^3 Risk-Adjusted Returns and Then by Confidence in Skill (M^3 Returns)

		Risk-Adjusted Performance		Luck vs. Skill
Fund No.	Inception	3-Year	10-Year	Since Inception
10	Jun 84	A	B	A
5	Mar 85	A	E	F
13	Feb 84	B	E	C
2	Aug 85	D	D	F
3	Aug 85	D	D	F
11	Aug 81	E	D	C
12	Mar 88	F	C	A
15	Jan 88	F	C	E
1	Aug 85	F	C	F
8	Oct 87	F	E	D
4	Mar 82	F	E	F
7	Aug 85	F	E	F
6	Sep 79	F	F	F
9	Dec 87	F	F	F
14	Sep 79	F	F	F

tracking error is arbitrary and does not change the rankings. The rankings are based on 3-year and 10-year M^3 outperformance and confidence in skill (since inception) on M^3 returns. What is striking in this table is the number of funds that underperform the passive alternative when appropriate risk adjustment is made. Only three funds have no F in this evaluation (funds 10, 11, and 13). Separately, it has been shown in Chapter 9 that rankings of funds can be reversed when one makes the comparison on risk-adjusted returns instead of raw returns (Modigliani and Modigliani 1997; Muralidhar 2000).

The above-mentioned papers focus on a static time dimension, whereas Table 10.5a provides a more dynamic time dimension to demonstrate how certain funds dominate others over extended periods on a risk-adjusted basis. For example, compare fund 6 with fund 10—the latter has an extremely consistent track record of risk-adjusted performance, though fund 6 has a better 10-year record. In Table 10.5b, the same funds are rerated based on since-inception skill first and then M^3 performance. Once again, the rankings differ, suggesting that the optimal choice of fund is very dependent on the individual's horizon

Table 10.5b
FirstRate Ratings First by Confidence in Skill (M^3 Returns) and Then by M^3 Risk-Adjusted Returns

| | | Risk-Adjusted Performance | | Luck vs. Skill |
| | | --- | --- | --- |
Fund No.	Inception	3-Year	10-Year	Since Inception
10	Jun 84	A	B	A
12	Mar 88	F	C	A
13	Feb 84	B	E	C
11	Aug 81	E	D	C
8	Oct 87	F	E	D
15	Jan 88	F	C	E
5	Mar 85	A	E	F
2	Aug 85	D	D	F
3	Aug 85	D	D	F
1	Aug 85	F	C	F
4	Mar 82	F	E	F
7	Aug 85	F	E	F
6	Sep 79	F	F	F
9	Dec 87	F	F	F
14	Sep 79	F	F	F

and objectives. A static five-star rating by Morningstar thus may not adequately capture such preferences, as identified in Sharpe (1998). However, correlation of the ranks is extremely high in this case: close to 0.8. This greater consistency in the rankings implies that investors can find a small group of funds that satisfy their objectives and time horizons (as opposed to the unadjusted return evaluation where ranks are influenced largely by the ordering of objectives).

Multiple Mutual Funds

The next extension is to look at the performance and rating of a portfolio of mutual funds. This is another shortcoming of the Morningstar rating, as it does not tell investors how a combination of funds will perform (this is possible through their rating method, but not offered to clients). In essence, if an investor wants to choose two funds to diversify investment styles, it may not be optimal to choose two five-star funds if they are very highly correlated. The investor would obviously want to combine funds. FirstRate lends itself to such an adjustment, demonstrated in Table 10.6. In this section, naïve combinations

Table 10.6
FirstRate Ratings for Multiple-Fund Portfolios Combining 1/3 of the Fund with 1/3 Each of Funds 5 and 10

Base Fund No.	Inception	Unadjusted			M^3 Returns			Skill: Raw Returns		
		3-Yr.	5-Yr.	10-Yr.	3-Yr.	5-Yr.	10-Yr.	3-Yr.	5-Yr.	10-Yr.
1	Aug 85	A	A	A	B	C	B	A	A	A
2	Aug 85	A	A	A	A	C	B	A	A	A
3	Aug 85	A	A	A	A	D	C	A	A	A
4	Mar 82	A	A	A	D	D	D	B	A	A
5	Mar 85	A	A	A	A	B	C	A	A	A
6	Sep 79	A	A	A	F	F	F	E	E	E
7	Aug 85	A	A	A	D	D	C	B	A	A
8	Oct 87	A	A	A	F	D	C	C	A	A
9	Dec 87	A	A	A	C	E	D	A	B	A
10	Jun 84	A	A	A	A	A	B	C	A	A
11	Aug 81	A	A	A	A	A	C	B	A	A
12	Mar 88	C	C	A	B	C	B	C	C	A
13	Feb 84	A	A	A	A	C	B	A	A	A
14	Sep 79	A	A	A	F	F	D	B	B	A
15	Jan 88	A	C	A	F	F	B	C	C	A

of funds are considered and their ratings, using different measures, are evaluated. Needless to say, this method lends itself to composite benchmarks as well (for example, 50 percent S&P 500 and 50 percent NASDAQ) either for individual funds or multiple-fund portfolios. The next chapter provides a more theoretically rigorous method of creating risk-adjusted multiple-manager portfolios.

Table 10.6 provides data assuming one-third of the investor's assets are invested in each of the original fund, fund 5, and fund 10, respectively. The reason for including funds 5 and 10 is their strong high confidence in skill and risk-adjusted performance. For simplicity, transactions costs of rebalancing are ignored. Moreover, the analysis is conducted using data for 10 years, which circumvents the problem of different inception dates, and all funds have data for this length of time. One interesting characteristic is that the returns of these funds are reasonably highly correlated with each other, with the lowest correlation being 0.895. Comparing Table 10.6 with Table 10.2 provides a very interesting set of results:

- The unadjusted performance ratings for all funds are as good, if not better, for all time horizons.

- The risk-adjusted performance ratings are as good, if not better, for all but one fund over all time horizons. On an individual basis, 14 funds had at least one E or F for risk-adjusted performance (given an approximately 6–7 percent tracking error budget) over the 3-year, 5-year, and 10-year horizons. This number of funds drops to four when the original fund is combined with funds 5 and 10.

- Skill ratings on the unadjusted returns are better (if not as good) for all but one fund (fund 6) over all time horizons. On an individual basis, nine funds had at least one E or F for skill over the 3-year, 5-year, and 10-year horizons. This number drops to one when the original fund is combined with the chosen two. Hence, diversification across funds makes the combination of funds more attractive relative to a passive fund.

- Even fund 5, chosen for its high confidence in skill, benefits from being combined with fund 10, chosen for its high risk-adjusted performance and vice versa. The ratings of these funds, combined with each other, are better than either fund in isolation.

- Fund 6 is worse off from a risk-adjusted and "luck" perspective when combined with these two funds. A possible reason is that its correlation with fund 5 is 0.98 and with 10 is 0.99; hence, there is little benefit from diversification.

The critical message from this section is that although individual funds may have unfavorable ratings, the ratings can improve substantially in a multiple-fund portfolio. Several commentators have made the case for passive management because many funds lack skill or performance, but they ignore the fact that a diversified pool of funds can do quite well relative to the passive alternative (Bogle 1998).[5] The approach taken here, although adequate, is naïve; Chapter 11 discusses optimal portfolio construction in a multiple-fund setting.

Percentile Rankings Versus Return-Based Rankings

Should the alphabet rating be applied to returns in an absolute sense or based on percentile rankings of mutual fund managers? There is nothing in this method to preclude the latter, as long as some distinction is made to ensure that funds are rated F if they underperform the passive alternative, regardless of percentile ranking. Using a percentile ranking for funds will probably appeal to those investors worried about performance relative to peers. This is more likely among institutional investors, as their compensation is often determined by performance relative to a peer group. The problems and information content of peer group comparisons are highlighted in Chapter 14, and suggest that percentile rankings should not be relevant to achieving personal investment goals. However, in this method, peer comparison can be implemented by the FirstRate rankings as demonstrated in Tables 10.4 and 10.5. Further, as demonstrated in Chapter 9 (Figure 9.5), percentile ranking after adjustment for risk, using the Morningstar method, does not provide adequate information about the skill of the manager.

Luck or Skill Versus Peer Group Average

A variation of using percentile rankings (rather than ranking returns) would be to ask whether the luck-or-skill measure should be applied relative to the average performance of the peer group or to a passive benchmark alternative. Once again, this is relevant for a very stylized utility function, but easily adapted in the FirstRate method. However, the issue is that 50 percent of the funds will be considered skillful and 50 percent unskillful, even if all exceed some index. The greater the clustering of fund performance, the more irrelevant peer comparisons will be. For example, if there are five funds with performance one basis point apart (if the lowest has performance 5 basis points less than the best), percentile ranking or peer group comparison may suggest one is preferred over the other. However, there is probably no reason to believe that the outperformance over the benchmark or the peer group is due to skill.

More important, the luck-or-skill technique will ideally be used to compare active management versus a "no-intervention" alternative and, hence, it would be more meaningful to compare individual mutual funds to their benchmark. Further, it would be difficult for the investor to replicate the peer group average on an ex-ante basis without purchasing all funds in small proportions, which is expensive and impractical. However, a number of developing countries in Latin America, which have privatized their social security systems, emphasize peer group comparison. The most effective benchmark for these, thus, is the peer group, in spite of all the flaws of such a comparison.

CAVEATS

The returns, volatilities, and correlations were estimated using a relatively long data series and were used to comment on skill or lack thereof.[6] Any ranking of funds based on the past is no comment on performance in the future, and a few years of good performance could change the profile dramatically. Such analyses need to be regularly updated when new information is available. In addition, some qualitative analysis is necessary to complement this analysis; some thoughts on these qualitative aspects are presented in Chapter 13.

In the case of the multiple-fund approach, allocations to the funds were held constant. This requires rebalancing, which could be expensive. However, the same method can be redesigned to account for different allocation strategies that an investor might choose.

Another caveat is that mutual fund managers engage in two activities to generate excess returns—timing allocation between risky assets and cash, and selecting an optimal portfolio of securities. This does not decouple the two, and it assumes that the average individual investor delegates both decisions to the mutual fund manager. Institutional investors who control asset allocation decisions and delegate security selection may want to conduct such analyses on a fully funded basis. Finally, although not explicitly stated, it is assumed that mutual fund returns should be compared on an after-fee (after-tax) basis.

SUMMARY

This chapter has developed a technique for rating and ranking mutual funds that is user-friendly, intuitive, transparent, and broad-based. More important, it provides greater clarity on the performance of funds over short and long horizons, and simultaneously evaluates a manager's skillfulness. This method demonstrates that the Morningstar rating, by cutting off data below 3 and beyond 10 years, may mask a fund's problems. Further, adjusting for skill may cause a rerating of funds. For example, though certain funds may have enjoyed an exceptional 10-year history, the confidence in a manager's skill and risk-adjusted excess returns are surprisingly low. This method is clearly beneficial to investors in DC or DB pension plans, who are keen to hire managers with strong performance—raw or risk-adjusted—and want to ensure that the managers are compensated for their skill rather than luck. More important, this method allows for the creation of multiple fund portfolios with more attractive ratings than those of individual funds in the portfolio. Hopefully, this ranking system lends itself to better fund selection and portfolio construction.

NOTES

1. I would like to thank Francis Vitagliano for pointing this out to me.

2. Here, each investor has a desired time preference. In the example in the text following this note, we examine 3 years and since inception, but it could be changed to 5 and 10 years or any other combination of the investor's choice.

3. The scheme is independent of the choice of benchmark and can even be changed to the 90-day T-bill. However, once an investor chooses this asset class the true choice is between a passive index fund with low fees or an active mutual fund, and not between funds and a riskless short-duration government security.

4. The M^3 method requires a target correlation to provide a target tracking error, and for simplicity we assume a target correlation of 0.9, which translates into approximately 6–7 percent tracking error for all four horizons. We also assume a risk-free rate of 5.5 percent.

5. This technique can also be applied to evaluate stock analysts. We can evaluate their success on a specific stock, as well as evaluate their recommendations in a specific sector.

6. We assume static allocations can be made to these mutual funds and benchmarks. In reality, the expected returns, volatilities, and correlations evolve daily. Therefore, an annual rebalancing would seem appropriate.

11

OPTIMAL RISK-ADJUSTED

PORTFOLIOS WITH

MULTIPLE MANAGERS

Arun S. Muralidhar

Previous chapters have demonstrated how current measures of risk-adjusted performance are insufficient for ranking investment managers or structuring portfolios and
provided an alternative measure called correlation-adjusted performance (or M^3). In
addition, using a naïve technique it was demonstrated how multiple-fund portfolios
could be created to outperform passive benchmarks. This chapter extends the analysis
for institutional and individual investors with multiple-manager portfolios. This technique facilitates optimal portfolio construction by combining the risk-free asset, the
benchmark, and many investment managers. Since managers are less than perfectly
correlated with each other, unattractive managers on a stand-alone basis may be chosen for their diversification properties and overall risk-adjusted performance can be
increased over that of the highest yielding manager. It is also shown that the case for
passive management is greatly diminished under this paradigm.

OVERVIEW

The goal of every institutional investor that selects investment managers is to
identify the best performing manager(s) of the many available for any asset

Adapted from Arun S. Muralidhar. "Optimal Risk-Adjusted Portfolios with Multiple Managers."
Journal of Portfolio Management, Volume 27, Number 3, Spring 2001.

class, and to ensure that in the future, this portfolio of active managers outperforms the benchmark on a risk-adjusted basis. Chapter 9 provided a methodology to measure the risk-adjusted performance of a manager and it also demonstrated how other measures such as the information ratio, the Sharpe ratio, or the M^2 measure may be inappropriate to adjust for risk.[1] The new measure accounted for differences in standard deviations and the correlation between portfolios and the benchmark, and the fact that institutional investors have a target relative risk.

The correlations between investment managers and the benchmarks they are measured against and the correlations among investment managers are important for two reasons—as a forward-looking risk measure and as a measure of covariance for optimal portfolio selection. By exploiting correlations in the former role, Chapter 9 demonstrated that the M^3 adjusts for differences in correlations and provides rankings of individual investment managers that are different from other techniques. This ranking was shown to be consistent with ranking managers based on confidence in skill. Further, this technique facilitates portfolio construction to achieve investors' objectives by combining an optimal fraction of the risk-free asset, the benchmark, and the risky investment manager. Not only is this a different paradigm and a form of three-fund separation, it also gives institutional investors optimal mixes of active and passive management based on market information and their target tracking error, rather than arbitrary biases on market efficiency. It also suggests that permitting leverage by either shorting the benchmark or the risk-free rate asset can be useful in increasing risk-adjusted performance.

THE PROBLEM

The average institutional investor rarely chooses only one manager, instead choosing a number of managers. In addition, most institutional investors attempt to budget overall active risk relative to the benchmark (or tracking error). Therefore, the problem is to combine the risk-free asset, the benchmark, and selected *multiple managers* in order to provide the highest correlation-adjusted performance within the target tracking error. In this situation the focus shifts to *correlation as a measure of covariance* for optimal diversification of managers. The difficulty here is that although the correlation of each investment manager with the benchmark is known, the uncertain variable is the correlation of a combination of investment managers with the benchmark as it depends on the weight of each manager in the composite. This information is needed to estimate the tracking error of the composite portfolio of risky investment managers.

THE SINGLE-MANAGER VERSUS THE MULTIPLE-MANAGER APPROACH

Assume that the investor (e.g., a pension fund) is willing to tolerate a certain target annualized tracking error around the benchmark, say a TE(target) of 700 basis points in the U.S. equity asset class or total portfolio. They essentially want to earn the highest risk-adjusted excess over the benchmark for a given tracking error and variance of the portfolio. One might be inclined to use mean-variance optimization to select managers that provide the highest absolute return subject to the tracking error constraint.[2] Maximizing absolute return is the wrong strategy. In essence, managers generate excess returns by deviating from benchmarks and the volatility of their portfolio and the correlation to the benchmark determine their tracking error. One wants to find managers that are most competent at using risk budgets. However, to normalize for tracking error across many managers, one must normalize for differences in volatility, as highlighted in Modigliani and Modigliani (1997), and in correlation (Muralidhar 2000). As a result, this normalization ensures that rankings based on correlation-adjusted performance are identical to rankings based on skill.

In the case of multiple-manager portfolios, the problem is similar to the earlier exposition on the M^3 measure, but requires minor respecification. Define K as the portfolio of investment managers, where w_i is the weight of the ith manager in K, $w_i \geq 0$ and $\sum_i w_i = 1$. Then, the investor must maximize

$$\max r(CAP - K) = \max[ar(K) + (1 - a - b)r(F) + br(B)]$$

$$(11.1)$$

subject to

$$\rho_{CAP-K,B} = \rho_{T,B} \tag{11.2}$$

$$\sigma_{CAP-K} = \sigma_B \tag{11.3}$$

where

$$\rho_{K,B} = \sum_i [w_i \rho_{i,B} \sigma_i] / \sigma_K \tag{11.4}$$

$$\rho_{CAP-K,B} = (a\rho_{K,B}\sigma_K + b\sigma_B) / \sigma_{CAP-K} \tag{11.4'}$$

$$r(K) = \sum_i w_i r(i) \tag{11.5}$$

$$\sigma_K = w^T \Gamma w \tag{11.6}$$

$$\sigma_{CAP-K} = a^2 \sigma_K^2 + 2ab\rho_{K,B}\sigma_B\sigma_K + b^2\sigma_B^2 \tag{11.6'}$$

where Γ is the variance-covariance matrix of returns of investment managers and w^T is the transpose of the matrix of weights of investment managers in K.

From Chapter 9, a (investment in active managers) and b (investment in the benchmark) are as follows:

$$a = +\sqrt{\frac{\sigma_B^2(1 - \rho_{T,B}^2)}{\sigma_K^2(1 - \rho_{K,B}^2)}} = \frac{\sigma_B}{\sigma_K}\sqrt{\frac{(1 - \rho_{T,B}^2)}{(1 - \rho_{K,B}^2)}} \tag{11.7}$$

$$b = \rho_{T,B} - a \times \frac{\sigma_K}{\sigma_B}\rho_{K,B} \tag{11.8}$$

$$b = \rho_{T,B} - \rho_{K,B}\sqrt{\frac{(1 - \rho_{T,B}^2)}{(1 - \rho_{K,B}^2)}} \tag{11.8'}$$

The optimal weight for each of the managers (w) is obtained from solving the above, which is easily done in a simple spreadsheet program.

CREATING OPTIMAL PORTFOLIOS USING THE M^3 MEASURE

This section examines the optimal composition of a U.S. equity portfolio for an investor that has seven investment managers on a short list of candidates for final selection. To facilitate data collection, monthly data on seven mutual

Table 11.1
Performance of Investment Managers Assuming 7% Target for Tracking Error

Manager (1)	Annualized Return (%) (2)	Annualized Std. Dev. (%) (3)	ρ (4)	a (5)	b (6)	(1−a−b) (7)	r(CAP) (%) (8)
F	5.50	0.00	0.00				
B	17.09	13.27	1.00				
1	33.24	27.57	0.71	0.35	0.35	0.30	19.18
2	25.63	24.93	0.77	0.42	0.25	0.33	16.92
3	25.04	25.02	0.73	0.40	0.31	0.29	16.86
4	24.08	21.33	0.80	0.53	0.18	0.29	17.41
5	21.90	13.84	0.84	0.89	0.08	0.03	21.07
6	21.61	14.37	0.83	0.84	0.10	0.05	20.27
7	20.77	14.00	0.89	1.04	−0.12	0.07	20.09

Note: Based on data from September 1989 through August 1999. F is the riskless asset, and B is the benchmark.

funds (as a proxy for investment managers for institutional investors) and the S&P 500 equity index (B) was obtained for the period September 1989 through August 1999. Assume that the risk-free rate (F) is 5.5 percent. For simplicity, it is assumed that these historical returns are an accurate representation of the investment managers' future return prospects.[3]

In Table 11.1 these managers, called managers 1–7, are ordered based on their unadjusted return; however, the relevant details for the calculation of the variables a and b for each of these managers is provided as are the values for these variables. The final column presents risk-adjusted returns or the r(CAP), assuming a 7 percent target tracking error ($\rho_{T,B} = 0.86$). An interesting conclusion is that for single-manager portfolios (even with strong performance) the case for passive management is quite strong as b is significantly greater than zero in nearly all cases. Table 11.2 provides the historical correlations between the returns of any two managers. Table 11.3 provides a simple ranking of the managers on an unadjusted and a correlation-adjusted basis, and it is interesting to note that investment managers 5, 6, and 7 are the three top-ranked investment managers using the M^3 approach. Although all portfolios outperform the S&P 500 on an unadjusted basis, the M^3 returns range from 21.07 percent for portfolio 5 to less than the benchmark return for portfolios 2 and 3.[4]

Table 11.2
Correlations Between Seven Managers', Benchmark, and Risk-Free Portfolios

Manager or Comparison	Portfolio								
	S&P 500	1	2	3	4	5	6	7	Risk-Free
S&P 500	1	0.71	0.77	0.73	0.8	0.84	0.83	0.89	0
1	0.71	1	0.923	0.88	0.77	0.685	0.74	0.728	0
2	0.77	0.923	1	0.946	0.908	0.823	0.874	0.86	0
3	0.73	0.88	0.946	1	0.905	0.798	0.815	0.856	0
4	0.8	0.77	0.908	0.905	1	0.819	0.893	0.934	0
5	0.84	0.685	0.823	0.798	0.819	1	0.888	0.837	0
6	0.83	0.74	0.874	0.815	0.893	0.888	1	0.94	0
7	0.89	0.728	0.86	0.856	0.934	0.837	0.94	1	0
Risk-free	0	0	0	0	0	0	0	0	1

Table 11.3
Ranking Managers Using Absolute Returns and M^3

Ranking	Unadjusted	M^3
First	1	5
Second	2	6
Third	3	7
Fourth	4	1
Fifth	5	4
Sixth	6	2
Seventh	7	3

Therefore, an institutional investor who had to choose a single manager on an absolute return basis would choose manager 1, but on a M^3 basis would choose manager 5. One would expect that an investor who had to choose multiple managers on an unadjusted basis (subject to the tracking error constraint) would be biased toward managers 1, 2, and 3, but on a M^3 basis would choose managers 5, 6, and 7.

Table 11.4 reports the composition of four portfolios across managers, the benchmark B, and the riskless asset F, and reports $r(CAP)$, standard deviations, correlations with the benchmark, and data on a, b, and $(1 - a - b)$. It also reports the confidence one could have that outperformance is skill-based using the Ambarish and Seigel (1996) technique. The data is provided under four scenarios: (a) maximizing $r(CAP)$ with no leverage permitted, column 2;

Table 11.4
Allocation to Investment Managers Under Different Optimization Scenarios

Manager or Statistic (1)	Optimize r(CAP), No Leverage (%) (2)	Optimize r(CAP) with Leverage (%) (3)	Optimize Return Subject to TE Constraint, No Leverage (%) (4)	Optimize Return Subject to TE Constraint with Leverage (%) (5)
F	10.9	9.2	2.57	16.52
B	0.0	−19.1	0.00	−13.38
1	13.3	10.5	0.00	20.27
2	0.0	0.0	0.00	0.00
3	0.0	0.0	0.00	0.00
4	0.0	0.0	0.00	0.00
5	75.7	58.6	80.00	38.64
6	0.0	0.0	7.41	0.00
7	0.0	40.8	10.02	37.95
r(CAP)	21.6	22.0	21.4	21.7
Std. dev.	13.27	13.27	13.27	13.27
$\rho_{K,B}$	0.86	0.90	0.86	0.89
a	0.89055	1.0986	0.9742	0.96854
b	6.8E-07	−0.1907	−0.0001	−0.1338
$(1 - a - b)$	0.10945	0.09214	0.02577	0.16527
Confidence in outperformance	97.89	99.56	97.45	99.04

Note: Target tracking error = 7% or target correlation to benchmark = 0.86.

(b) maximizing $r(CAP)$ with leverage permitted, column 3; (c) maximizing the unadjusted return subject to the tracking error constraint and with no leverage, column 4;[5] and (d) maximizing the unadjusted return subject to the tracking error constraint and with leverage, column 5.

The reasons for choosing these four scenarios are (1) to show the benefit of leverage;[6] (2) to provide alternatives for institutional investors who may be prevented from engaging in leverage for regulatory reasons; and (3) to demonstrate that an investor would be better off maximizing $r(CAP)$ than raw returns, as the latter, on a risk-adjusted basis, is less likely to be optimal. The first point is verified by noting that the levered strategies have higher risk-adjusted returns than the unlevered strategies. The third point is verified by comparing the $r(CAP)$ of columns 2 versus 4, and 3 versus 5. Optimizing $r(CAP)$ and permitting leverage provides the highest risk-adjusted return of

22 percent (column 3). Therefore, maximizing returns subject to a tracking error constraint is not a simple replacement for maximizing risk-adjusted performance, as the first strategy may not take risk in the most efficient manner vis-à-vis the benchmark.

Additionally, the following interesting observations can be made:

- Since the managers are less than perfectly correlated, the $r(CAP)$ from an optimized multiple-manager portfolio is higher than that of the best-ranked manager (manager 5).[7]

- Managers 2, 3, and 4, which have the lowest CAP rank, are not selected under these four simulations.

- Manager 6 is not selected when leverage is permitted, and when leverage is not permitted, manager 6 receives an allocation only for a suboptimal portfolio (column 4).

- The coefficient for the actively managed portfolio (variable a) is on average higher than under the single-manager case, and the coefficient for the benchmark (variable b) is negative or zero, suggesting that with these managers and holding an optimal combination of multiple managers, the case for passive management is weakened, and if anything should be used for leverage opportunities only.

- Investing in the riskless asset is dictated by the fact that the target volatility is lower than that of any one manager, as is the target tracking error.

- The two lowest correlation coefficients are between managers 1 and 5 (0.685) and managers 1 and 7 (0.728), which may explain why managers 1, 5, and 7 are part of the optimal basket (column 3) and why manager 6 is not selected.

- Manager 5 is an especially good manager not only because it has the highest individual $r(CAP)$, caused by low volatility and a high correlation with the S&P 500, but also because it has a weak set of correlations with other managers. A somewhat similar case can be made for manager 7. Hence, where leverage is precluded, the allocations from manager 7 are largely transferred to manager 5 (comparing columns 3 and 2).

- Manager 1, with the highest unadjusted return and volatility and the lowest correlation with the S&P 500, and as a consequence the fourth highest $r(CAP)$, is selected largely because of its low correlation with manager 5 and 7. However, the optimal basket with leverage would hold only 10.5 percent in manager 1. On an unlevered basis, the allocation to manager 1 increases marginally 13.3 percent. However, in the approach where absolute return is maximized subject to a tracking error constraint (column 5), this allocation could be as high as 20 percent.

- Optimizing returns subject to a tracking error constraint gives a lower confidence in skill than maximizing the correlation-adjusted performance under the same constraints.

- Investing through a single active manager is not optimal for this tracking error budget; otherwise it would have been selected in simulations 3 and 4.

EXTENSIONS

This technique was used for U.S. equity managers, but nothing in this technique precludes its use for other asset classes or across asset classes. In addition, retail investors who seek to hold a portfolio of mutual funds to achieve some investment goal could use such a technique. This technique would work as long as investors are delegating investment decisions to an agent (i.e., investment or mutual fund manager) and seek to control the risk that they take relative to a given benchmark.

SUMMARY

Chapter 9 demonstrated how previously used measures of risk-adjusted performance such as the Sharpe ratio, the information ratio, and the M^2 measure are inadequate to rank investment managers or structure portfolios. A new measure was proposed—the M^3 measure—which demonstrated that it is important not only to adjust for differences in standard deviation between a portfolio and a benchmark, but also to adjust for the fact that different correlations imply different relative risk and possibly insufficient return for such risk. This chapter extended the analysis by demonstrating how institutional or individual investors might combine many investment managers, the benchmark, and the risk-free asset to achieve the highest risk-adjusted return for given volatility and correlation constraints.

In testing this with actual performance data it was possible to show that the manager that had the highest M^3 rank was likely to be part of an optimal multiple manager portfolio, even if it did not have the highest absolute return. The investment managers with the highest absolute return need not be part of the optimal portfolio, especially if they have a low risk-adjusted performance. However, if they are poorly correlated with other managers with a higher risk-adjusted performance, their case for being included is greatly enhanced. Further, although on a single-manager basis there is some case for passive management, on a multiple-manager basis the case for active management is greatly enhanced.

Too often investors choose investment managers on the basis of the highest returns over a historical period, and advertisements for many of these managers are biased toward reporting absolute returns only. This analysis has demonstrated that not only is it important to calculate the risk-adjusted performance of individual managers, but that an investor who is likely to choose multiple managers should look at how correlated these managers are with the benchmark and with other managers that are candidates for selection. By using the technique described here, investors should construct portfolios using an optimal combination of the benchmark, riskless asset, and risky investment managers. This also enhances the confidence they have in the skill embedded in the portfolio. It may still turn out that the highest absolute return manager is a part of the optimal portfolio, but it would be a surprise if that manager commands as large a share as if the investor did not adjust for risk.

SOLUTION TO CORRELATION OF PORTFOLIO OF MULTIPLE

FUNDS WITH BENCHMARK

Define portfolio X as the composite of many mutual funds. The problem for the investor is to maximize the following:

$$r(CAP - X) = ar(X) + (1 - a - b) \times r(F) + br(B) \qquad (A11.1.1)$$

subject to a given target tracking error and variance where $r(X) = \sum_i w_i \, r(i)$, w_i is the weight of the ith mutual fund (and the sum of their weights is equal to unity) and $r(i)$ is its return, and a and b are as defined in the chapter.

Assume two mutual funds—mutual fund 1 and 2, defined by standard deviations σ_1 and σ_2 and correlations $\rho_{1,B}$ and $\rho_{2,B}$ with the benchmark. Assume further that the correlation between these two mutual funds is $\rho_{1,2}$. Assume further that w_1 and w_2 are the respective weights in portfolio X.

$$\sigma_X^2 = w_1^2 \sigma_1^2 + 2 w_1 w_2 \rho_{1,2} \sigma_1 \sigma_2 = w_2^2 \sigma_2^2 \qquad (A11.1.2)$$

$$TE(X)^2 = \sigma_X^2 - 2 \rho_{X,B} \sigma_X \sigma_B + \sigma_B^2 \qquad (A11.1.3)$$

Also,

$$TE(X)^2 = w_1^2 \sigma_1^2 + w_2^2 \sigma_2^2 + \sigma_B^2 - 2 w_1 \rho_{1,B} \sigma_1 \sigma_B$$
$$- 2 w_2 \rho_{2,B} \sigma_2 \sigma_B + 2 w_1 w_2 \rho_{1,2} \sigma_1 \sigma_2 \qquad (A111.4)$$

Using (A11.1.2),

$$= \sigma_X^2 + \sigma_B^2 - 2 [w_1 \rho_{1,B} \sigma_1 + w_2 \rho_{2,B} \sigma_2] \sigma_B \qquad (A11.1.5)$$

Combining (A11.1.3) and (A11.1.5),

$$\rho_{X,B} \sigma_X = [w_1 \rho_{1,B} \sigma_1 + w_2 \rho_{2,B} \sigma_2] \qquad (A11.1.6)$$

or alternatively,

$$\rho_{X,B} = [w_1 \rho_{1,B} \sigma_1 + w_2 \rho_{2,B} \sigma_2] / \sigma_X \qquad (A11.1.7)$$

The extension to multiple mutual funds is trivial; namely, that

$$\rho_{X,B} = \sum_i [w_i \rho_{i,B} \sigma_i] / \sigma_X \qquad (A11.1.8)$$

Now, the investor solves for a, b, and w_i, and the allocation to each mutual fund is $a \times w_i$.

1. The information ratio is the ratio of excess returns over the benchmark to the standard deviation of the excess returns. The Sharpe ratio is the ratio of excess returns over the risk-free rate to the standard deviation of the portfolio. For the M^2 measure see Chapter 9, or Modigliani and Modigliani (1997).

2. See Markowitz (1959) and Waring and Castille (1998) for this specific extension.

3. This issue is addressed in greater detail in Muralidhar (1999c).

4. In Muralidhar (1999c) such results are used to show why the information ratio, the Sharpe ratio, and the M^2 measure are inadequate to rank portfolios.

5. In Table 11.4, the optimizer was unable to satisfy this constraint entirely and hence we report a marginal negative value for b for completeness. This is the Waring and Castille (1998) technique.

6. See also Modigliani and Modigliani (1997), Muralidhar and Van der Wouden (2000), and Muralidhar (1999c).

7. This is a trivial result, as one would expect the benefits of diversification to pay off.

12

THE GREATER FOOL THEORY OF ASSET MANAGEMENT OR WHERE A FUND SHOULD TAKE RISK

Arun S. Muralidhar

This chapter evaluates opportunities for active management across asset classes. It examines two manager databases with different but partially overlapping periods. The analysis suggests that in order to pursue active management in most asset classes (U.S. equity large cap, U.S. fixed income, non-U.S. equity, and non-U.S. fixed income), one must believe there are those who select poorly performing managers or that historical accidents in benchmark construction, such as the extreme valuation of Japan, will be repeated. Where active management appears to add value on an absolute and risk-adjusted basis (U.S. equity mid and small cap, emerging markets equity, currencies, and high-yield bonds), one must believe the inefficiencies in benchmark construction or the market are likely to continue, in order to budget for risk in these asset classes. In addition, it appears the average tracking error in these asset classes is high, but confidence in outperformance is also high and risk-adjusted excess returns are positive. Manager selection, monitoring, and management are the keys to success.

Adapted from Arun S. Muralidhar and Robert Weary. "The Greater Fool Theory of Asset Management." Investment Management Department Working Paper Series, The World Bank, September 1998; adapted from Arun S. Muralidhar and Robertus Prajogi. "Persistence of Manager Performance with Implications for Allocating Risk." Unpublished working paper, 2001. Table 12.1 and Figures 12.1 through 12.3 are derived from Muralidhar and Weary(1998); Table 12.4 is from David Blake, as credited on page 266; all others are from Muralidhar and Prajogi (2001).

OVERVIEW

Previous chapters demonstrated that active management outperforms passive management on a risk-adjusted basis, if the plan sponsor or individual selects multiple managers/mutual funds. This was predicated on short-lists of managers with strong performance and the ability to have hindsight in recognizing a good manager.

Unresolved questions include these:

1. In which asset class is this likely to be most advantageous?
2. In which asset class is one likely to find the greatest persistence in return and high skill?
3. What characteristics of managers can give adequate information about persistence?

This chapter undertakes to answer the first two questions and leaves the third question to future research. For simplicity, the chapter looks at asset classes in isolation and ignores the fact that taking risk in some asset classes, where alpha is low, may be beneficial in an overall portfolio if the marginal contribution to risk is negative.

Two manager universes are examined: Wilshire Associates and Plan Sponsor Network.[1] This chapter examines whether conclusions on excess and risk-adjusted excess returns are consistent across the different manager databases that the average plan sponsor has access to. The problem is that these databases largely contain data on publicly traded markets and it is not possible to evaluate asset classes such as currencies, private equity, hedge funds/absolute return strategies, and real estate. In addition, no established benchmark exists for currency markets, so the plan sponsor has to rely on data either from clients with multiple managers or very generic databases maintained by consultants.

The data set considers the maximum possible number of managers for as far back as possible. The following asset classes were examined for the Wilshire database: U.S. equities—large-cap (USLC), mid-cap (USMC), and small-cap (USSC); international large-cap equities (INTL); emerging market equities (EME); U.S. high-grade fixed income (USFI); non-U.S. high-grade fixed income unhedged (GFI); and high-yield bonds (HY). Background information on this analysis is provided in Tables A12.1.1 and A12.1.2 in Appendix 12.1.

All of the above, except USMC, GFI, and HY, were evaluated for the Plan Sponsor Network database.

WILSHIRE DATABASE

After examining the Wilshire database, Muralidhar and Weary (1998) concluded that, *on average* and after fees, there is little or no excess return from active management in most major asset classes, such as for USLC, USFI, INTL, and GFI. The average excess return in international developed markets is largely explained by an aberration in the benchmarks, which unduly overweighted Japan in the early 1990s. However, the average is positive for USMC, USSC, EME, and HY (see Figure 12.1 and Table 12.1). Participants in these markets seek positive excess returns (unlike currency), and this is probably the case for these four asset classes, as the efficiency of these benchmarks can be called into question, especially the emerging market indices.[2]

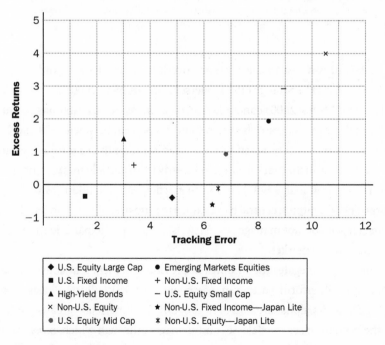

Figure 12.1 Tracking Error Versus Excess Returns in All Asset Classes

Note: Returns are net of fees.

Table 12.1

Details on Asset Classes in the Wilshire Database

	USLC	USMC	USSC	INTL	EME	USFI	GFI	HY
Managers	251	78	124	67	33	222	22	38
Benchmark	S&P 500	S&P Midcap	Russell 2000	MSCI EAFE	MSCI EMG Free	Salomon BIG	Salomon Non-U.S. Govt.	Salomon High-Yield
No. of years	10	5	10	10	5	10	5	5
Excess gross returns (%)	0.06	1.47	3.7	4.57	2.81	−0.09	1.01	1.93
Excess net returns (%)	−0.42	0.91	2.94	3.97	1.93	−0.37	0.63	1.45
Average tracking error (%)	4.8	6.9	8.9	10.5	8.4	1.6	3.4	3.0
Information ratio	−0.09	0.13	0.33	0.38	0.23	−0.23	0.19	0.48
Confidence in skill (%)	38.9	61.6	85.1	88.2	69.4	23.3	61.6	86

Note: Abbreviations used: U.S. equities—large cap (USLC), mid cap (USMC), and small cap (USSC); international large cap equities (INTL); emerging market equities (EME); U.S. high-grade fixed income (USFI); non-U.S. high-grade fixed income unhedged (GFI); and high-yield bonds (HY).

This is in contrast to the currency overlay market. Recent studies on the currency market by Strange (1998), Hersey and Minnick (2000), and Baldridge, Meath, and Myers (2000) conclude that, on average, the industry has produced an annualized excess return between 1 and 1.5 percent between 1989 and 2000. However, currencies are a medium of exchange rather than a pure asset; hence, the inefficiency in the market is derived clearly from participants with nonprofit motives (Muralidhar 1999). Nonprofit participants include passive hedgers (corporate treasurers); central banks; tourists; and investment bond and equity managers who do not manage currency risk. These participants lend their balance sheet to the market.

None of this negates the findings in previous chapters that active management can outperform passive management on a risk-adjusted basis, even if average industry alphas are zero or negative. If anything, it lays greater emphasis on the need to select asset classes and managers through which excess returns can be captured in the most effective manner. In effect, this analysis suggests that, in many asset classes, alpha is a scarce commodity and its acquisition by one plan sponsor probably means another must have negative excess returns. Alternatively, plan sponsors must find regulatory reasons, inefficiencies in benchmarks or non-profit participants to justify why an asset class (or even a hedge fund strategy) will provide consistent excess returns over the benchmark.

The Wilshire database suggests that, on average, there is substantial variability of excess returns in all asset classes (tracking error). This in turn suggests that, on an industry basis, active management in certain asset classes leads to substantial relative risk with little or no value added (Figure 12.1 and Table 12.1). However, there are clearly winners and losers. Although some fund managers outperform and others underperform, most plan sponsors would argue they are capable of selecting the good managers. Unless there are inherent inefficiencies in benchmarks or markets, for every basis point of outperformance experienced by a plan sponsor in most asset classes, there is a plan sponsor who gives it up. This is the greater fool theory—there must be a greater fool in selecting a manager for every one of us that believes we can select a manager or managers who will outperform.[3] This also suggests it is not an easy task to outperform benchmarks through manager selection, and plan sponsors need to actively monitor their manager allocations.[4] However, tools for the active management of manager allocations are not readily available to the average plan sponsor.

ANALYSIS

The managers mentioned here will remain anonymous. But in all asset classes, active managers were evaluated against commonly used benchmarks. Within major asset classes, the results are largely independent of which benchmark is used, given the high correlation and similarity of expected returns of the different benchmarks.[5] The average excess returns (both gross and net of fees), tracking error, information ratio net of fees, and confidence in skill on a net of fees basis were then calculated. This chapter assumes the results are size independent (all fund managers manage the same amount of assets), and recognizes this is not necessarily true. In the non-U.S. asset classes, where applicable, the data was compared based on unhedged returns, as they were easier to obtain. For asset classes with relatively shorter histories, such as USMC, EME, GFI, and HY, only 5 years of data (December 1992 to December 1997) was analyzed. In all other cases, 10 years of data (from December 1987 to December 1997) was used.

In creating a universe for analysis, a number of biases can occur.[6] One is survivorship bias, which results from the tendency of poorly performing managers to drop out over time. A recent multiasset class study noted that survivorship bias raised the average return of the remaining members of the universe substantially. For example, in the USLC sector it increased by 50 basis points, in the small-cap sector by 78 basis points, in the INTL sector by 173 basis points, and in the USFI sector by 14 basis points.[7] Therefore, if the performance of managers who dropped out was included, the analysis would have shown lower average excess returns than those noted.

An analysis of each of the asset class follows.

U.S. Equity Large Capitalization

Three capitalization sectors—large, mid-, and small—of the U.S. equity market were examined. In the large-cap sector, the returns of 251 active managers were analyzed against the S&P 500 index. On average, these managers returned only 6 basis points of excess return, gross of fees. The average fees charged for active management of large-cap (with an allocation of $100 million) were calculated, with the assistance of Wilshire Associates. Active management fees averaged 48 basis points. Therefore, net of fees, these managers underperformed the S&P 500 by 42 basis points, for an average tracking error of 4.8 percent (see Figure 12.2). The confidence in skill for this data set is less than 50 percent, suggesting a lack of skill, on average.

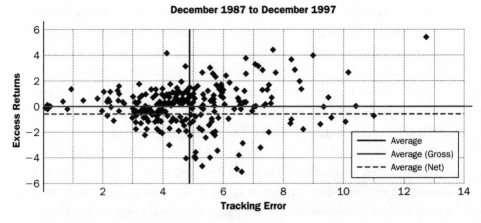

Figure 12.2   Large-Cap U.S. Equity Managers

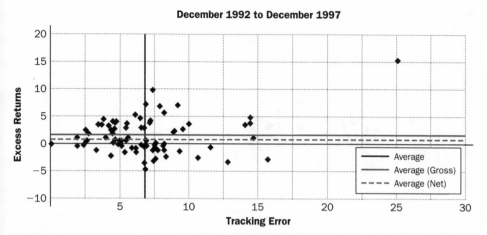

Figure 12.3   Mid-Cap U.S. Equity Managers

U.S. Equity Mid-Capitalization

The returns of 78 active mid-cap managers were analyzed against the S&P Mid Cap index. On average, these managers returned 147 basis points of excess returns, gross of fees. (Active management fees average 56 basis points.) Net of fees, active management in the mid-cap sector outperformed the benchmark by 91 basis points (see Figure 12.3). Although the average mid-cap manager adds value over the benchmark, he does so at the expense of risk. In this section, for simplicity the information ratio is used as a measure of risk-adjusted performance. Tracking error in the mid-cap sector averages 6.9 percent versus 4.8 percent in the large-cap sector. Further analysis reveals that the extra tracking error is worthwhile. A comparison of managers' information ratios from the large- and mid-cap sectors shows that the average information ratio of the large-cap managers is 0.0, and the average of the mid-cap managers is 0.3.[8] The higher average in the mid-cap sector indicates that these managers provide more excess return per unit of tracking error. As a result, there is higher confidence in skill, net of fees (despite the shorter data set), but this is still low at approximately 60 percent.

U.S. Equity Small Capitalization

The returns of 124 active managers were analyzed against the Russell 2000 index. On average, these managers returned 370 basis points of excess returns, gross

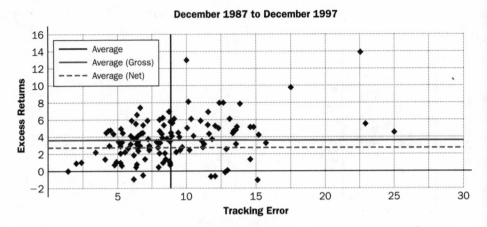

Figure 12.4 Small-Cap U.S. Equity Managers

of fees. (Active management fees average 76 basis points.) Net of fees, active management in this sector outperformed the benchmark by 294 basis points (see Figure 12.4). As in the mid-cap sector, the average small-cap manager added value over the benchmark, but at higher levels of risk. Again, the average of the managers' information ratio in the large cap-sector is 0.0, versus 0.4 in the small-cap sector. Although the small-cap sector has the highest tracking error within U.S. equities, it also rewards the plan sponsor with the highest excess return for each extra unit of tracking error. (The tracking error in the small-cap sector averages 8.9 percent.) Further, confidence in skill, net of fees, is very high at 85 percent.

Non-U.S. Equity

The returns of 67 active INTL managers were analyzed against the MSCI EAFE index. On average, these managers returned 457 basis points of excess returns, gross of fees. Active management fees averaged 60 basis points, with an allocation of $100 million. Net of fees, the average INTL manager returned just under 400 basis points of excess, but with a high level of risk (see Figure 12.5). Tracking error averaged 10.5 percent, for an information ratio of 0.38; confidence in skill was 88 percent.

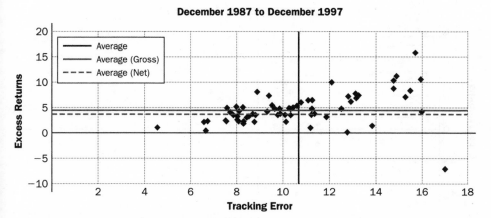

Figure 12.5 Non-U.S. Equity Managers

Adjustment for Japan

Many plan sponsors underweighted Japan either explicitly or by using GDP-weighted benchmarks. Therefore, the analysis is conducted for an Japan-Lite index, in which the Japan weight was fixed at 17.7 percent for the entire period.[9] In this case, the managers returned only 45 basis points of excess returns, gross of fees. Net of fees, these same managers underperform the Japan-Lite index by 15 basis points, with a lower tracking error, compared to the MSCI EAFE index (see Figure 12.6). Against the Japan-Lite index, the tracking error is only

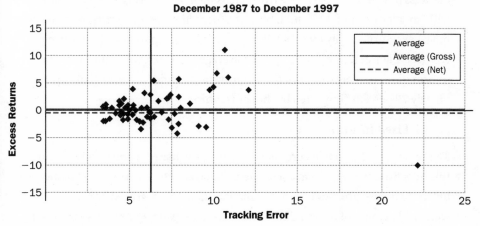

Figure 12.6 Non-U.S. Equity Managers Versus Japan-Lite

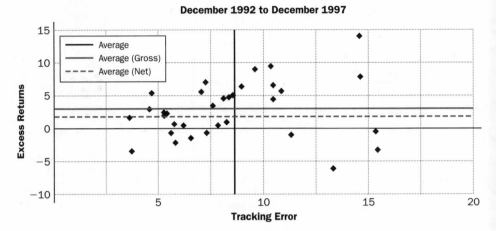

Figure 12.7 Emerging Markets Equity Managers

6.5 percent, and confidence in skill is less than 50 percent. In other words, the managers' high excess returns against the MSCI EAFE are explained by the managers' *skillful* bet against Japan. Against an Japan-Lite index, these managers' excess returns disappear.

Emerging Markets Equity

The returns of 33 active emerging market managers were reviewed against the MSCI EMG Free index. On average, these managers returned 281 basis points of excess returns gross of fees. Active management fees averaged 88 basis points, with an allocation of $100 million. Net of fees, the average emerging market manager returned only over 190 basis points of excess returns, with fairly high risk (see Figure 12.7). Tracking error averaged 8.4 percent, with an average information ratio net of fees of 0.23, and average confidence in skill of approximately 70 percent (impacted by the shorter history).

U.S. Fixed Income

The returns of 222 active core managers were evaluated against the Salomon Brothers Broad index. On average, these managers underperformed the index by 9 basis points, gross of fees. Active management fees averaged 28 basis points with an allocation of $100 million. Net of fees, the average core active manager underperformed the index by 37 basis points, at a lower level of risk (see

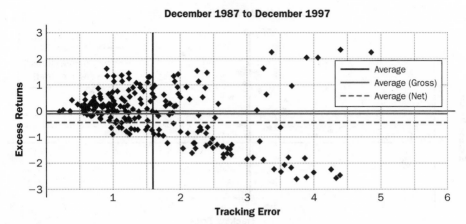

Figure 12.8 U.S. Fixed Income Managers

Figure 12.8). Tracking error averaged only 1.6 percent. The heavier concentration in the northwest quadrant suggests that restricting tracking error would potentially lead to higher information ratios and excess returns. There is clearly a skill issue in the total universe, making it imperative that sponsors evaluate managers and control with great care.

Non-U.S. Fixed Income

The returns of 22 active non-U.S. fixed income managers were compared with the Salomon Brothers Non-U.S. Government index (unhedged). On average, these managers returned 101 basis points of excess returns, gross of fees. Active management fees averaged 38 basis points with a $100 million allocation. Net of fees, the average non-U.S. fixed income manger returned an excess of 63 basis points, and a tracking error of 3.4 percent (see Figure 12.9).

Adjustment for Japan

As for the INTL managers, the analysis of the non-U.S. fixed income managers was redone against a Japan-Lite benchmark, with a 20.0 percent weight to Japan versus a 26.0 percent weight in the Salomon Brothers Non-U.S. Government index.[10] These managers underperformed the benchmark by 24 basis points, gross of fees, against the Japan-Lite benchmark. Net of fees, the managers underperformed the benchmark by 62 basis points, at a higher level of

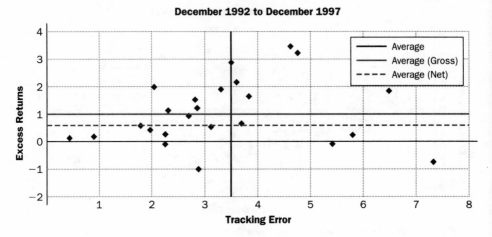

Figure 12.9 Non-U.S. Fixed Income Managers

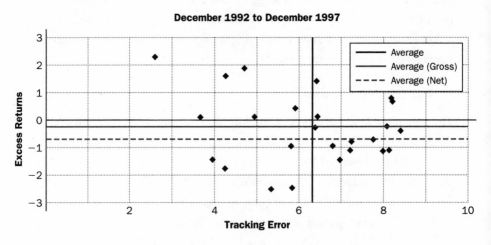

Figure 12.10 Non-U.S. Fixed Income Managers Versus Japan-Lite Index

risk (see Figure 12.10). Tracking error was 6.3 percent. Although the tracking error was higher against the Japan-Lite benchmark, it is probably safe to conclude that most non-U.S. fixed income mangers made a bet against Japan. Hence, the excess returns are higher against the Salomon Brothers Non-U.S. Government index than against a Japan-Lite index.

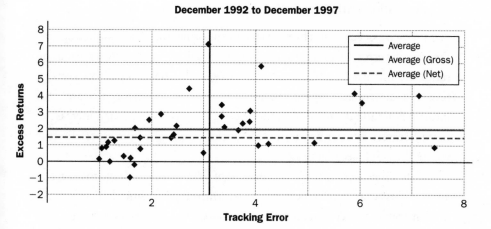

Figure 12.11   High-Yield Bonds Managers

High-Yield Bonds

The returns of 38 active high-yield managers were analyzed versus the Salomon Brothers High Yield index. On average, these managers returned 193 basis points of excess return, gross of fees. Active management fees averaged 48 basis points, with an allocation of $100 million. Net of fees, the average high-yield manager returned an excess of 145 basis points, with very low risk (see Figure 12.11). Tracking error averaged 3.0 percent, and again, despite the short data history and fees, confidence in skill was very high at 86 percent.

EXTENSIONS

To further support these results, risk-adjusted performance was examined. First, the relationship between the information ratio and tracking error was examined to determine whether a linear relationship exists. The information ratio is used because the possibility of leverage is ignored, as are combinations of these managers with the risk-free asset and the benchmark (as per the M^3 method). This is relevant, as others have suggested that the active-passive choice (in terms of risk allocation) can be made assuming that information ratios are independent of tracking error.[11] The M^3 method is used to risk-adjust return of the Plan Sponsor Network database.

Information Ratio Versus Tracking Error

Within each asset class and by manager, the information ratio is plotted against the tracking error. Contrary to the assumptions in a recent study, information ratios are impacted as tracking error increases.[12] This analysis, on average, reveals a downward sloping relationship—as tracking error increases, the information ratio decreases. In other words, there is no associated increase in reward (excess return) per extra unit of risk taken. This was especially true within the USFI (see Figure 12.12).

The findings were similar, irrespective of whether the average manager in an asset class underperformed or outperformed the benchmark. Figure 12.13 demonstrates that, even within the U.S. equity mid-cap sector (in which the average manager outperforms the benchmark) a downward-sloping linear relationship between the information ratio and tracking error is experienced.[13] This has important implications for plan sponsors who are compensated based on their information ratios, as excessive risk taking by managers in certain asset classes can lead to underperforming the target information ratio.

Currencies provide an interesting deviation from these results. The history of the currency management business goes back no further than the late 1980s.

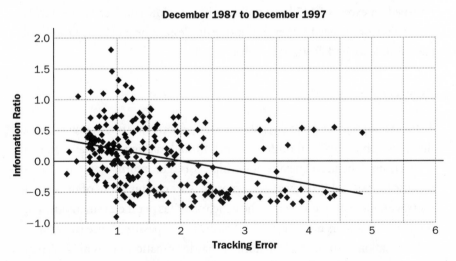

Figure 12.12 U.S. Fixed Income—Information Ratio Versus Tracking Error

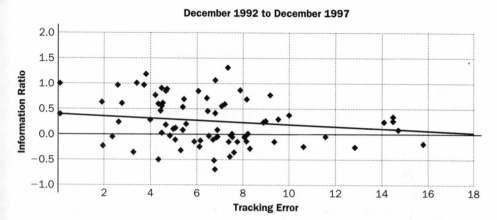

Figure 12.13   U.S. Equity Mid-Cap—Information Ratio Versus Tracking Error

However, for mandates with as little as 5 years of performance, confidence in skill on a gross basis is extremely high at 80 to 99 percent (Muralidhar 1999). In addition, the relationship between information ratios and tracking error appears to be different. Muralidhar and Richmond (1999) include a chart on JP Morgan Flemings Asset Management results. This chart demonstrates that as managers are permitted to take greater tracking error, the information ratio increases. This is possibly because there are many nonprofit players in the currency markets, such as corporate treasurers and central banks, who provide a backstop for active managers. Hence greater tracking error implies a relaxation of constraints and, therefore, a better opportunity set with better information ratios. This is an unusual area where greater tracking error implies leverage, which is demonstrated to improve the welfare of the average investor. On an industry basis, using data from Strange (1998), this result is not as compelling, as the dataset is biased towards managers who have not created absolute return strategies.

SUMMARY

On average (using the Wilshire database), after fees there is little or no excess return from active management in most asset classes except USMC, USSC,

EME, and HY. It appears that excess returns exist where benchmarks are not liquid or efficient, rather than from a market inefficiency (as in the case of currencies). With the exception of HY, positive excess return is associated with high tracking error. However, confidence in skill (on a net of fees basis) in USMC and EME is low due to the short data history.

Therefore, in most liquid markets, one must believe that others choose bad managers if one believes he can pick managers who will outperform.[14] Furthermore, in the international bond and equity markets, the average manager outperformed the benchmark by a single bet against Japan. In both cases, against a Japan-Lite index, the average manager underperforms. On average, there is a downward-sloping relationship between the information ratio and tracking error—as tracking error increases the information ratio decreases (less reward per unit of risk). In a simplistic sense, to justify selection of active managers in certain asset classes, investment professionals must believe there is a "fool" elsewhere in the industry who is making a poor choice. This is the greater fool theory.

THE PLAN SPONSOR DATABASE

The previous sections present a rather dim perspective on the average prospects for active management in USLC, USFI, INTL and GFI. Data from the Plan Sponsor database is used to see if this result is true (with the exception of GFI) across manager databases.[15] In addition, the M^3 measure is used to evaluate the risk-adjusted return. In using M^3 within asset classes, the average $r(CAP)$ for each asset class is analyzed, assuming the average tracking error as the target. The average $r(CAP)$ for all asset classes is also estimated assuming the same target tracking error of 10 percent, to compare across asset classes for the most attractive asset class. The only constraint is the inability to achieve this target tracking error in USFI because of the nature of the asset class. In other words, the analysis assists investors in budgeting active risk in the most effective manner. However, the ability to capture this alpha requires the selection of managers who have persistent alpha or risk-adjusted returns, and assumes that sponsors can find ways to identify these managers. This will be pursued in future research.

THE DATA

This section is derived extensively from Muralidhar and Prajogi (2001). The techniques highlighted previously are applied to the following asset classes: USLC, USSC, INTL, EME, and USFI. Data are derived from the Plan Sponsor Network database, taking 10-year performance for different funds, except for EME, where only 5 years of data is available. (This data is for the period ending June 2000.) Table 12.2 summarizes information on the various asset classes, including the number of managers, the benchmark to which they were compared, and data history. Once again, in the interests of confidentiality, the names of the funds are not provided.

There are a few key differences across the databases: the Plan Sponsor database has more recent data; there are fewer managers in the USLC and more in USFI in the Wilshire database, although the rest are largely the same; and results

Table 12.2
The Plan Sponsor Network Database (Through December 2000)

	USLC	USSC	INTL	EME	USFI
Managers	394	109	72	32	127
Benchmark	S&P 500	Russell 2000	MSCI EAFE	MSCI EMG Free	Lehman Aggregate
Number of years	10	10	10	5	10
Average annualized benchmark return (%)	17.79	13.56	8.28	0.99	7.82
Average annualized std. dev. of benchmark (%)	13.66	19.99	15.94	27.20	4.46
Average annualized gross excess returns (%)	−0.14	4.62	3.63	5.17	0.57
Average tracking error (%)	6.13	11.15	9.03	9.96	1.16
Average M^3 excess (%)	−1.38	3.65	3.48	5.41	0.43
Average information ratio	−0.04	0.38	0.38	0.51	0.49
M^3 excess assuming 10% tracking error (%)	−3.40	4.62	3.75	5.53	N/A
Confidence in skill (%)	44.84	78.00	83.38	79.12	82.45

Note: Abbreviations used: U.S. equities—large cap (USLC) and small cap (USSC); international large cap equities (INTL); emerging market equities (EME); U.S. high-grade fixed income (USFI).

are generally the same except in USFI, which changes sign to positive average (gross and net) alpha and much higher confidence in skill, suggesting the more recent history has been favorable to this asset class. In addition, there is higher emerging equity alpha and a higher confidence in skill in the Plan Sponsor database despite the various crises that managers have had to contend with. However, with the exception of EME and USFI, the information ratios are largely the same.

There is a tendency among investors to select managers of asset classes with the highest absolute excess returns. This may be justified if risk adjustment is not an objective. It is important to note that a unit of excess return (for the same time period) is not equal to the same confidence in skill across asset classes. For example, a 3.97 percent alpha in USLC is equal to 86.61 percent confidence, whereas 3.58 percent alpha in INTL is equal to 89.42 percent confidence in skill (even though the latter has a higher average tracking error). In addition, although the average small-cap alpha is equal to 4.62 percent (compared to INTL of 3.63 percent), the confidence in skill is 78 percent compared to INTL of 83.4 percent. However, the USSC asset class has a higher average tracking error and higher volatility. Finally, bond managers have a lower average alpha than small-cap managers, but higher confidence in skill.

The M^3 measure is used as it normalizes alphas for risk and provides rankings consistent with rankings based on skill. USFI is excluded because it is a low tracking error asset class. If one assumes the plan sponsor has a 10 percent tracking error budget that they would like to allocate to a single asset class with the highest $r(CAP)$, EME and USSC would be the preferred areas to spend the budget, as the Japan issue biases INTL.

ANALYSIS

Should plan sponsors blindly buy into these asset classes or is more diligence required? The asset classes are evaluated in greater detail to calculate the spread between the top-performing and worst-performing managers, as this could have an impact on the ability to access unadjusted or risk-adjusted alpha. Table 12.3 provides quartile breaks across all asset classes.

For each quartile and asset class average, the table provides excess returns, information ratios, and the degree of confidence in skill. In addition to these

Table 12.3

Details on Asset Classes–Plan Sponsor Network Database

Mean		USLC	USSC	INTL	EM Equity	USFI
Alpha (%)	All	−0.14	4.62	3.63	5.17	0.57
	First Quartile	3.97	12.46	7.80	10.42	1.39
	Second Quartile	0.54	4.38	3.58	6.38	0.63
	Third Quartile	−1.20	1.87	2.44	2.98	0.30
	Fourth Quartile	−3.91	−0.51	0.72	0.90	−0.04
	Range (1Q–4Q)	7.87	12.96	7.08	9.52	1.42
Tracking error (%)	All	6.31	11.15	9.03	9.96	1.16
	First Quartile	8.22	17.53	13.13	11.65	1.83
	Second Quartile	4.35	9.28	9.03	12.90	1.20
	Third Quartile	5.46	8.27	7.76	8.45	0.87
	Fourth Quartile	7.17	9.30	6.19	6.85	0.73
	Range (1Q–4Q)	1.05	8.24	6.93	4.80	1.11
Information ratio	All	−0.04	0.38	0.38	0.51	0.49
	First Quartile	0.49	0.71	0.62	0.95	0.88
	Second Quartile	0.18	0.52	0.41	0.57	0.60
	Third Quartile	−0.24	0.27	0.33	0.36	0.39
	Fourth Quartile	−0.57	0.00	0.14	0.15	0.06
	Range (1Q–4Q)	1.06	0.72	0.49	0.80	0.82
Confidence (%)	All	44.84	78.00	83.38	79.12	82.45
	First Quartile	86.61	93.89	94.55	94.17	97.73
	Second Quartile	64.62	88.81	89.42	80.90	93.94
	Third Quartile	22.53	79.80	84.82	77.78	85.19
	Fourth Quartile	5.41	48.91	64.72	63.62	52.00
	Range (1Q–4Q)	81.20	44.98	29.83	30.56	45.73
Number of managers	All	394	109	72	32	127
	First Quartile	99	28	18	8	32
	Second Quartile	98	27	18	8	32
	Third Quartile	99	27	18	8	32
	Fourth Quartile	98	27	18	8	31

SOURCE: Plan Sponsor Network (PSN). Ten-year manager performance (gross of fees) ending June 2000.

statistics, Figures 12.14 (A through E) plots the excess return against confidence in skill for the average, and the lowest and highest quartile for each asset class. The most striking results for confidence in skills are these:

- There is wide dispersion between the first and fourth quartile within USLC (81.2 percent), which suggests that manager selection in this asset class needs to be undertaken with great care.

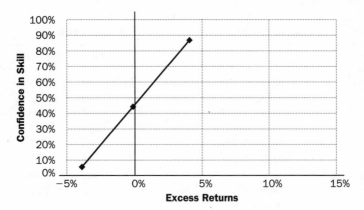

(A) U.S. Large Cap

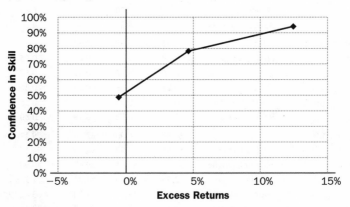

(B) U.S. Small Cap

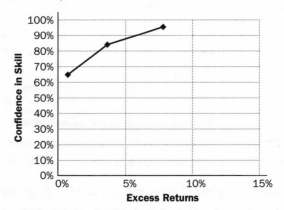

(C) International Equity

Figure 12.14 Confidence in Skill versus Excess Returns in Different Asset Classes (*figure continues*)

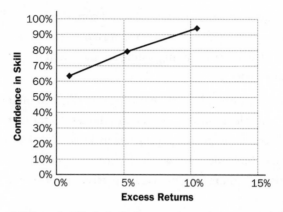

(D) Emerging Markets Equity

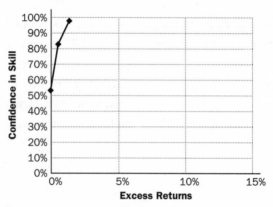

(E) U.S. High-Grade Fixed Income

Figure 12.14 Confidence in Skill versus Excess Returns in Different Asset Classes (*continued*)

- By comparison with USLC, USSC has a larger dispersion of returns but a greater clustering of skill. This clustering is largely because of the positive average alpha for small-cap managers.

- Similarly, comparing USLC and INTL managers, there is the same range of excess but greater clustering of skill in INTL, once again due to the average alpha.

- Excluding emerging markets equities, it appears that a wider range of information ratios correspond to a wider range of confidence in skill.

- Within quartile breaks, there is a linear relationship between excess returns and confidence in skill, as demonstrated in Figure 12.14. The same is true of the information ratio and confidence in skill, as expected and as shown in Table 12.3. However, it is interesting that tracking error does not have this pattern, suggesting an inefficient use of tracking error budgets by managers.

- Though not reported here, if quartiling is performed on information ratios or confidence in skill or even M^3, the results for each quartile are strikingly similar along the parameters in Table 12.3. This result has interesting implications for whether information ratio or confidence in skill statistics is more informative for persistence of alpha.

DATA ON OTHER COUNTRIES

Blake (2000) provides data on the performance of UK pension funds in comparison with the market for the 1986–1994 period. Although details are not provided on individual managers, the averages are quite revealing (Table 12.4). The results are very similar to those of the United States; namely, excess return opportunities appear to be in international assets. In addition, manager selection and management is critical to achieving alpha, as industry averages are likely to give only benchmark returns.

SUMMARY

To summarize the results across both databases, investors would be well advised to consider budgeting risk to asset classes where the payoff (unadjusted and risk-adjusted) and confidence in skill is high and concentrated. This would

Table 12.4
Performance of UK Pension Funds (1986–1994)

	UK Equities	Int'l Equities	UK Bonds	Int'l Bonds	UK Property
Average annualized benchmark return (%)	13.30	11.11	10.35	8.64	9.00
Average pension fund return (%)	12.97	11.23	10.76	10.03	9.52
Average outperformance (%)	−0.33	0.12	0.41	1.39	0.52
Percentage of outperformers (%)	44.8	39.8	77.3	68.8	39.1

SOURCE: David Blake. "Does It Matter What Type of Pension You Have?" *The Economic Journal*, February 2000, 110: F46–81, Table 7.

favor USSC, EME to some extent, INTL (with the previous caveat on Japan), and USMC over USLC. Within USLC, there is a high degree of confidence in the performance of certain styles, and investors may be biased toward selecting first-quartile managers. However, because past performance is no guarantee of future performance, one has to be careful about simple generalizations. Plan sponsors need to determine whether there is persistence in performance or skill, and whether information ratios, M^3, or data on skill can provide any

INVESTMENT TRUTHS

■ *There appear to be excess returns (raw and risk-adjusted) from four asset classes—U.S. small and mid cap, emerging market equity, and high-yield bonds—and from currencies. This may be a result of inefficiencies in markets or benchmarks.*

■ *There appears to be a high degree of confidence in skill of managers (on average) in U.S. small-cap and emerging market equity classes, which is sustained over time. In high-yield bonds, despite the short history, there appears to be confidence in skill.*

■ *In the case of international large-cap equities and non-U.S. high-grade fixed income, the case was predicated on whether deviating from the Japan weight is considered skillful or an obvious bet.*

■ *The information ratio appears to decrease as tracking error increases. Therefore, plan sponsors interested in high information ratios may want to budget risk to managers.*

■ *In some asset classes, there is a wide dispersion in skill, and selecting managers who demonstrate persistence in unadjusted and risk-adjusted performance is critical. Alternatively, where persistence is limited, plan sponsors should consider tactical allocations across managers (over time).*

information about the persistence in outperformance. Gupta and others (1999) demonstrate that the information ratio provides investors with some indication of the persistence in alpha. This is an interesting area for future research, as the objectives of investors can go beyond pure alpha, and numerous parameters need to be evaluated to determine their efficacy in identifying portfolios that satisfy these objectives. Alternatively, plan sponsors may need to tactically allocate across managers to achieve the best possible outcome.

Certain investment truths can be extracted from this work, as shown in the previous page box.

Clearly, then, when plan sponsors select asset classes to budget risk and select managers, they must clearly define their objectives: are they interested in raw excess returns or risk-adjusted returns? Is skill measured through the skill measure here or is consistency of outperformance on a raw basis important? Do plan sponsors feel they have adequate skill to select a single manager or multiple managers to outperform the benchmark on an unadjusted or a risk-adjusted basis? Once again, one shoe cannot fit all, and sponsors need to ensure that risk is taken in areas where they are most compensated, and that the overall objectives are reached. In addition, plan sponsors should be able to justify why they expect excess returns from an assest class or manager, and this analysis suggests that some assest classes may offer opportunities because of the objectives of the other participants or the nature of benchmarks (or in some cases regulations). However, manager selection and maintenance will be critical in all asset classes to achieve excess returns.

BACKGROUND INFORMATION FOR

CHAPTER ANALYSIS

Table A12.1.1
Additional Details on Wilshire Database

Asset Class	Benchmark	Number of Managers	Time Period	Data Periods	Average Fees[a]
U.S. equity (large cap)	S&P 500	251	12/87–12/97	Quarterly	49 bps
U.S. equity (mid cap)	S&P Mid	78	12/92–12/97	Quarterly	56 bps
U.S. equity (small cap)	Russell 2000	124	12/87–12/97	Quarterly	76 bps
U.S. fixed income (core)	SB BIG	222	12/87–12/97	Quarterly	28 bps
High-yield bonds	SB HY	38	12/92–12/97	Quarterly	46 bps
Non-U.S. equity	MSCI EAFE	67	12/87–12/97	Quarterly	60 bps
Non-U.S. equity	Japan-Lite[b]	67	12/87–12/97	Quarterly	60 bps
Emerging markets equity	MSCI EMG Free	33	12/92–12/97	Quarterly	88 bps
Non-U.S. fixed income (unhedged)	SB Non-U.S. Govt	22	12/92–12/97	Quarterly	38 bps
Non-U.S. fixed income (unhedged)	Japan-Lite Policy[c]	22	12/92–12/97	Quarterly	38 bps

[a]With a $100 million allocation for active management, as provided by Wilshire Associates.
[b]Weights: Japan (17.7%), EAFE Europe (64.3%), EAFE Pacific ex-Japan (12.8%), Canada (2.7%), and emerging market countries (2.6%).
[c]Weights: Japan (20.0%), Europe (73.2%), Pacific ex-Japan (1.6%), and Canada (5.2%).

Table A12.1.2
Excess Returns, Tracking Error, and Information Ratios—Wilshire Database

Asset Class	Tracking Error (%)	Excess Return[a] (bps)	Information Ratio
U.S. equity (large-cap)	4.8	−42	0.0
U.S. equity (mid-cap)	6.9	91	0.3
U.S. equity (small-cap)	8.9	294	0.4
U.S. fixed income (core)	1.6	−37	0.0
High-yield bonds	3.0	145	0.3
Non-U.S. equity	10.5	397	0.4
Non-U.S. equity (Japan-Lite)	6.5	−15	0.0
Emerging markets equity	8.4	193	0.3
Non-U.S. fixed income	3.4	101	0.3
Non-U.S. fixed income (Japan-Lite)	6.3	−62	0.0

[a]Net of fees.

1. The Wilshire database is examined in Muralidhar and Weary (1998a) and the Plan Sponsor database is reviewed in Muralidhar and Prajogi (2001).

2. We have no proof of the inefficiency of these indices, but hypothesize based on both the volatility and relative "immaturity" of these sectors.

3. Also known as the "Nimrod factor"—a term used by undergraduates at M.I.T. In every course graded on a curve, there is someone who misread the question, did not answer the right number of questions, or forgot to turn the question paper over, etc. These are the Nimrods who will probably get a C or worse. To get a grade better than a C, one has to make sure one is not the Nimrod!

4. We ignore outperformance through tactical asset allocation or through management of manager allocations.

5. Where available, we tested the asset classes against alternate comparable benchmarks and noted no significant change in the results.

6. See, for example, Ankrim (1998).

7. Ibid.

8. The information ratio is simply the managers' annualized average excess return over benchmark divided by the managers' tracking error.

9. Other differences between the benchmarks include: a 2.6 percent weight to emerging market equities (versus a zero weight in MSCI-EAFE), a slightly lower weight to EAFE Europe at 64.3 percent (versus 67.2 percent for MSCI-EAFE), a 2.7 percent weight to Canada (versus a zero weight for MSCI-EAFE), and a higher weight to EAFE Pacific ex-Japan at 12.8 percent (versus 6.0 percent for MSCI-EAFE), as of December 31, 1997. This was the World Bank's own benchmark to account for exclusion of certain countries, and cross-holdings in Japan.

10. The Nordic countries, United Kingdom, Canada, and Australia are comparable between the two indices, with the weight to continental Europe increased by 6.0 percent in the Japan-Lite index, as of August 1, 1998.

11. See Demakis (1997).

12. Ibid.

13. In the USLC and INTL sectors, there is a slightly positive slope. Statistical tests of significance of the slope can be done if it is of interest.

14. Given Ambarish and Seigel (1996), the ability to divine the skill from the noise for any one manager requires a time horizon longer than the average manager has actually been in existence, further exacerbating the selection problem.

15. There have been extensive discussions of budgeting risk in funds, but none to date have budgeted risk based on skill in generating excess returns.

13

QUALITATIVE ASPECTS OF MANAGER SELECTION

Arun S. Muralidhar

Previous chapters highlighted quantitative tools by which managers can be evaluated and asset classes in which risk may be taken. In selecting a manager, basic due diligence must be conducted and specific procedures must be followed. This chapter highlights certain qualitative aspects of manager selection, including establishing financial stability, organizational structure, commitment of resources to the business, investment philosophy and process, research, and willingness to train and share research with the client. Applying a consistent process for manager selection is likely to lead to effective implementation of the investment policy.

OVERVIEW

Previous chapters looked at the quantitative aspects of budgeting risks to asset classes and to selecting investment managers or mutual funds. However, there are qualitative aspects to manager selection that cannot be understated. No quantitative evaluation can capture the fundamental stability of an investment process that a strong due-diligence process can identify. This chapter examines

Adapted from Arun S. Muralidhar. "Manager Selection." Investment Management Department Working Paper Series, The World Bank, March 1998.

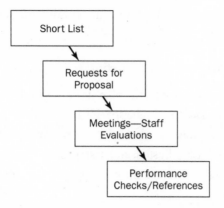

Figure 13.1 Process for Manager Selection

the process of evaluation and selection of external managers. As highlighted in Kutler (1997), one can look at the process as following four key steps:

1. Establishing a short list based on previous quantitative analyses
2. Evaluating additional details through the request-for-proposal (RFP) process
3. On-site meetings to clarify additional issues
4. Performance and reference checks.[1]

The goal of the entire process (Figure 13.1) is to ensure that the expectations of the plan sponsor and the managers are made transparent and are reflected clearly in the guidelines and contracts signed by both parties.

Maintaining Data and Creating Short Lists

Investment officers must regularly update their databases on the methodology and performance of a large universe of managers. This can be achieved by getting the data directly from managers or from data vendors (as highlighted in Chapter 12). These databases can then be distilled into short lists for consideration, should the plan sponsor decide to hire a new manager. Methods to create such short lists have been identified in Chapters 9 through 11, by evaluating the raw and risk-adjusted performance and the confidence in skill and consistency/ persistence in returns.

Requests for Proposal or Information

At the time of a manager search, the plan sponsor should send out a brief RFP and request the manager to provide specific information. There are four main areas to be evaluated: the organization itself; the investment process; performance, absolute and risk-adjusted; and costs or fees. The key attributes of each area are briefly described later in the chapter.

Meetings with Staff

Short-listed managers should be invited to make a presentation to the investment team about their proposals as to how the mandate will be implemented. In addition to investment performance, staff must evaluate how willing a manager would be to train staff, engage in joint research, and join in other noninvestment activities such as systems development.

A potential manager must then be visited for due diligence. Separately, due diligence should include reference checks for performance and quality of interaction between client and manager. During the due-diligence visit, the plan sponsor should spend time watching how portfolios are structured and implemented. One caveat: manager selection is more of an art than a science, as there is no guarantee that a manager, once selected, will never perform poorly.

The Organization

Try to discern the investment agent's financial stability. An analysis of the organization's capitalization and corporate structure would be useful. It is also critical to evaluate the background and experience of management and staff and the success of the organization in ensuring stability and retaining its best staff. Companies with a large percentage of new staff and high turnover are likely to experience problems in the future. However, turnover could be good if skills have been upgraded. Other success factors to examine are assets under management; asset growth; low account turnover; and quality of clients (for example, large and sophisticated clients are an indication of a strong

> **Organization**
> • Commitment to Investment Business
> • Financial Stability
> • Experience of Management and Staff
> • Turnover
> • Asset Growth

Figure 13.2   Issues Pertaining to the Organization

organization). These help to determine whether a firm is committed to investment management or does it merely as an ancillary to its core business. In some OECD countries, pension assets were managed by trust banks and insurance companies; given the poor performance by these managers, the trend in these countries has been to shift these assets to professional asset managers. Figure 13.2 summarizes organizational issues to consider in selecting an investment management firm.

Investment Process

The second stage of the analysis is to look at the clarity of the investment decision-making process within an organization. A clearly articulated investment philosophy and process is likely to provide consistent performance. The investment process could be either quantitative or qualitative (fundamental analysis of either the economy or an individual stock). However, it should demonstrate where the manager believes there is an inefficiency in the asset class or benchmarks. For example, Chapter 12 highlighted the inefficiency inherent in creating global indices that managers could exploit. In addition, currency overlay managers argue that this is a market where there are a number of nonprofit players (central banks, corporate treasurers, individuals, and investment managers who do not seek profit from foreign exchange transactions in purchasing foreign securities). This is critical in asset classes where average excess returns are zero.

The manager must then describe in detail the tools they utilize to exploit such inefficiencies. These tools could be either quantitative or qualitative, and although there is a tendency to believe that quantitative processes are not arbitrary, there is a fair amount of qualitative judgment that must go into creating the model. In addition, purely quantitative processes can be slow to adapt to

```
┌─────────────────────────────────────────┐
│ Investment Process                        │
│ • Clarity of Decision-Making Process      │
│ • Implementation of Best Ideas            │
│ • Top Down Versus Bottom Up               │
│ • Research                                │
│ • Risk Budgeting and Management           │
│ • Quantitative Versus Qualitative         │
└─────────────────────────────────────────┘
```

Figure 13.3   Issues Pertaining to Investment
Process

changes in market regime. In this analysis, one looks to establishing not only how investment decisions are made to buy and sell securities, but also who makes the decisions. In some organizations, decisions are made by a committee, whereas in others responsibility for the decision is delegated to individual portfolio managers. Both these models can be successful as long as there is a good way to ensure implementation of the best investment ideas. This must be complemented by an effective internal risk allocation and management process. Finally, it is important to determine the emphasis on and quality of research and the willingness of the organization to share the research with clients. Institutions with strong research capabilities can also be used to train internal staff.

An investment firm's approach to these aspects of the investment process, summarized in Figure 13.3, is a good indicator of skill.

Performance

Firms should be required to provide performance of a live account relative to different benchmarks (rather than composites). Dispersion of performance returns across similar mandates is an indication of poor implementation of the investment process and controls. If plan sponsors have extensive data on different markets, they can determine what risks were taken to achieve these results and determine whether the risk-adjusted performance is acceptable. Further, plan sponsors should want to know when an institutional investor has recently fired its external manager; this could suggest internal or performance problems not reflected in the data it provides. In countries where this business is only beginning, one is not likely to find a history long enough to be able to reach reasonable conclusions. If a manager has an acceptable philosophy but a limited history, require initial mandates that have relatively low risk (even passive mandates, if they have some clearly specified benchmark). Once the organization demonstrates it can achieve acceptable performance, risk tolerance can be increased and the manager can be given more freedom in investment decisions.

Costs and Fees

Plan sponsors should be conscious about costs for both internally and externally managed portfolios. For external managers, the plan sponsor should evaluate fees to ensure they are fair. For example, in a number of developing countries that have set up investment companies, it appears that a bulk of the costs can be attributed to marketing-related expenses. One would expect such companies to incur marketing costs; however, when these costs are far in excess of investment-related costs, it may indicate an inefficient allocation of resources. Related to this topic, plan sponsors should also seek to identify whether these managers receive any commissions from brokers (either in cash or kind). This has become an important topic for pension plans in the United States, and many plans have tried to capture these commissions directly by creating a list of preferred brokers. However, external managers would argue that these arrangements may not lead to the best execution in purchasing and selling securities. In short, the total fees should be used to look at after-fee performance relative to the benchmarks.

In summary, plan sponsors must look at the strength of an organization, quality of internal staff, investment process, and after-fees performance.

Implementation Issues

Once a manager is selected, other important implementation issues include developing and implementing contracts and guidelines for managers. This should be an area where staff devotes considerable effort. Contracts and guidelines are the legally sound ways to ensure that mandates implemented by external managers are in line with the risk tolerance of the sponsor, and that adequate indemnification is provided should there be fraud or negligence by the external manager. In addition, these contracts should specify requirements for risk management (for example, any tracking error guidelines), accounting

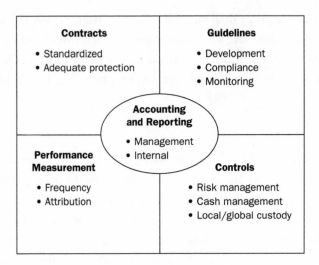

Figure 13.4 Implementation Issues

reports, and, most importantly, the performance reporting to staff. Figure 13.4 summarizes these issues, which were first introduced in Chapter 1.

In reviewing one fund, an advisory group discovered that the investment managers received performance reports only once a quarter. Further, the manner in which performance was reported was not clear, making it difficult to evaluate how the portfolio performed relative to its benchmark. A quick analysis showed that the manager lost 3 percent of the fund over 5 years and charged 1 percent in fees per year for doing so. External managers should report the performance of the portfolio and reasons for both under- or overperformance within a few business days of the end of each month. This could be followed by a more detailed evaluation later in the month. If performance lags behind benchmarks, either for the entire portfolio or for specific managers, then corrective measures can be taken by changing allocations or replacing managers. Further, it is important to evaluate the risks taken by the managers and to compare these to the performance. It is also important to stress that risk monitoring requires fairly sophisticated staff and computer software, as demonstrated before. Given the importance of risk management to the overall stability of the pension system, at least one staff member should be designated and trained to perform this function effectively.

SUMMARY

Managers should have qualified staff, clear responsibilities, and a good, clearly specified investment process and implementation procedures. Contracts and guidelines need to be developed and updated regularly to take into account changes in the markets. Thereafter, performance, costs, and risks need to be monitored frequently to ensure compliance. Finally, plan sponsors must ensure they work with financially secure firms.

1. See also Mennis and Clark (1983) and Kehrer (1991).

V

PEER COMPARISON

14

ESTABLISHING A PEER COMPARATOR UNIVERSE FOR AN INSTITUTIONAL INVESTOR

Arun S. Muralidhar and Khin Mala U

An objective way to establish an asset manager's ability to manage portfolios is to compare their performance to their policy benchmark and to their peers over relevant time periods. A pension plan's overall performance is composed of the policy benchmark return plus the relative excess return. In the pension fund/large institutional investor industry, the quality and precision of the peer evaluation is clouded by the following: (1) the comparisons do not distinguish between the performance of the policy benchmark and the relative excess return generated by the plan sponsors from deviating from their benchmarks; and (2) no attempt has been made to create the appropriate peer comparator universe by which to gauge the performance of a specific plan. This chapter corrects for the various problems and provides plans with an innovative approach to peer comparison.

OVERVIEW

Let us assume a pension plan has implemented all the previous recommendations for optimal investment and funding policy, manager selection and risk taking. One can legitimately ask: How well has the group performed relative to

Adapted from Arun S. Muralidhar and Khin Mala U. "Establishing a Peer Comparator Universe for an Institutional Investor." *Journal of Pension Plan Investing*, Volume 1, Number 4, Spring 1997.

the available opportunities? An objective way to establish the ability of plan sponsors to manage portfolios is to compare their performance to their policy benchmark and their peers, over relevant time periods.[1] More important, at all times the overall performance of the plan is composed of the policy benchmark returns plus the relative excess returns. In the pension fund/large institutional investor industry, the quality and precision of peer evaluation is clouded by the following: (1) the comparisons do not distinguish between the performance of the policy benchmark and relative excess returns generated by the plan sponsors from deviating from the benchmarks;[2] and (2) no attempt is made to create a peer comparator universe by which to gauge the performance of a given plan. Instead, the actual performance of a plan[3] is compared to that of a generic group of plans.

Of the two, the more serious problem for most plans has been the peer universe by which to measure respective policy benchmarks. In the past, a plan, regardless of orientation, has been compared to other U.S. pension plans and endowments, with the universe being determined by a minimum market value size (such as plans with a market value above or below $1 billion). However, that does not take into account the different risk characteristics of the various plans and runs into the classic "apples and oranges" problem. The question for an international plan such as the World Bank's (also referred to as the IBRD) is whether these peer comparisons are appropriate as the Bank's benchmark asset allocation, specifically the allocation to non-U.S. assets, is significantly different from those of the U.S. plans.[4] For example, the target allocation to non-U.S. equities was 39%, which was a high allocation relative to plans domiciled in the United States. However, the allocation was in some part a reflection of foreign currency liabilities.

This chapter attempts to correct this and outlines a simple method to establish a peer comparator universe for the policy benchmark and the excess return (or value added) relative to that benchmark. This approach is independent of the labels attached to either the type of plan or the amount invested in specific asset classes. Specifically, peer comparison is conducted after adjusting for risk rather than the size/market value of the plan or the amount invested in a particular asset class.

The remainder of the chapter discusses the need for peer comparison, explains the present methodology adopted by the industry, identifies shortcomings, and describes in detail the proposed alternative method. For ease of exposition, there are two different discussions for the evaluation of benchmark performance and the excess return relative to the benchmark.

Need for Peer Comparison

Plans select policy benchmarks either to maximize expected returns for a given level of risk (such as an efficient portfolio in the standard mean-variance paradigm) or because the risk-return profile of the portfolio assures sponsors that the various asset-liability risks are managed with some prespecified probability. Although performance relative to the benchmark is useful to determine the ability of the staff overseeing the plan, an objective method of evaluating how market opportunities are exploited is to see how other institutions in the same situation fare over a reasonable period of time. Any performance below the median of the appropriate peer universe is an indication that further review of staff and/or processes is required. It has already been shown in Chapters 5 and 7 that active management can lower asset-liability risk, even if there is no excess return. This chapter assumes that generating excess returns is an objective.

An alternative view of the need for peer comparison is driven by the core objective of the institution affiliated with these plans. In some cases, the oversight committee might specifically include a requirement that the investment team must match or outperform peers. This is usually true where underperformers harm the competitive ability of the institution. This could apply to corporations or educational endowments, where a competitive edge could be secured by freeing up funds that could otherwise be contributed to a pension plan or provide the institution more funds to attract staff or improve facilities.[5]

Current Peer Comparisons

The present methodology for a large plan involves submitting the policy benchmark and actual portfolio performance data to the vendors, who then identify the decile in which these portfolios would lie relative to all actual portfolio performances for plans with market values in excess of $1 billion for periods as short as one quarter and as long as 10 years. For example, a ranking of the World Bank's pension plan relative to peers, as prepared by Trust Universe Comparison Service (TUCS), is provided in Table 14.1. The extreme swing

Table 14.1
An Example of Current Peer Comparison and Ranking

	Q1 1996	1995	1994	1990–1995
World Bank returns	4.0%	16.7%	−2.1%	12.6%
World Bank policy benchmark	4.3%	22.2%	−0.4%	12.3%
TUCS[a] median	3.2%	24.7%	−0.2%	13.3%
TUCS decile ranking	2	10	10	7

[a]TUCS: Trust Universe Comparison Service.

in the decile ranking from 1995 to 1996 suggests some problems with this method. Often, plan sponsors may make internal adjustments to these analyses by establishing a subgroup of peers who have policy allocations similar to their own or those that represent similar institutions, such as endowments, public funds, and international organizations.

Problems with Current Peer Comparisons

The first obvious fault in the current process of peer comparison is the lack of distinction between performance attributable to the policy benchmark and excess return relative to the benchmark. The plan sponsor generates excess returns by deviating from the benchmark (through asset mix decisions and selection of managers). Therefore, in any period, a plan sponsor who underperforms a well-performing benchmark by a significant margin could be considered superior to a plan sponsor who outperforms a mediocre-performing benchmark for that period. Under the proposed scheme, the "apples" are separated from the "oranges" and, by recognizing that actual performance is equal to the policy return and excess return, plans are evaluated separately on the performance of their policy benchmark and the excess return added relative to a benchmark.[6]

The second problem with the current method is the screening process used to establish the appropriate peer comparator universe for either the policy benchmark evaluation or the excess return comparison. This method does not account for different risk tolerances of the respective committees in selecting policy benchmarks or excess return targets. As a result, plans with very different risk profiles are compared to each other.

The third problem is that the comparison is based on criteria established ex-post (based on the size of the plan) as opposed to ex-ante (after identifying the appropriate selection criteria).

Chapters 1 and 3 demonstrated multiple financial objectives that committees would like to achieve. If peer comparison is conducted with the above-mentioned process, it could result in an inappropriate asset allocation policy. Therefore, some attempt must be made to correct this to prevent funds from being forced into inefficient allocations.

At the most basic level, regardless of the multiple-objective specification, the policy benchmark, given long-term expectations about expected returns and volatilities of asset classes, could be represented as a portfolio with a given target expected return and volatility. For example, consider some reasonable assumptions on long-term expected returns and the variance-covariance matrix for some basic asset classes. For simplicity, the assumptions from Chapters 3 and 4 for asset classes are retained.[7] Using these assumptions, the World Bank's past policy implied an expected return of 9.52%, with a standard deviation of these returns of 11.93%. The expected return and risk of other plans based on their asset class allocations are provided in Table 14.3 and plotted in Figure 14.1.[8] These funds have been grouped into the following categories: international organizations (INT); U.S. corporates (COR); U.S. endowments (END); U.S. public funds (PF); and U.S. foundations (FND). One interesting observation is that even with limited data there is some clustering of results across sponsors in each of these groups. This clustering indicates that investment policies may be similar within groups, very different across groups, and in both cases irrelevant to size.

A NEW APPROACH

For convenience, the peer comparison of policy benchmarks and excess return is reviewed separately. For both analyses the same three questions are posed:

1. Who should be selected ex-ante as a peer?
2. How will the comparison be conducted?
3. What is the relevant time frame for this report card to be meaningful?

Comparison of Policy Benchmarks

Selection of Peers

Table 14.3 and Figure 14.1 demonstrate that although the long-term objectives (and liabilities) of different plans may not be aligned with those of the World Bank, the target risk-return preference of the plan sponsor is revealed through an analysis of their respective policy benchmarks.[9] Because a plan is likely to include a policy benchmark that minimizes the probability of funding embarrassments, the benchmark probably will unique to its liability structure and markedly different from other plans. However, the willingness to target a specific expected return and risk point is not markedly different from that of other plans. Therefore, for all institutions in general, and specifically for the World Bank, it would be more appropriate to establish, ex-ante, a peer comparator universe composed of plans whose policy portfolios lie in an acceptable neighborhood to the World Bank's point in risk-return space. In the case of endowments and corporations that explicitly define the objective as tracking peers, the policy portfolios should, and appear to be, very similar (Figure 14.1).

The process to establish the universe for the policy benchmark for a plan like the World Bank's can be easily understood as a progression of some simple steps.

Step 1. Create a table with long-term expected returns and a variance-covariance matrix for all asset classes. This data set should ideally include asset classes to which some plans may have no target exposure (such as commodities), but to which other plans may have made some long-term allocation (see Table 14.2). In some cases, specific asset classes such as hedge funds or event arbitrage cannot be modeled, but Step 2 assumes that such allocations are carved out from other asset classes, such as U.S. equities or private equities.

Step 2. Create a database of plan sponsor information by including all plans with assets in excess of $1 billion, without distinguishing between trusts, endowments, foundations, pension funds, or even nationality of the plans (see Table 14.3). Ideally, this data should include the target asset class weights in their policy benchmarks as well as permissible ranges across asset classes for asset mix decisions, as they will be needed for the second analysis.

Table 14.2

Data on Asset Classes for Peer Comparison

Asset Classes	Expected Returns (%)	Standard Deviations (%)	Correlations							
			USEQ	NUSEQ	USFI	NUSFI	HY	RE	PE	Cash
U.S. equities	10.5	15.0	1.0	0.5	0.4	0.1	0.5	0.1	0.4	0.1
Non-U.S. equities	10.5	19.7	0.5	1.0	0.2	0.4	0.2	0.1	0.1	−0.2
U.S. fixed income	6.5	5.2	0.4	0.2	1.0	0.2	0.3	0.0	0.0	0.1
Non-U.S. fixed income	6.5	12.6	0.1	0.4	0.2	1.0	0.0	0.0	0.0	−0.1
High-yield bonds	8.0	9.8	0.5	0.2	0.3	0.0	1.0	0.0	0.0	−0.2
Real estate	7.0	18.0	0.1	0.1	0.0	0.0	0.0	1.0	0.0	0.1
Private equity	10.5	27.0	0.4	0.1	0.0	0.0	0.0	0.0	1.0	0.0
Cash	5.2	1.4	0.1	−0.2	0.1	−0.1	−0.2	0.1	0.0	1.0

Step 3. Using the data gathered in previous steps, determine the expected benchmark return and benchmark standard deviation (risk) of all plans (see Table 14.3).[10]

Step 4. Set up ranges around the benchmark portfolio to establish which plans will be clearly excluded from the peer universe. For simplicity, we propose a range of plus or minus 1 percent around the benchmark risk target of the World Bank. Using the old World Bank benchmark portfolio as an example, this would include all plans whose standard deviation of benchmark returns are between 10.93 percent and 12.93 percent (Figure 14.1). From the limited sample in Table 14.3, this would result in only one international organization (INT1), one corporate (COR1), and four endowments for universities (END1, END3, END4, and END5) being included as peers for the policy benchmark. In a more expansive universe of plans, there would be many more peers.

Step 5. Instead of using the percentage weight allocated to each asset class as a means of determining the peers, establish the contribution to total benchmark risk of each asset class, as discussed in Chapter 8. It is quite possible that two plans with different allocations to Non-U.S. Equities (NUSEQ) could have identical contributions to total benchmark risk from NUSEQ, because of the interaction of this asset class with others in the portfolio. This calculation allows the plan sponsor to step back from unnecessary constraints to restrict the percentage allocation to individual asset classes so as to resemble

Table 14.3
Benchmark Composition for Different Funds

Asset Classes	World Bank	International Organization		Corporations				Endowments					Public Funds		Foundations			
		INT1[a]	INT2[b]	COR1	COR2	COR3	COR4	END1[c]	END2[d]	END3	END4[e]	END5[f]	PF1	PF2	FND1	FND2[g]	FND3[h]	FND4
U.S. equities	30.0	28.7	50.0	55.0	35.0	45.0	55.0	41.1	24.4	58.6	29.2	34.2	39.0	36.0	47.0	36.6	38.7	71.7
Non-U.S. equities	39.0	36.3	10.0	18.0	25.0	15.0	15.0	20.0	12.5	14.2	12.9	22.9	5.0	15.0	13.8	19.4	15.9	1.6
U.S. fixed income	7.0	9.1	15.0	22.0	22.5	17.0	25.0	12.8	12.2	12.6	12.8	11.4	54.0	24.0	20.0	13.9	34.9	10.1
Non-U.S. fixed income	11.0	9.1	0.0	0.0	5.0	5.0	0.0	4.1	0.0	0.8	5.2	0.0	0.0	5.0	6.0	6.5	0.0	0.0
High-yield bonds	2.0	0.0	0.0	0.0	0.0	0.0	0.0	4.4	10.5	0.0	1.1	1.6	0.0	11.0	0.0	1.9	0.0	0.0
Real estate	6.0	8.0	0.0	0.0	5.0	8.0	5.0	4.9	13.5	1.3	6.3	14.9	2.0	7.0	2.3	1.5	0.1	0.4
Private equity	5.0	8.3	15.0	0.0	7.5	10.0	0.0	14.5	25.1	8.3	27.5	14.4	0.0	0.0	3.1	12.5	10.4	0.0
Cash	0.0	0.5	10.0	5.0	0.0	0.0	0.0	-1.8	1.8	4.2	5.0	0.6	0.0	2.0	7.8	7.7	0.0	16.2
Total	100.0	100.0	100.0	100.0	100.0	100.0	100.0	100.0	100.0	100.0	100.0	100.0	100.0	100.0	100.0	100.0	100.0	100.0
Expected return	9.5	9.5	9.4	9.4	9.2	9.3	9.3	9.6	9.2	9.7	9.3	9.5	8.3	8.7	9.0	9.2	9.1	9.2
Risk	11.9	11.1	9.7	11.0	10.4	10.6	10.8	11.1	9.9	11.7	10.9	11.1	8.0	8.8	9.2	9.2	9.1	9.6

[a] Private equities includes 7.9% hedge funds.
[b] Private equities includes 15% other.
[c] U.S. equities includes 1.6% oil & gas; private equities includes 2.5% other.
[d] Private equities includes 0.6% hedge funds, 0.3% other; 5.7% event arbitrage; U.S. equities includes 2.9% oil & gas.
[e] Private equities includes 18.6% hedge funds & 0.4% other; U.S. equities includes 0.8% oil & gas.
[f] U.S. equities includes 0.2% oil & gas; private equities includes 3.2% other.
[g] Private equities includes 6.7% other.
[h] Private equities includes 10.4% other; U.S. fixed income includes non-U.S. fixed income and cash.

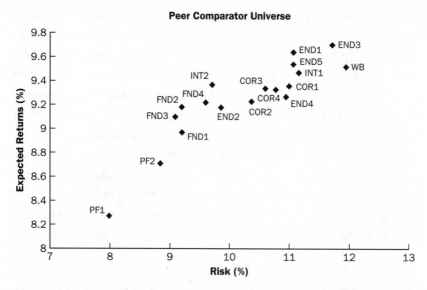

Figure 14.1   Expected Performance and Risk of Benchmarks for Different Funds

peers.[11] This is not a major step, but it is useful for ex-post analysis. This analysis would also ensure that two plans with different target allocations to the various asset classes could be considered peers as long as they have similar risk characteristics.

Step 6. More important, although plans may have identical long-term risk-return points, the performance of their benchmark portfolios may or may not be correlated in the short term. Based on the analysis in Step 5, and simulations of all portfolios, one should segregate the set of peer portfolios into three buckets based on the correlation of other plans' benchmark policies to that of their own; namely high (correlation coefficient 0.68–1), medium (correlation coefficient 0.33–0.67), or low (correlation coefficient 0.0–0.32). If all plans had the same liabilities, one could interpret lower correlations to indicate that the objective functions (in meeting alternative asset-liability management criteria) are quite different for the plans. Differences in liabilities make the correlation more tricky to interpret.

Peer Comparison and Degree of Precision

Step 7. Rank the performance of policy benchmarks as is presently conducted for actual performance. However, the oversight committee should be made aware of the degree of precision that can be derived from such an analysis and the minimum period required to separate the signal from the noise of performance data. In this framework, luck and skill would relate to the ability to select appropriate target weights in establishing a benchmark with the highest return for a given level of risk. It is critical to do this step as it tempers (ex-ante) the expectations of the oversight committee. Tables 14.4, 14.5, and 14.6 use the methodology in Chapter 9 to estimate the relevance of a comparison of the previous World Bank policy portfolio with those of the INT1, END1, and COR1, respectively, over a range of 1 year to 30 years, for different correlation assumptions. (As correlations have not been estimated due to the unavailability of data, these results are presented for the different peers to demonstrate the impact of different correlation outcomes.) The uncertainty constant

Table 14.4

Comparing the IBRD to an International Plan (INT1): Confidence Estimates Based on Correlation, for Different Periods

Time (Years)	Uncertainty Constant	% Signal (100% = Perfect)	Time (Years)	Uncertainty Constant	% Signal (100% = Perfect)
Correlation = 1			**Correlation = 0.33**		
1	0.05	52	1	0.00	50
2	0.07	53	2	0.00	50
3	0.09	54	3	0.01	50
5	0.12	55	5	0.01	50
8	0.15	56	8	0.01	50
10	0.16	57	10	0.01	50
15	0.20	58	15	0.01	50
20	0.23	59	20	0.01	51
30	0.29	61	30	0.02	51
Correlation = 0.67					
1	0.00	50			
2	0.01	50			
3	0.01	50			
5	0.01	50			
8	0.01	50			
10	0.01	51			
15	0.02	51			
20	0.02	51			
30	0.02	51			

Note: For all three correlations, the mean returns are 9.5% for both INT1 and IBRD, and the standard deviations are 11.1% for INT1 and 11.9% for IBRD.

Table 14.5

Comparing the IBRD to an Endowment Fund (END1): Confidence Estimates
Based on Correlation, for Different Periods

Time (Years)	Uncertainty Constant	% Signal (100% = Perfect)	Time (Years)	Uncertainty Constant	% Signal (100% = Perfect)
Correlation = 1			**Correlation = 0.33**		
1	0.25	60	1	0.02	51
2	0.36	64	2	0.02	51
3	0.44	67	3	0.03	51
5	0.56	71	5	0.04	51
8	0.71	76	8	0.05	52
10	0.79	79	10	0.05	52
15	0.97	83	15	0.06	53
20	1.12	87	20	0.07	53
30	1.38	92	30	0.09	54
Correlation = 0.67					
1	0.02	51			
2	0.03	51			
3	0.04	52			
5	0.05	52			
8	0.07	53			
10	0.07	53			
15	0.09	54			
20	0.11	54			
30	0.13	55			

Note: For all three correlations, the mean returns are 9.6% for END1 and 9.5% for IBRD, and the standard deviations are 11.1% for END1 and 11.9% for IBRD.

is the parameter 'K' in Chapter 9. The tables show that if the correlation is below 0.68, the data has approximately 50 percent signal to 50 percent noise for all periods, making it difficult to determine whether the investment team was skillful or lucky in selecting a benchmark that outperforms peers. If the correlation is high, in cases like the END1 comparison (Table 14.5), any outperformance data has a significant signal even after 5 years. However, in cases like the INT1 and COR1 comparisons (Tables 14.4 and 14.6), when the correlation is high, there is a fair amount of noise even after 30 years. This analysis allows for an estimate of confidence for each comparison (such as for comparison of 1-year, 3-year, and 5-year performance), with peer plans in different correlation buckets.

Step 8. Finally, the proposed approach assumes that policies remain unchanged. This may not seem to be a reasonable assumption, but the policy

Table 14.6

Comparing the IBRD to a Corporate Fund (COR1): Confidence Estimates
Based on Correlation, for Different Periods

Time (Years)	Uncertainty Constant	% Signal (100% = Perfect)	Time (Years)	Uncertainty Constant	% Signal (100% = Perfect)
Correlation = 1			Correlation = 0.33		
1	0.05	52	1	0.00	50
2	0.07	53	2	0.01	50
3	0.09	54	3	0.01	50
5	0.12	55	5	0.01	50
8	0.15	56	8	0.01	50
10	0.16	57	10	0.01	50
15	0.20	58	15	0.01	51
20	0.23	59	20	0.02	51
30	0.29	61	30	0.02	51
Correlation = 0.67					
1	0.01	50			
2	0.01	50			
3	0.01	50			
5	0.01	50			
8	0.02	51			
10	0.02	51			
15	0.02	51			
20	0.02	51			
30	0.03	51			

Note: For all three correlations, the mean returns are 9.4% for COR1 and 9.5% for IBRD, and the standard deviations are 11.0% for COR1 and 11.9% for IBRD.

benchmarks and the performance of the universe of plans must be tracked on a regular basis to update the database for any changes. Any plan that makes changes to its policy benchmark, which would place it in or exclude it from the desired cluster, would be a candidate for inclusion into or exclusion from this peer universe for the policy benchmark. In addition, a similar analysis can be conducted for each asset class.

Comparisons of Excess Returns

Selection of Peers

The problem in establishing this universe is to determine ex-ante a reasonable expected excess return for a plan, and a corresponding variance or standard

Table 14.7
Comparison of Simulated Tracking Error for Permissible Ranges

	Mean (bps)	Fifth Percentile (bps)	Ninety-Fifth Percentile (bps)	Tracking Error (bps)	Information Ratio
World Bank	74	142	5	41	1.82
INT1	57	114	3	34	1.67
END1	44	109	−12	39	1.13
COR1	64	129	10	39	1.64

deviation for that expected excess return (tracking error). This is the most difficult step, as staff must identify the subset of plans with the same distribution of feasible excess returns from tactical deviations vis-à-vis the World Bank.

In many cases, the range data may be difficult to procure, as some plans may not have explicit ranges or may not be willing to divulge such information. However, where such data is available, establish the distribution of excess returns by simulating possible portfolios within these constraints. Given the limited data available on policy benchmarks and permissible ranges, 500 possible random deviations from the benchmark portfolio on historical data were simulated. Estimates were made on the mean excess return and standard deviation of excess returns of these data points for the World Bank, INT1, END1, and COR1.[12] Table 14.7 gives the results of these simulations.

More important, from this set, identify a subset whose tactical risk tolerance (that is, tracking error generated from the range provided to plan sponsors with respect to the decisions to underweight and overweight individual asset classes) is similar. In the case of the limited sample of three other plans, the tracking errors are within a range of 7 bps. whereas the mean expected excess returns ranges from 44 bps (END1) to 74 bps (IBRD).[13] It is useful to determine the correlations for the excess return data across these plans.

Peer Comparison and Degree of Precision

Once again, perform peer comparison by ranking all the plans for the different horizons based on realized excess returns relative to benchmarks. As Tables 14.8

Table 14.8

Comparing Excess Returns for the IBRD and a Corporate Fund: Confidence
Estimates Based on Correlation, for Different Periods

Time (Years)	Uncertainty Constant	% Signal (100% = Perfect)	Time (Years)	Uncertainty Constant	% Signal (100% = Perfect)
Correlation = 1			Correlation = 0.33		
1	5.00	100	1	0.22	59
2	7.07	100	2	0.30	62
3	8.65	100	3	0.37	65
5	11.17	100	5	0.48	69
8	14.13	100	8	0.61	73
10	15.80	100	10	0.68	75
15	19.35	100	15	0.84	80
20	22.34	100	20	0.96	83
30	27.36	100	30	1.18	88
Correlation = 0.67					
1	0.31	62			
2	0.43	67			
3	0.53	70			
5	0.69	75			
8	0.87	81			
10	0.97	83			
15	1.19	88			
20	1.37	92			
30	1.68	95			

Note: For all three correlations, the mean returns are 0.6% for COR1 and 0.7% for IBRD, and the standard
deviations are 0.4% for both COR1 and IBRD.

through 14.10 demonstrate, in contrast to the benchmark policy comparisons,
excess return comparisons for plans with similar tactical risk tolerances are
meaningful over short periods of time, regardless of correlation.

CAVEATS AND EXTENSIONS

Because the method assumed that the plan sponsor conducted the evaluation,
it runs the risk that the assumptions are specific only to the plan sponsor, such
as estimates of expected returns, volatilities, and correlations. Therefore, it is
quite possible that an institution that is considered a peer may not consider the

Table 14.9

Comparing Excess Returns for the IBRD and an Endowment Fund: Confidence
Estimates Based on Correlation, for Different Periods

Time (Years)	Uncertainty Constant	% Signal (100% = Perfect)	Time (Years)	Uncertainty Constant	% Signal (100% = Perfect)
Correlation = 1			Correlation = 0.33		
1	15.00	100	1	0.65	74
2	21.21	100	2	0.92	82
3	25.97	100	3	1.12	87
5	33.53	100	5	1.45	93
8	42.42	100	8	1.83	97
10	47.42	100	10	2.05	98
15	58.08	100	15	2.51	99
20	67.06	100	20	2.89	100
30	82.14	100	30	3.55	100
Correlation = 0.67					
1	0.92	82			
2	1.30	90			
3	1.60	94			
5	2.06	98			
8	2.61	100			
10	2.91	100			
15	3.57	100			
20	4.12	100			
30	5.05	100			

Note: For all three correlations, the mean returns are 0.4% for COR1 and 0.7% for IBRD, and the standard deviations are 0.4% for both COR1 and IBRD.

plan sponsor to be a peer of the plan. In addition, all possible asset classes need to be identified and utilized in generating these estimates. Ideally, a vendor will take on such responsibilities with a consistent set of data, thereby eliminating any idiosyncrasies from the process and expanding the number of institutions included. Also, expectations of potential excess return are based on tactical asset allocation and cannot capture what the plan hopes to achieve from manager selection. It is implicitly assumed that all plans have identical expectations. Finally, the analysis presented here does not depend on the type of investment business, but on the tolerance for risk/return and active tactical risk. Therefore, this method can be used for any investment portfolios within an organization.

Table 14.10

Comparing Excess Returns for the IBRD and an International Plan: Confidence
Estimates Based on Correlation, for Different Periods

Time (Years)	Uncertainty Constant	% Signal (100% = Perfect)	Time (Years)	Uncertainty Constant	% Signal (100% = Perfect)
Correlation = 1			Correlation = 0.33		
1	5.00	100	1	0.22	59
2	7.07	100	2	0.30	62
3	8.65	100	3	0.37	65
5	11.17	100	5	0.48	69
8	14.13	100	8	0.61	73
10	15.80	100	10	0.68	75
15	19.35	100	15	0.84	80
20	22.34	100	20	0.96	83
30	27.36	100	30	1.18	88
Correlation = 0.67					
1	0.31	62			
2	0.43	67			
3	0.53	70			
5	0.69	75			
8	0.87	81			
10	0.97	83			
15	1.19	88			
20	1.37	92			
30	1.68	95			

Note: For all three correlations, the mean returns are 0.6% for COR1 and 0.7% for IBRD, and the standard deviations are 0.4% for both COR1 and IBRD.

SUMMARY

This chapter highlighted the investment truths summarized in the accompanying box.

The new approach thus proposes that the peer comparator universe for the benchmark of a plan be composed of plans with policy portfolios within a pre-specified cluster in risk-return space, around the policy portfolio of the plan, without necessarily adjusting for size or type of plan or the allocation to any specific asset class. However, it is proposed that differences in allocations to various asset classes be used to temper and direct expectations of the oversight committee, rather than to create the peer universe. Hence, two plans with different target allocations to the various asset classes can be considered peers if

INVESTMENT TRUTHS

- *Current methods of peer comparison are flawed because they do not distinguish between benchmark performance and excess over benchmark.*

- *Peers for the benchmark and excess return comparison need to be selected based on risk characteristics rather than the size of assets.*

- *Short-term peer comparisons (i.e., comparisons based on less than 5 years) for benchmarks have a significant amount of noise (up to 40 percent of the outperformance) even for very similar plans.*

- *Comparisons for excess return are meaningful over short periods, even for very dissimilar plans.*

they meet the risk criteria outlined here. For the comparison of excess returns, institutions will be included as peers based on the tracking error permitted by the committees. On that basis, it is quite possible that the universe for the policy benchmark and the excess return encompass different plans. This clearly argues for revamping the present method of doing peer analysis.

1. We address appropriate time periods for analysis later in the chapter.

2. We assume that the policy benchmark establishes long-term asset class allocations based on expected long-term asset class returns. To the extent that target allocations are changed, in this context we consider it a change in policy. Plans attempt to add positive relative excess returns by under- or overweighting asset classes (asset mix decisions) based on short-term return expectations and select investment managers to outperform market indices. These decisions generate risk relative to the benchmark. Research shows that up to 90% of overall return can be attributed to the policy benchmark (Brinson, Singer, and Beebower 1991).

3. For simplicity, assume all endowments, trusts, and pension plans are referred to as "plans."

4. The World Bank reviewed its asset policy for implementation in 1997. For this chapter, we use the policy allocation effective between 1991 and 1996.

5. We extend thanks to Messrs. Verne Sedlacek and Michael Pradko of the Harvard Management Co., Inc., for pointing this out to us.

6. In addition to overall plan rankings, the vendors also provide decile rankings within specific asset classes (e.g., U.S. equities, and non-U.S. equities). This data is useful, but once again to the extent that different plans have different benchmarks for the same asset class, the comparison is inadequate in its present form. For example, within U.S. equities, a plan may adhere to the Wilshire 5000, while other plans may follow the S&P 500. We ignore this problem for now, but it can be corrected in a similar fashion. However, to the extent that alternative benchmarks are very highly correlated, the present methodology is acceptable.

7. These long-term assumptions would normally be used to establish target weights and were tested against those of investment management companies and consultants and found to be within reasonable bands of consistency.

8. This is a limited database; the plans in Table 14.3 were selected at random, based on data availability to illustrate the point. We thank Cambridge Associates and The Northern Trust Company for providing us with the policy information of large plans (pension for public and private organizations, endowments, foundations and trusts) on a "no names" basis.

9. The caveat here is that we have had to compress different allocations into broad asset classes and hence allocations to hedge funds, and event arbitrage are included in private equities (for their risk characteristics). At this stage, commodities are included under U.S. equities. This can be overcome in a more detailed analysis.

10. When viewing these portfolios in risk-return space, it is not possible to conclude that portfolios not on the "efficient frontier" are inferior as they could be motivated by asset-liability management considerations and by different expected returns or variance-covariance assumptions. We thank Mr. David Wilton for this point and will address this later.

11. The analogy to risk management for currency overlay is worth pointing out as one could ignore hedge ratio ranges as a means of controlling risk, and instead monitor only the portfolio tracking error and contribution to total tracking error of any bet. See Mashayekhi-Beschloss and Muralidhar (1996).

12. Ideally, we would have like to perform this analysis on all plans. This estimate only captures the expected excess return from overweighting or underweighting asset classes and not manager selection.

13. In this section, selection is based on risk of the actual portfolio relative to the respective benchmarks. Should the absolute risk of the benchmark and actual portfolio be a more important measure of risk for a plan, an alternative method would have been to plot the efficient frontier using the data in Table 14.2. Then, for any plan, the expected excess return that can be achieved without increasing the absolute risk would be the vertical distance (along the expected return axis) between the policy portfolio and the efficient frontier. This is clearly a more difficult method to implement.

REFERENCES

Ambachtsheer, K.P. 1997. Pension Fund Governance, Operations and Value Creation, in *Pension Fund Investment Management,* ed. F. Fabozzi, Frank Fabozzi Associates, New Hope, Pa.

Ambachtsheer, K.P., R. Capelle and T. Scheibelhut. 1998. Improving Pension Fund Performance. *Financial Analysts Journal,* 54(6):15–21.

Ambachtsheer, K.P., and D. Ezra. 1998. *Pension Fund Excellence: Creating Value for Stakeholders,* Wiley, New York.

Ambarish, R., and Seigel, L. 1996. Time Is the Essence. *Risk,* August 1996, 9(8).

Ankrim, E. 1998. Peer Relative Active Portfolio Performance: It's Even Worse Than We Thought. *The Journal of Portfolio Management,* 2(4), Summer.

Arnott, R. 1990. Managing the Asset Mix—Decisions and Consequences, in *Pension Fund Investment Management: A Handbook for Sponsors and their Advisors,* eds. F. Fabozzi and N. Mencher, Probus, Chicago.

Arnott, R., and P. Bernstein. 1990. Defining and Managing Pension Fund Risk, in *Pension Fund Investment Management: A Handbook for Sponsors and their Advisors,* eds. F. Fabozzi and N. Mencher, Probus, Chicago.

Asad-Syed, K., A. Muralidhar and R.J.P. van der Wouden. 1998. Determination of Replacement Rates for Savings Schemes, *The World Bank IMD Model Development Paper 1,* World Bank, Washington DC.

Asad-Syed, K., and A. Muralidhar. 1998. An Asset Liability Approach to Value-at-Risk. *Investment Management Department Working Paper Series 98-023,* World Bank, Washington DC.

Asad-Syed, K., A. Muralidhar and P. Pasquariello. 2000. Understanding Risk—Estimating the Contribution to Total Risk of Individual Bets. *Unpublished Working Paper.*

Bader, L.N. 1995. The Financial Executive's Guide to Pension Plans—1995 Edition. *Salomon Brothers United States Investment Research-Pension Services.* New York, January.

Bailey, J.V. 1997. Investment Policy: The Missing Link, in *Pension Fund Investment Management,* ed. F. Fabozzi, Frank Fabozzi Associates, New Hope, Pa.

Balana, A., and R. Weary. 1998. A Decision-Based Approach to Performance Attribution. *Investment Management Department Working Paper Series,* World Bank, Washington, DC.

Baldridge, J., B. Meath and H. Myers. 2000. Capturing Alpha Through Active Currency Overlay. *Frank Russell Research Commentary,* May.

Barclays Global Investors. 1998. Futures vs. Physicals: Implementing an International Portfolio for the US Investor. *Investment Insights,* March.

Baz, J., F. Breedon, V. Naik and J. Peress. 1999. Optimal Currency Portfolios: Trading on the Forward Bias. *Lehman Brothers Analytical Research Series,* October.

Bensman, M. 1996. Brave New World Bank. *Institutional Investor Magazine,* September 1.

Black, F. 1989. Universal Hedging: Optimizing Currency Risk and Reward in International Equity Portfolios. *Financial Analysts Journal,* July/August.

Blake, D. 2000. Does It Matter What Type of Pension You Have? *The Economic Journal,* 110 (February): F46–81.

Blake D., A.J.G. Cairns and K. Dowd. 2000. Optimal Dynamic Asset Allocation for Defined Benefit Pension Plans. *The Pensions Institute Discussion Paper PI-0003,* Birkbeck College, London, February.

Blume, M. 1998. An Anatomy of Morningstar Ratings. *Financial Analysts Journal,* 54(2):19–27.

Bodie Z., A.J. Marcus and R.C. Merton. 1988. Defined Benefit Versus Defined Contribution Pension Plans: What Are the Real Trade-offs. In *Pensions in the U.S. Economy,* by Z. Bodie, J.B. Shoven and D.A. Wise, University of Chicago Press, pp. 139–162.

Bodie, Z., R.C. Merton and W.F. Samuelson. 1992. Labor Supply Flexibility and Portfolio Choice in a Life Cycle Model. *Journal of Economic Dynamics and Control,* 16:427–449, July/October.

Boender, Guus C.E. 1997. A Hybrid Simulation/Optimization Scenario Model for Asset/Liability Management. *European Journal of Operations Research*, 99:126–135.

Boender, Guus C.E. 1998. Optimal Rebalancing for Defined Benefit Pension Plans. *Erasmus University Working Paper*, Rotterdam.

Boender, G.C.E., and F. Heemskerk. 1995. A Static Scenario Optimization Model for Asset/Liability Management of Defined Benefit Plans. *Report 9512/A Econometric Institute, Erasmus University Working Paper*, Rotterdam.

Boender, G.C.E., B. Oldenkamp and M. Vos. 1997. Solvency Insurance with Optioned Portfolios: An Empirical Investigation. *Proceedings of the 7th International AFIR Colloquium*, Australia.

Boender, G.C.E., P.C. van Aalst and F. Heemskerk. 1999. Modeling and Management of Assets and Liabilities of Pension Plans in the Netherlands, in *Worldwide Asset-Liability Modeling*, eds. W.T. Ziemba and J. Mulvey. Cambridge University Press.

Boender, G.C.E., and M. Vos. 2000. Risk-Return Budgeting at Pension Plans, in *Risk Budgeting: A Cutting Edge Approach to Enhancing Fund Management*, ed. R. Layard-Liesching. Institutional Investor, May, pp. 80–88.

Bogle, J.C. 1998. The First Index Fund. In *Indexing for Maximum Investment Results*, ed. A.S. Neubert, Glenlake.

Brennan, M. 1993. Agency and Asset Pricing. *Anderson Graduate School of Management Working Paper*, Los Angeles, May.

Brinson, G.P., B.D. Singer and G.L. Beebower. 1991. Determinants of Portfolio Performance II: An Update. *Financial Analysts Journal*, 47(3):40–48.

Burton, E. 1996. Derivatives: Is There a Future for Them in Pension Funds. *Presentation to Pensions and Investments Investment Management Conference*, Washington DC, December.

Chicago Board of Exchange. 1998. ERISA Pension Funds and Listed Options: Portfolio Management Strategies. *The Chicago Board of Exchange Investor Series*, No. 4.

Chung, K., and M. Granito. 2000. Characteristics of Manager Excess Return. *JP Morgan Flemings Asset Management—Strategic Investment Advisory Note*, New York, October.

Chung, K., M. Granito and R. Prajogi. 2001. U.S. Corporate Pension Financial Performance: Review and Outlook 2001. *JP Morgan Fleming Asset Management—Strategic Investment Advisory Note*, New York, February.

Damato, K. 1996. Morningstar Edges Toward One-Year Ratings. *Wall Street Journal,* April 5:C1.

De Bever, L., W. Kozun and B. Zvan. 2000. Risk Budgeting in a Pension Fund, in *Risk Budgeting, A New Approach to Investing,* ed. L. Rahl, Risk Books, London.

De Marco, M., and T. Petzel. 2000. Risk Budgeting with Conditional Risk Tolerance, in *Risk Budgeting, A New Approach to Investing,* ed. L. Rahl, Risk Books, London.

Dert, C. L. 1995. Asset Liability Management for Pension Funds. Ph.D. thesis, Erasmus University, Rotterdam.

Demakis, D. 1997. Optimization of Active Risk Across Asset Classes. *Rogers Casey Research Insights.*

Divecha, A., and R. Grinold. 1990. How Sponsors Can Use Normal Portfolios, in *Pension Fund Investment Management: A Handbook for Sponsors and their Advisors,* eds. F. Fabozzi and N. Mencher, Probus, Chicago.

Dynkin, L., J. Hyman and W. Wu. 1997. Replicating Index Returns with Treasury Futures. *Lehman Brothers Fixed Income Research,* November.

England, R.S. 2001. The Hole in ERISA. *Plan Sponsor Magazine,* January.

Ezra, D.D. 1991. Asset Allocation by Surplus Optimization. *Financial Analysts Journal,* 47(1):51–57.

Gibson III, L. 1997. Managing Firmwide Risk for Pension Funds, in *Pension Fund Investment Management,* ed. F. Fabozzi, Frank Fabozzi Associates, New Hope, Pa.

Graham, J.R., and C.R. Harvey. 1997. Grading the Performance of Market Timing Newsletters. *Financial Analysts Journal,* 53(6):54–66.

Grinold, R. 1990. The Sponsor's View of Risk, in *Pension Fund Investment Management: A Handbook for Sponsors and their Advisors,* eds. F. Fabozzi and N. Mencher, Probus, Chicago.

Grinold, R., and R. Meese. 2000. Strategic Asset Allocation and International Investing. *Journal of Portfolio Management,* 27(1):53–60.

Gupta, F., R. Prajogi and E. Stubbs. 1999. The Information Ratio and Performance—Implications for Tracking Error Budgeting. *Journal of Portfolio Management,* Fall, 26(1).

Hammond, D.R. 1997. Establishing Performance-Related Termination Thresholds for Investment Management, in *Pension Fund Investment Management,* ed. F. Fabozzi, Frank Fabozzi Associates, New Hope, Pa.

Harvard Business School. 1983. GTE Corporation (A). *Harvard Business School*, Harvard University Press, Cambridge, Mass.

Harvard Business School. 1986. GTE Corporation (B). *Harvard Business School*, Harvard University Press, Cambridge, Mass.

Harvard Business School. 1993. GTE Corporation (C). *Harvard Business School*, Harvard University Press, Cambridge, Mass.

Hersey, B., and J. Minnick. 2000. Active Managers Generating Positive Excess Returns over Benchmarks. *Global Pensions,* February.

Hill, J. 1998. Derivatives in Equity Portfolios. *Derivatives in Portfolio Management,* Goldman Sachs Research.

Hulbert, M. 2001. Same Yardsticks, Different Races. *The New York Times,* January 7: BU20.

Hunter, R. 1998. Derivatives? Not There. *Derivatives Strategy.* December.

Ibbotson, R.G., and Brinson, G. P. 1993. Global Investing, in *Guide to the World's Capital Markets,* McGraw-Hill, pp. 88–89.

Kehrer, D. 1991. *The Pension Plan Investor: A Guide for Fund Managers and Sponsors in Today's Complex and Uncertain Times,* Probus, Chicago.

Krishnamurthi, S., A. Muralidhar and R.J.P. van der Wouden. 1998a. Pension Investment Decisions. *The World Bank Investment Management Department Working Paper 98-001,* Washington, DC, May.

Krishnamurthi, S., A. Muralidhar and R.J.P. van der Wouden. 1998b. An Asset-Liability Analysis of Retirement Plans. *The World Bank Investment Management Department Working Paper 98-004,* Washington, DC, May.

Kutler, V.A. 1997. Money Manager Selection: A Top-Down Approach, in *Pension Fund Investment Management,* ed. F. Fabozzi, Frank Fabozzi Associates, New Hope, Pa.

Laubscher, P., A. Muralidhar and M. Reynolds. 2001. A Primer on Performance for Currency Overlay. *Journal of Management Performance,* forthcoming.

Leibowitz M., L. Bader and S. Kogelman. 1992. Asset Allocation Under Liability Uncertainty. *Journal of Fixed Income,* 2(2):7–20.

Leibowitz, M., L. Bader and S. Kogelman. 1996. *Return Targets and Shortfall Risks: Studies in Strategic Asset Allocation.* Irwin Professional Publications, Chicago.

Litterman, R. 1996. Hot Spots™ and Hedges. *Goldman Sachs Risk Management Series,* October.

Logue, D.E., and J.S. Rader. 1997. *Managing Pension Plans: A Comprehensive Guide to Improving Plan Performance (Financial Management Association*

Survey and Synthesis Series), Harvard Business School Press, Cambridge, Mass.

MacBeth, J.D., D.C. Emanuel and C.E. Heatter. 1994. An Investment Strategy for Defined Benefit Plans. *Financial Analysts Journal*, 50(3):34–41.

Mantel, J., and D. Bowers. 1999. European Pension Reforms. *Merrill Lynch European Strategy*, September.

Markowitz, H. 1959. *Portfolio Selection.* Wiley, New York.

Mashayekhi-Beschloss, A., and Muralidhar, A. 1996. Managing the Implementation Risks of a Currency Overlay. *Journal of Pension Plan Investing*, Winter, 1(3):79–93.

Mehrzad, K., and A. Muralidhar. 2000. Risk Control and Active Currency Management. *Investments and Pensions—Europe*, September.

Mennis, E.A., and C.D. Clark. 1983. Understanding Corporate Pension Plans, *Financial Analysts Research Foundation*, Charlottesville, Va.

Menssen, M.J. 1997. Appendix: Illustration of an Investment Policy, in *Pension Fund Investment Management*, ed. F. Fabozzi, Frank Fabozzi Associates, New Hope, Pa.

Modigliani, F., and A. Ando. 1963. The Lifecycle Hypothesis of Savings: Aggregated Implications and Tests, *American Economic Review*, 53:55–84.

Modigliani, F., and R. Brumberg. 1954. Utility Analysis and the Consumption Function—An Interpretation of Cross Section Data, in *Post-Keynesian Economics*, ed. K.K. Kurihara, Rutgers University Press, New Brunswick, N.J.

Modigliani, F., and L. Modigliani. 1997. Risk-Adjusted Performance. *The Journal of Portfolio Management*, 23(2):45–54.

Modigliani, F., and A. Muralidhar. 1998. Latin American Pension Reforms—A Critique. *MIT Sloan School of Management Working Paper*, August.

Modigliani, L. 1998. Risk-Adjusted Performance. *Morgan Stanley Dean Witter Research.*

Mulvey, J., and W.T. Ziemba (eds). 1999. *Worldwide Asset-Liability Modeling.* Cambridge University Press, Cambridge, U.K.

Muralidhar, A. 1998a. Manager Selection. *The World Bank Investment Management Department Working Paper*, Washington, DC, March.

Muralidhar, A. 1998b. Managing Pension Funds Efficiently. *The World Bank Investment Management Department Working Paper*, Washington, DC, July.

Muralidhar, A. 1999a. Luck or Skill? *Investments and Pensions—Europe*, September.

Muralidhar, A. 1999b. The Death of the CAPM. *Unpublished Working Paper.*

Muralidhar, A. 1999c. Reforming Pension Reform: The Importance of Guaranteed Return Products. *Unpublished Working Paper.*

Muralidhar, A. 2000. Risk-Adjusted Performance—The Correlation Correction. *Financial Analysts Journal,* 56(5):63–71.

Muralidhar, A. 2001. Optimal Risk-Adjusted Portfolios with Multiple Managers. *Journal of Portfolio Management,* 27(3):97–104.

Muralidhar, A., and S. Muralidhar. 2001. A Better Approach to Rating Mutual Funds—The Importance of Skill. *Unpublished Working Paper.*

Muralidhar, A., and P. Pasquariello. 2001. Views: Use and Abuse. *Journal of Asset Management,* 2(1):47–55.

Muralidhar, A., and R. Prajogi. 2001. Persistence of Manager Performance with Implications for Allocating Risk. *Unpublished Working Paper.*

Muralidhar, A., R. Prajogi and R.J.P. van der Wouden. 2000. An Asset-Liability Analysis of the Currency Decision for Pension Plans. *Derivatives Quarterly,* 7(2).

Muralidhar, A., and M. Tsumagari. 1998. Derivative Strategies. *The World Bank Investment Management Department Working Paper,* Washington, DC, August.

Muralidhar, A., and M. Tsumagari. 1999. Action Stations. *Futures and OTC World,* April.

Muralidhar, A., and K.M. U. 1997. Establishing a Peer Comparator Universe for an Institutional Investor. *Journal of Pension Plan Investing,* 1(4). Spring.

Muralidhar, A., and R.J.P. van der Wouden. 1998a. Reforming Pension Reform— The Case for Contributory Defined Benefit Second Pillars. *The World Bank Investment Management Department Working Paper,* Washington, DC, May.

Muralidhar, A., and R.J.P. van der Wouden. 1998b. Welfare Costs of Defined Contribution Plans—The Case for an Alternative Scheme. *The World Bank Investment Management Department Working Paper,* Washington, DC, May.

Muralidhar, A., and R.J.P. van der Wouden. 2000. Optimal ALM Strategies for Defined Benefit Plans. *Journal of Risk,* 2(2):47–69.

Muralidhar, A., and R. Weary. 1998a. The Greater Fool Theory of Asset Management. *The World Bank Investment Management Department Working Paper,* Washington, DC, September.

Muralidhar, A. and R. Weary. 1998b. The Case for an Improved Non-US Equity Benchmark. *The World Bank Investment Management Department Working Paper,* Washington, DC, September.

Mutual Fund Fact Book, 1999, Investment Company Institute, May.

Myners Review of Institutional Investment, National Association of Pension Funds, UK.

Nakovick, N. 1999. Management Strategies in a Changing Market, in *Perspectives on Investment Management of Public Pension Funds,* ed. F. Fabozzi, Frank Fabozzi Associates, New Hope, Pa.

Nesbitt, S.L. 1991. Currency Hedging Rules for Plan Sponsors. *Financial Analysts Journal,* 47(2):73–81.

Perold, A.F., and E.C. Schulman. 1988. The Free Lunch in Currency Hedging: Implications for Investment Policy and Performance Standards. *Financial Analysts Journal,* 44(3):45–52.

Peskin, M. 1997. Asset Allocation and Funding Policy for Corporate-Sponsored Defined-Benefit Pension Plans. *Journal of Portfolio Management,* 23(2):66–73.

Philips, T.K. 1997. Measures of Risk for Portfolio Optimization and Asset/ Liability Modeling, in *Pension Fund Investment Management,* ed. F. Fabozzi, Frank Fabozzi Associates, New Hope, Pa.

Philips, T.K. 1999. The Pros and Cons of Indexing Pension Assets, in *Perspectives on Investment Management of Public Pension Funds,* ed. F. Fabozzi, Frank Fabozzi Associates, New Hope, Pa.

Philips, T.K., and E. Yashchin. 1999. Monitoring Manager Performance Using Statistical Process Control. *Unpublished Working Paper.*

Rahl, L. 2000. Risk Budgeting: The Next Step of the Risk Management Journey— The Veteran's Perspective, in *Risk Budgeting, A New Approach to Investing,* ed. L. Rahl, Risk Books, London.

Reinert, T. 2000. Practical Active Currency Management for Global Equity Portfolios. *Journal of Portfolio Management,* 26(4):41–48.

Risk Standards for Institutional Investment Managers and Institutional Investors by Risk Standards Working Group, composed of Suzanne Brenner of The Rockefeller Foundation, Kevin Bryne of The Equitable Companies, Christopher J. Campisano of the Xerox Corporation, Mary Cottrill of CalPERS, Michael deMarco of GTE Investment Management, Jon Lukomnik of City of New York Office of the Comptroller, Richard Rose of San Diego County Employees' Retirement Association, David Russ of the Pacific Telesis Group, James Seymour of The Common Fund, Kathy Wassmann of R.R. Donnelley & Sons Co, and Gregory Williamson of the Amoco Corporation.

Roll, R. 1992. A Mean/Variance Analysis of Tracking Error. *Journal of Portfolio Management,* 18(4):13–23.

Ryan, R. 1997. Pension Liabilities: The True Objectives, in *Pension Fund Investment Management,* ed. F. Fabozzi, Frank Fabozzi Associates, New Hope, Pa.

Sharpe, W. 1964. Capital Asset Prices: A Theory of Market Equilibrium Under Conditions of Risk. *The Journal of Finance,* 19(3).

Sharpe, W. 1990. Asset Allocation, in *Managing Investment Portfolios—A Dynamic Process,* eds. J. Magin and D. Tuttle, 7-1–7-70, Warren, Gorham and Camont, New York.

Sharpe, W. 1994. The Sharpe Ratio. *Journal of Portfolio Management,* 20(1): 49–59.

Sharpe, W. 1998. Morningstar's Risk-Adjusted Ratings. *Financial Analysts Journal,* 54(4):21–33.

Sharpe, W.F., G. Alexander, and J. Bailey. 1998. *Investments.* Prentice Hall, Englewood Cliffs, N.J.

Sharpe, W.F., and L.G. Tint. 1990. Liabilities: A New Approach. *Journal of Portfolio Management,* 16(2):5–10.

Simons, K. 1998. Risk-Adjusted Performance of Mutual Funds. *New England Economic Review,* September/October, pp. 33–48.

Singer, B. 1996. Valuation of Portfolio Performance: Aggregate Return and Risk Analysis. *Journal of Portfolio Measurement,* 1(1).

Sortino, F.A., and R. van der Meer. 1991. Downside Risk. *Journal of Portfolio Management,* 17(4):27–32.

Strange, B. 1998. Currency Overlay Managers Show Consistency. *Pensions and Investments,* June 15.

Surz, R. 1997. Computer-aided Pension Investment Decision-Making, in *Pension Fund Investment Management,* ed. F. Fabozzi, Frank Fabozzi Associates, New Hope, Pa.

Tobin, J. 1958. Liquidity Preference as a Behavior Towards Risk *Review of Economic Studies,* February, pp. 65–86.

Tsumagari, M. 1998. Optimal Ranges for Tactical Asset Allocation. *Investment Management Department Working Paper Series,* World Bank, Washington, DC.

Van der Meer, R., and M. Smink. 1998. Applying Downside Risk to ALM—A Pension Fund Case Study. *Journal of Portfolio Measurement.* 2(3).

Vos, M. 1997. The Use of Optioned Portfolios in Asset-Liability Management for Pension Plans (in Dutch). Master's Thesis, Erasmus University, Rotterdam.

Ward, J.F. 1999. Internal Versus External Management, in *Perspectives on Investment Management of Public Pension Funds,* ed. F. Fabozzi, Frank Fabozzi Associates, New Hope, Pa.

Waring, B., and C. Castille. 1998. A Framework for Optimal Manager Structure. *Barclays Global Investment Insight,* 1(2).

Winkelman, K. 2000. Risk Budgeting: Managing Active Risk at the Total Fund Level, in *Risk Budgeting: A New Approach to Investing,* ed. L. Rahl, Risk Books, London.

Winkelman, K., R. Litterman, J. Longerstaey, and J. Rosengarten. 2000. Risk Budgeting for Active Investment Managers, in *Risk Budgeting: A New Approach to Investing,* ed. L. Rahl, Risk Books, London.

World Bank. 1994. Averting the Old Age Crisis. *World Bank Policy Research Report.* Oxford: University Press, New York.

Zwanenburg, M.W. 1998. The Added Value of Exotic Optioned Portfolios in Asset-Liability Management (in Dutch). Master's Thesis, Erasmus University, Rotterdam.

THE AUTHOR

Arun S. Muralidhar is a Managing Director at FX Concepts and has extensive interactions with investment management clients. Before joining FX Concepts, he was a Managing Director and Head of Currency Research at J.P. Morgan Fleming Asset Management. Prior to J.P. Morgan, he was a Member of the Investment Management Committee and Head of Research at the World Bank, where he helped manage over $40 billion in funds. He was hired by the World Bank in 1992 as a member of the Young Professionals Program. Dr. Muralidhar holds a Ph.D. in Managerial Economics from the MIT Sloan School of Management (1992) and a B.A. from Wabash College (1988). He has taught in the M.I.T. Sloan Fellows Executive Program and has been a guest lecturer at the M.I.T. Sloan School of Management for Professor Franco Modigliani. Dr. Muralidhar has written many papers on pension finance and social security reform (along with Professor Modigliani) and has spoken at pension fund and central bank conferences around the world.

INDEX